D1016914

COLLABORATIVE INTELLIGENCE

COLLABORATIVE
INTELLIGENCE

THINKING WITH PEOPLE
WHO THINK DIFFERENTLY

Dawna Markova, Ph.D. | Angie McArthur

SPIEGEL & GRAU

NEW YORK

Copyright © 2015 by Dawna Markova, Ph.D., and Angie McArthur

Published in the United States by Spiegel & Grau,
an imprint of Random House, a division of
Penguin Random House LLC, New York.

SPIEGEL & GRAU and the HOUSE colophon are
registered trademarks of Penguin Random House LLC.

ISBN 978-0-8129-9490-2
eBook ISBN 978-0-8129-9491-9

Printed in the United States of America on acid-free paper

spiegelandgrau.com
randomhousebooks.com

246897531

First Edition

Book design by Casey Hampton

To the Possibilists who have come before us,
who stand next to us, and who will follow us

We have no choice but to think together, ponder together, in groups and communities. The question is how to do this, how to come together and think and hear each other in order to touch, and be touched by, the intelligence we need.

—Jacob Needleman

AUTHORS' NOTE

This book has grown out of many years of our individual and collective experience. And while all stories and examples are based on actual events, many of the places, names, and specific details regarding the individuals we have worked with have been changed. In addition, some of the stories are based on composites of several individuals.

In support of what we can all make possible,

Dawna and Angie

CONTENTS

STRATEGY 3—
INQUIRY: BRIDGING OUR DIFFERENCES

STRATEGY 4—
MIND SHARE: CREATING A COLLABORATIVE FUTURE

CONCLUSION

APPENDIX

COLLABORATIVE INTELLIGENCE

OUT OF THE DARKNESS

Farmers used to think that it was in the nature of chickens to peck at one another, that they were basically loners, unsocial animals that couldn't mingle without being nasty. On some farms, their beaks were clipped, but this only made it more difficult for the chickens to eat—which made them hungrier, so they pecked at themselves and one another even more. Then a chicken farmer somewhere noticed something exquisitely simple that changed everything: Chicken coops were dark, and the absence of light was what was causing the chickens to peck at themselves and one another. As soon as that farmer introduced a light source into his coops, his chickens stopped pecking—it was as simple as that.

People are not all that different. When we don't know what our minds need to think well together, we are like chickens pecking around in the dark. This isn't as far afield as it might seem: When we are communicating and thinking well together, our faces actually "light up." When our minds don't get enough light, our thinking breaks down and we begin to peck at ourselves and one another.

Humans can no longer afford to think in division and darkness. Collaborative intelligence is the light that is necessary for our individual and collective survival. We have no choice now but to think together.

INTRODUCTION

There is a new story waiting for our voice. It is the story of human possibility, of what people are capable of when we come together. Many of us carry this story inside but are afraid to speak it. We tell ourselves we're crazy. But in fact we represent the new sanity— the ideas and practices that can create a future worth living.

—Meg Wheatley

The most significant gift our species brings to the world is our capacity to think. The most significant danger our species brings to the world is our inability to think with those who think differently. I've been writing this book for forty years. It has formed and re-formed itself into thirteen other books. It has moved with me from house to house in manila folders: from the lakeshores of Vermont, to the mountains of Utah, to the foothills of California, and now to the side of a volcano in the middle of the Pacific Ocean. It was in my mind and heart when I was twenty, teaching children who were labeled as having learning disabilities in the migrant labor camps of Florida. It came back when I was in private practice as a psychotherapist in Norwich, Vermont. It resurfaced when I was training psychologists and social workers on the East Coast, in the Midwest, and on the West Coast. It nagged at me when I was an adviser to CEOs of global corporations. The need to write this book has been driven by what all of us should have been taught and never were: how to access the full range of the unique intelligence that is within us and between us.

Now that I am seventy-three years old, I can only say it is for this I have come. My life has been, in one way or another, about collaboration. This obsession of mine has taken on new importance as it has become clear that to stay competitive in our global economy, we must learn how to think collaboratively and innovatively. But if you have ever sat through a mind-numbing meeting, or tried to influence a colleague's view on a project, or had a recurring argument with a family member, or struggled to participate in a community project, you have recognized that most of us actually don't know how to think well together. I have attended endless years of education and professional training. Never once did anyone bring up the subject of learning *how* to collaborate.

We habitually misread people and therefore miscommunicate with them. We blame and belittle one another and ourselves because we have not been trained to notice the effect we have on one another or to fluidly shift the ways we communicate to accommodate others. We take for granted that intelligence occurs within our own minds. We don't realize that it also occurs *between* us. What keeps us from communicating effectively is that most of us don't know how to think with people who think differently than we do.

In the past decade, neuroscientists have learned some remarkable things about the human mind and brain, things that can directly increase our capacity to relate to others. As these new understandings emerge, we are realizing how deeply we affect other people. We can grow one another's capacity as well as diminish it. Despite our unending love affair with digital devices, we still crave face-to-face connection with other people. Too often we find ourselves working alone, through our screens, cut off from the regular sources of renewal and inspiration that only collaboration can bring.

I began my career as a clinical psychologist and educator, with a special fascination with cognitive neuroscience. I was trained to measure intelligence as something static, a noun, a "thing," like a cup. The experts told me that some of us are born smart, with a big cup, and others not so smart, with a little cup. A teacher's job was to fill that cup, or so I was instructed while mine was being filled in school. I paid for my oh-so-expensive graduate school education by teaching the "impossible" children that everyone else had given up on. I never questioned the size of their cups. Each and every one of them taught me that intelligence is a verb, not a noun. As with tending a garden, it requires cultivation. All that mattered to me was discovering how they *were* smart. Only then could I help them bring that capacity to the challenges they faced.

For the past fifty years I have devoted my work and career to helping people discover their unique intelligence, teaching corporate leaders, parents, educators, and children about "intellectual diversity." We are accustomed to considering diversity through the lens of race, gender, and culture, but most of us are unaware that there is also a range of differences in how we think. When I met Angie McArthur, a specialist in multi-dimensional communication (who eventually became my daughter-in-law), I realized how much more this body of work could grow in collaboration with her expertise and experience.

I was raised as an expat in the Middle East, the second of four daughters, and spent my childhood exploring remote corners of the world. I had to learn to build bridges between people, to see the whole of any issue, to inquire and cross-pollinate ideas from one person to the next. Many people think of in-laws as adversaries, but Dawna and I are joined in a shared mission: the constant search for what it takes for people to focus on what connects them rather than what divides them.

We have spent the last thirteen years as professional thinking partners to CEOs and the senior leadership teams of some of the world's largest corporations, exploring all aspects of intellectual diversity. When Dawna and I asked executives from such companies as Royal Dutch Shell, PepsiCo, Frito-Lay, Harley-Davidson, Merck, and Intel what their biggest challenge was, the most common response was "People." They said they needed to learn in real time how to collaborate more effectively, to create a collective goal of excellence in the midst of rapid change, and to foster greater alignment among their employees and colleagues. The most significant work we have done with these clients, therefore, has been to develop strategies and practices that make it possible to unleash each person's potential and to think across habitual divides. We teach them how to maximize the value of their intellectual diversity. We call this collaborative intelligence.

Your collaborative-intelligence quotient, which we will refer to as "CQ" throughout this book, is a measure of your ability to think with others on behalf of what matters to us all. To access that intelligence, we must learn to dignify the differences in how we think and use them to face complex challenges. Given the friction we often experience when we try to think with those who think differently, that task may seem impossible. We celebrate diversity in sports and the arts, but even the relatively recent concept that humans have "multiple intelligences," as articulated by developmental psychologist Howard Gardner of Harvard, is of very limited use, because we haven't been trained to value and utilize those diverse capacities. Peter Senge, author of *The Fifth Discipline,* estimates that the IQ of a group can actually drop by more than 30 percent compared to the IQ of individuals in the group. The numbing and dumbing down that happen when we try to think together are astounding. But never have we needed collaboration more.

We are living in an age of complexity, chaos, and collapse. Every significant conversation between us seems to be a tug-of-war between polarities. Black or white. Red or blue. We don't know, or have forgotten, how to think together about the possibility of purple. We tear ourselves apart with the mistaken belief that

we must decide between two opposing forces: independence or interdependence. We believe we have to either stand on our own two feet as individuals to make a mark and achieve recognition or sacrifice our uniqueness and perspective in order to accommodate a larger whole—a company, a family, a community.

Imagine that you are holding a rope, one end in each hand, pulling it in opposite directions. Who are the adversaries or adversarial forces in your life right now that pull you apart? Most minds, most leaders, and most organizations are stuck in this position. *The harder we pull away from one another, the more tightly stuck we become.* The only way to resolve this, in fact, is to take the pressure off and allow the ends of the rope to bend toward each other by asking the question: "How can the real needs of *each* of these opposing forces be met?" In this way, we free our minds to think together about how to "make ends meet" until we form a circle.

We know intuitively that the only way we get through challenging times is together. During the Second World War, there was a street in London where certain families had not spoken to one another for decades. They held on to resentments of transgressions long past, from one generation to the next. As London was mercilessly bombarded during the Blitz, these families were forced to share the same air-raid shelter. Faced with a common mortal threat, they forgot their grievances in no time at all. Friendships were struck. People who had not spoken for years began to support and help one another, swap jokes, and laugh together.

Many of the barriers keeping us apart are actually optional, present only in our minds. When our lives depend on it, the barriers dissolve and we draw on the innate hardwiring we have to connect. Remember the first days after September 11? As a society, we experienced a visceral longing to connect, to help, to offer whatever we had—prayers, talents, resources—to those most directly affected. We instantly changed our habitual individuated ways of thinking. What appeared at first glance to be separate and polarized human needs came into balance, if only for a short time.

HINGE TIME: SHIFTING FROM A MARKET-SHARE TO A MIND-SHARE MENTALITY

We are living in a hinge time. We have been educated for a time that no longer exists. Leaders today are confronted with vastly different challenges from the ones of their predecessors, who were taught how to be right but not how to be effective with other people. They had been trained for a "market share" economy. We are now entering a "mind share" world, no longer just dealing with analytic and procedural problems that require rational solutions. We're being asked to think together in ways that are innovative and relational. People who have never met are being forced to come up with breakthrough solutions to complex problems. We must work and think across continents, cultures, time zones, and temperaments.

In the market-share way of thinking, value is determined by shortage—I have it and you don't. Objects are valued according to their scarcity—diamonds, for example. Market-share mentality solves problems by asking our minds to think practically, analytically, and procedurally. We break down challenges into small pieces and arrange them neatly in sequential order, hoping the solution will make itself apparent. A question is asked and our brains shoot back an answer: Ready, aim, fire. We focus our individual and collective attention on deficits—cognitive, emotional, and financial.

When we think this way, we bifurcate. We get stuck at the ends of the rope: Either I'm right or you are. Select one answer or the other. A leader is a hero who has clawed his way up the ladder of success and accumulated the most power over others. Success is measured in assets accrued.

Former U.S. IKEA CEO Göran Carstedt calls the opposite approach a mind-share mentality. Wealth is created and carried by ideas and relationships more than by transactions. When *things* carry value, if I have one and give it away, I lose something. But when *ideas* carry value, everything is turned upside down. When you have a good idea and I have a good idea and we exchange them, you walk away with two new ideas and I also have two new ideas. *The more we share, the more we have.* Our capacity to generate, share, and enact ideas becomes most valuable.

A mind-share world necessitates that we learn to use influence with others rather than power over them. This is especially crucial now because, in the age of rapidly formed "Velcro teams," where people across continents work together remotely for a short period of time, influence, not power, is needed to get breakthrough work done. Mind share also requires developing the capacity within ourselves to be influenced by others and using skillful collaboration to create forward movement. In this way, leadership becomes a verb, *to host*, rather than a noun, *the hero*. Ultimately, in a mind-share world, those who are most flexible in their thinking will be those who have the most influence.

While market share requires that we answer questions quickly and expertly, mind share requires that we know how to ask the kinds of questions that open our own and others' minds to new possibilities. Market share determines who is right and who is wrong. Mind share asks what is possible. This kind of inquiry encourages the brain to wonder. It is wonder that creates the fertile conditions that generate ideas and build bridges between seemingly opposing thoughts.

In his bestselling book *A Whole New Mind*, Daniel Pink wrote that we can't solve today's and tomorrow's problems with yesterday's ways of thinking. Because most of us have only been educated in the market-share mentality, our problem-solving abilities, our communication skills, and our capacity to bend that rope and bridge differences haven't evolved quickly enough to sustain us. We have been taught that the one who pulls hardest wins. We have been trained to use thinking strategies that result in one side or the other losing: needing to be right, resolving differences by eradicating them, controlling the other person, retaliating by getting even, and withdrawing resources. These strategies use power over others: power to provoke, protect, procure, preserve.

Collaborative intelligence (CQ) is a critical component of mind share, because it allows you to recognize what expertise is present and what is missing. Imagine a forty-five-minute phone call with a group of people you have never met from around the world; it begins with everyone announcing their thinking talents, their blind spots, and how you can most effectively communicate with them. This would give you, in effect, an operating manual for one another's minds, and as the meeting progressed you could easily avoid counterproductive assumptions that you would normally attribute to personality. Think of this book as that operating manual which helps you understand the differences in how the people around you think.

In a study on collaborative advantage published in the *Harvard Business Review*, Rosabeth Moss Kanter observed thirty-seven companies and their partners from eleven parts of the world. She and her associates found that North American companies, more than others, "take a narrow, opportunistic view of relationships" and "frequently neglect the political, cultural, organizational, and human aspects of the partnership." She concluded that collaborative alliances "require a dense web of interpersonal connections and internal infrastructures."

It is tempting to make the mistake of thinking that one of these mentalities is good and the other bad. In this hinge time, both market-share and mind-share mentalities are needed to balance each other; we must learn to collaborate as well as compete.

Alan S. Cohen, an expert on networks who has launched several start-ups, describes this relationship as follows: "In Silicon Valley, 'collaboration' is defined as something you do with another colleague or company to achieve greatness." Silicon Valley continues to thrive by finding new ways to solve bigger problems faster and by employing new strategies that create forward movement. This does not mean competition is absent or that ideas do not sometimes clash. But in addition to the heated competition, meaningful collaboration happens, because these companies share a common goal: to serve the customer the best product or service possible.

Companies may try to best one another in one market *and* work together in another. Microsoft Windows running on Apple's Macs is an example. Another is the way LinkedIn, the leading professional-networking site, at times competes with headhunters and at other times is used by headhunters, as described in an article by Thomas Friedman:

> "Sure, competition here is sharp-elbowed," said Reid Hoffman, co-founder and executive chairman of LinkedIn. "But no one can succeed by themselves. Apple today is totally focused on how it can better work with its [applications] developer community." It cannot thrive without them. "The only way you can achieve something magnificent is by working with other people," said Hoffman. "There is lots of co-opetition." LinkedIn competes with headhunters and is used by headhunters.
>
> With collaboration, one plus one can often turn out to be four, says Jeff Weiner, the CEO of LinkedIn, adding: "I will always work with you—if I know we'll get to four. You can't build great products alone."

RATE YOUR CQ

The following assessment will help you evaluate the quality of collaboration between you and the people you spend the most time with at work. It will serve as a benchmark, because we will be asking you to repeat this assessment at the conclusion of the book, to gauge what has grown between you.

Instructions

- Identify the five people with whom you currently spend the most time at work.
- Write their names across the top of the chart below. (This chart and the other tools can be downloaded from our website: CQthebook.com.)
- Next, estimate the approximate percentage of time in any given week that you spend with each person and write it below his or her name.
- Rate the collaboration between you and this person on a scale of 1 to 5 through the lens of each of the four qualities in the far left column (1 being lowest, 5 being highest).
- Tally the columns.

QUALITY	NAME	NAME	NAME	NAME	NAME
Respect: How much admiration and sense of each other's value exists between you.					
Aliveness: How much "zest," vitality, and energy there is between you.					
Understanding: How secure you feel in communicating your needs, fears, ideas, and enthusiasm.					
Growth: How much you grow each other's capacity for exploring new possibilities and ideas.					
TOTAL					

Interpreting the Results

The qualities listed in the left column enrich collaborative thinking. We adapted them from the work of the Jean Baker Miller Training Institute (JBMTI) at the Wellesley Centers for Women. Their research, combined with ours, posits that people can grow in relationships over the course of their entire lives. A low score (10 or below per person) on the chart above indicates where learning and new approaches are needed.

A high overall score (15 or higher per person) indicates a relationship that is both rewarding and collaborative. This assessment offers you a way to begin to compare your relationships and transfer what you learn from one that is high-scoring and fulfilling to one that is depleting.

Each of these people influences the way your brain does or does not grow. You probably know intuitively that spending a lot of time with someone who is frenzied makes you feel anxious. Likewise, when you are with someone who is serene and centered, you most likely feel calmer and more at ease. But we haven't known until recently how profound an effect others have on the way our brains are wired. We either grow or diminish our capacity through those people with whom we spend the most time.

PARTNERING WITH THE POSSIBLE: ACTIVATING THE FOUR STRATEGIES OF CQ

I always laugh when asked if I am a coach, because sports have never been where my gifts lie. I can't throw a ball or handle a racket, and have always been last to be asked to join an athletic team. Some people have perfect pitch; others can analyze financial trends. The only talent I've ever had is the ability to help others think well.

Angie is not a coach either. To survive and thrive in foreign places, she had to become authentically curious and adapt quickly, and this became her gift. She often could not use words to create connections, so she learned to use gestures, actions, and multi-sensory communication as ways to embrace and bridge differences.

Professional Thinking Partners™ is the name of our company and the term Angie and I use to define the work we are passionate about doing. We have used the strategies in this book to help and support sales teams around the world to expand their influence and deepen their relationships with customers. We've helped individuals, teams, companies, and governments to begin to think across habitual divides. Through our work, the Nigerian oil ministry can now think collaboratively with Royal Dutch Shell after decades of being adversaries; the senior leadership team of Frito-Lay now thinks together about how their products can nourish children; the global leaders of GE Capital think innovatively about the market challenges they are facing; the senior leadership team of Bolthouse Farms transformed a ninety-five-year-old business into a market-leading innovator.

Collaborative intelligence is the flow of energy and information within and between us. To help senior leaders gain access to that intelligence, Angie and I, along with our colleagues, have developed four thinking strategies and breakthrough practices that bridge the practical and the possible. In the pages that follow, we will be sharing examples of how we have implemented the CQ program with leaders we fondly call "the Possibilists." Each of them came to understand that collaborative intelligence is unrelated to the smarts and drive that helped them get into the top ten percent of the top ten business schools in the world. After mastering our strategies, the Possibilists recognized that significant changes in their organizations' ability to learn and thrive couldn't begin until deep changes occurred in how individuals were thinking and acting. This book is dedicated to helping you learn to think as a Possibilist.

What is challenging the organization or community that you care deeply about? We each experience a longing to make a difference and a longing to belong to a larger whole. Like any other capacity, influence is a powerful force that can lie dormant, but it can also be cultivated to grow. Too many of us turn away from using our influence to create change because we just don't know how to bridge the differences between us.

ARE YOU EFFECTIVE?

What is important about this quiz is not the overall score. Each question will heighten your awareness of a different aspect of CQ that you can grow. We invite you to use the quiz as a benchmark by taking it now and then again at the end of the book to measure how you have expanded your effectiveness with others.

EFFECTIVENESS OF YOUR CQ	
Please respond to the following statements on a scale of 0–10 (0 = Not at all; 10 = Great)	Rating
1. The ease with which I contribute ideas in meetings	
2. The frequency with which I share my talents and resources with other team members	
3. The frequency with which other members offer their talents and resources to me and one another	
4. From my perspective, the opportunity for a minority opinion in team meetings to be considered and accepted	
5. The frequency with which I think cross-functionally	
6. The options for different participation styles I create in meetings—visual, auditory, kinesthetic, etc.	
7. My knowledge of which talents and resources each person brings to the team and how to leverage them fully	
8. My effectiveness with challenging clients/customers/co-workers	
9. My ability to get people to act together	
10. My ability to get people to think effectively together	

The information in this book will help you understand the specific contribution you can make and teach you the most effective way to express it. You will learn to recognize the thinking talents of those around you. You will know how to open your mind to achieve what you want to make possible. Most important, you will know how to make the most of the intellectual diversity that surrounds you in the same way that a conductor, though silent, leads the different instruments of an orchestra to play a symphony.

In the chapters that follow, Angie and I invite you to become a Possibilist by increasing your awareness of how you and those around you are thinking, particularly those who think differently from you. You have to understand how to tune and play the instrument of your own mind first and then expand your awareness so that you can be influenced by the diversity of those around you. As you master this, you develop the capacity to bring out their best, and they yours. The ultimate goal is to recognize and be able to say, "I think better when I think with you."

What is the breakthrough you most want to see happen in the next year? What do you imagine could be possible if you were truly collaborating with those who stand beside you? What effect would that have on those who will follow you?

Angie and I have asked ourselves those same questions. In writing this book, we have thought of ourselves as your "thinking partners," guiding you to explore different ways to relate to the people and the problems in your life as you master the four essential strategies of CQ.

THE FOUR ESSENTIAL STRATEGIES OF CQ

1. **Mind Patterns:** Your mind pattern is the unique way that you process and respond to information. We will teach you to identify and maximize your own mind pattern and to recognize the mind patterns of others.
2. **Thinking Talents:** These are the specific ways of approaching challenges that energize your brain and come naturally to you. Identifying these talents and your blind spots, as

well as those of your colleagues, is key to more effective collaboration.

3. **Inquiry:** This is the unique way that you frame questions and consider possibilities. By identifying your own preferences, as well as the styles of those around you, you open yourself to widening your perspective and become a better thinking partner.

4. **Mind Share:** Mind share encompasses the mindset shift required to generate alignment within your team. We will show you how to aim your individual and collective attention, intention, and imagination in order to create this.

BREAKTHROUGH PRACTICES

To learn the most difficult things our brains ever have to master—walking and talking—we don't distinguish learning in our bodies from learning in our heads. As we get older, the culture of classrooms, training sessions, and business meetings teaches us that learning involves memorizing facts and digesting abstract theories. We learn to recite the bits and pieces we have accumulated, but we're not actually taught to *do* anything differently, particularly in real-life situations where there is conflict and pressure to perform in the midst of complexity and uncertainty. When we disconnect learning from our bodies, we can't embody what we've learned. If we physically experience the strategy, on the other hand, and practice it deliberately, it will be immediate, effective, and available to us when we most need it. We call these "breakthrough practices."

When we first introduced breakthrough practices in the leadership seminars we facilitated with Peter Senge at the Center for Organizational Learning at MIT's Sloan School of Management, some people thought they were the "exercise" portion of the program and wanted to know when they were going to get to the "real stuff." As they experienced the practices, however, they began to make very interesting discoveries, such as where in their bodies they held themselves back from extending their influence or how it felt physically to depend on others and also to have others depend on them. They became aware of how they habitually used power rather than influence to meet challenges. We could almost hear the doors of their minds creaking open. Conflict with colleagues turned into a subject of curiosity rather than a problem to be avoided. It became obvious that physically experiencing a new understanding made the concept readily accessible. "Of all the stuff I learned about systems thinking and mental models," wrote the head of R&D at a large telecommunications company, "nothing was so directly useful to me as the embodiment practice that helped me become aware of what happens to me physically during a meeting."

We are used to seeing what we expect to see, hearing what we expect to hear, and doing what we expect to do. However, these habits can make us numb and limit our potential. They offer comfort without challenge, reassurance without insight, and certainty without imagination.

- Most breakdowns are a result of habitual thinking.
- Most breakups are a result of habitual thinking.
- Most breakthroughs are a result of non-habitual thinking.

Throughout the book, we will present you with a few select breakthrough practices. They will not cause you stress, but they will ask you to stretch. You have been reading about habitual and non-habitual thinking; now let's experience that concept in an embodied way with a practice I first learned from physicist, black-belt martial artist, and founder of psychophysical re-education Moshe Feldenkrais.

BREAKTHROUGH PRACTICE: THINKING ALIVE

Fold your hands by interlacing the fingers as you have done habitually since you were a well-behaved young child.

- Now bring your attention to the *way* you are doing this. Is the right thumb on top of the left or the left on top of right?
- Next, unfold your fingers and refold them in the opposite, non-habitual way (i.e., if right was on top of left, put left on top of right, or vice versa).
- Go back and forth between the two ways while asking yourself: Which feels most comfortable? Which feels most awkward? Which feels most secure? Which one helps you be the most aware of the spaces between your fingers? Which helps your hands feel the most alive to you?

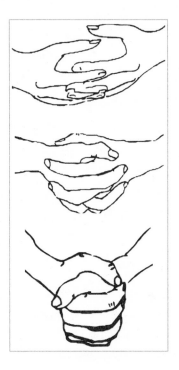

When I learned this practice, I was amazed to discover that what was awkward could in fact make me feel more aware and alive. Up until that moment, I had been trained to avoid feeling awkward at all costs. Because I wanted to feel secure and comfortable, I lived within a box of habitual thinking, until I discovered this little practice. I realized that I actually felt safer in the non-habitual position, because I was more aware in the "awkward folding" and I could unlace my hands faster to respond to a challenge. Was this true for you? Use this practice whenever you want to remind yourself to risk thinking in a new way.

THE MONKEY TRAP

On an island not so far from here, the local people became very annoyed at the pesky monkeys who lived in the trees surrounding their village and wreaked havoc on their orderly gardens. A clever village elder created a small bamboo cage and placed a banana inside it, then hung it on the edge of his property. Late that afternoon, a monkey reached in and grabbed the banana. When he tried to pull it out between the narrow ribs of the cage, his hand was stuck. All he had to do to get free was to release the banana and slide his little hand out. But that evening, when the elder came to check the trap, the monkey was hanging from it, still clutching that banana, even though it meant the loss of his own freedom.

Many of us are just like that monkey. We grasp on to something that tantalizes us, and even when we realize that to be free we have to let go, we hold on nonetheless. One of the things that most commonly trap us is the habitual pattern of our own thinking—the limiting stories we tell ourselves about who we are and what our capacities are.

MIND PATTERNS

Thinking about Thinking

THINK   **MIND PATTERNS**   TALENTS   INQUIRY   MIND SHARE   CQ

Understanding the
unique way you
think, learn, and
communicate

RECOGNIZING HOW YOUR MIND WORKS

Each mind has its own method.
—Ralph Waldo Emerson

I never heard my father say, "I love you." He said many things to me in his lifetime, but never that. My mother collected newspaper clippings that chronicled his journey from inner-city street fighter to CEO of a major Chicago corporation. He often said he regretted never having a son who could inherit the knowledge he'd gathered as he climbed the corporate ladder. My father lacked one skill, however, and it was his greatest secret and most profound shame. Every day after school I would go to his huge office. My feet would leave prints in the plush burgundy carpeting as I approached his immense mahogany desk and pulled myself up onto the leather swivel chair. The only things on the shining desktop were a large reel-to-reel tape recorder and a very thick pile of documents held in place by a crystal paperweight carved with the company insignia. Day after day, I pushed the button on the tape recorder and began to read the papers, one by one, into the microphone. Then, when I had finished, I slipped my hand under the big black-and-green blotter and found the quarter my father had left me so I could buy a hot fudge sundae on the way home. No one ever found out about this ritual. It was our secret. No one ever found out that he couldn't read a word.

During the ten years I read and recorded for my father in his office, our conversations grew deeper and more engaging: We actually became thinking partners. He loved my questions, and I loved learning how he managed to inspire so many people. He explained to me that in a leader, no quality was more important than the ability to recognize and develop the capacity of each person, the particular way he or she brings value to the world. As I write this, his words still resonate: "Remember this secret, Dawna: Talent attracts capital far more than capital attracts talent."

I knew my father was intelligent in specific ways. As I became increasingly curious about why my father—a man who could stand before a thousand people and deliver a speech, who could "read" the gifts of all of his employees—couldn't read, I was driven to understand how his mind worked.

The notion that we use different "operating systems" to think has been at the center of my work for the last fifty years. I uncovered it in the 1970s while I was shuttling back and forth from graduate school at Columbia to a classroom in Harlem, where I was teaching forty kids, many with rat bites on their cheeks and folders full of labels about how they were disabled. I adored these children. Each one was a precious riddle that asked, "What can be possible for this child?"

Then I met a lanky researcher at NYU named E. Roy John, who was measuring certain brain-wave frequencies associated with general psychological processes. He originated a field of study called neurometrics, which used a computer and an EEG to monitor what was going on in the brain while a person was thinking. Meanwhile, I was searching for the best reading method to use with my students: the sight method, phonics, or an experiential approach. I brought several children to his lab and connected them to his equipment. What I observed, to put it simply, was that if I gave Johnny written information to look at, his brain produced more beta waves, indicating he was concentrating. But when I gave Jimmy the same information, his brain produced more alpha waves, which indicated a daydream state. Even more confusing was that when I presented the same visual information to Jason, his brain produced more theta waves, which is a very spaced-out state. How could this be? The kind of input was determining the kind of attention that each student's brain was producing. I brought in more children and shifted to auditory input—sounds and verbal words. When she was listening or talking, Jenny's brain got very focused, but Jessie's daydreamed, and Julia's spaced out completely. Now my confusion opened up into curiosity. I tried kinesthetic input, having the kids play with clay and move around. For some children, this produced more beta waves; for others, more alpha waves; and for still others, more theta waves. What I hadn't realized until that point was: 1) Input from the outside caused the children's brains to shift from focused attention to a daydream or creative state. Their different states of attention were being produced by the different kinds of input they were exposed to. 2) There is no one way of "paying attention." The brain uses all three states to learn and think.

Through this and other experiences, I became convinced that the question is not "Are you smart?" but "How *are* you smart?" This awareness, coupled with the work I was studying on shifting states of attention in clinical hypnotherapy, led me to create a system for understanding different patterns of thinking, learning, and communicating, which I call "mind patterns." Tens of thousands of individuals around the world now use this model in education, business, and family relationships to learn and collaborate more effectively.

The first strategy of CQ is recognizing mind patterns. This chapter and the next are the planks you will lay to help bridge differences between you and your intellectually diverse colleagues. Initially, you need to learn how to recognize the unique and specific way *you* process information. Knowing this will make learning, unlearning, digesting, and expressing information more natural. It will also help you design a working environment and develop new habits that evoke your best thinking. This understanding will challenge you to open your mind and grow your natural curiosity and capacity.

This information is meant to increase your curiosity about and your awareness of how you are affected by different experiences and how you can be most effective with others. It is based on what is called "theory-in-use and action research," meaning that neuroscientists haven't yet definitively pinpointed how the brain processes information, but we can make observations and hypotheses based on extensive experience in the field. This knowledge will increase your awareness of the conditions that maximize how you think, learn, and communicate. It does *not* describe personality (although many of the characteristics of a person's mind pattern are often incorrectly attributed to that). Identifying the particular sequence your mind uses to shift attention will enable you to notice how your and other people's thinking is affected by different kinds of input.

At the back of the book, there is an appendix with more-detailed information on how to use your mind pattern in many work situations and a guide for how you can best interact and communicate with other patterns.

As thinkers, all of us are stuck in our own ruts and habits, and we are reluctant to move beyond them. You need to know how to create the conditions where you can let go and open up to what can be possible. You need to learn—and unlearn—with others constantly. This can be more challenging than it seems. One thing that distinguishes a boss from a leader is the ability to suspend belief and disbelief so that innovations and new processes will have a chance to emerge. In the beginning, all of our clients identified themselves as open-minded people, but not one of them understood the specific combination of conditions that was necessary to open his or her own mind.

HOW DO YOU PAY ATTENTION TO ATTENTION?

The first step in recognizing your mind pattern is noticing your attention and then coming to understand its three different states and what triggers each one. Attention literally means how we attend to things, what we notice in the world we inhabit and the people we encounter. It regulates the flow of information within and between us. It is fluid. We can all aim it, follow it, or shift it, but each of us does that in a different way.

Attention, like water, has several different "forms" or states. It can be "*focused*," or solid as a cube of ice. This is a state where you give your attention to only one thing and ignore the rest of what is going on around you. Attention can also be in a "*sorting*" or mediating state, shifting from inner awareness to outer and back again, sorting and digesting information. You may experience this as confusion or weighing two options, such as, "On the one hand . . . but on the other hand . . ." Attention can also be "*open*," creative, daydreaming, and diffuse, where you get in touch with memories, images, and ideas and transform them into new patterns, thoughts, or insights. For instance, think of a time when you were in the shower and an idea just "popped" into your mind, or you had an "aha" moment.

Let's explore each state in more detail:

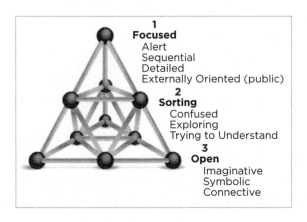

1
Focused
Alert
Sequential
Detailed
Externally Oriented (public)
2
Sorting
Confused
Exploring
Trying to Understand
3
Open
Imaginative
Symbolic
Connective

1. FOCUSED ATTENTION

This describes the conscious state of mind where your brain is producing more beta waves. Your thoughts become certain and form into solid beliefs. You are very directed; you concentrate on what is in front of you: your computer screen, the other person's voice, the hammer in your hand. This is the state of attention best suited for:

- Concentrating on accomplishing tasks.
- Decision-making.
- Attending to details and timelines.

2. SORTING ATTENTION

This describes the subconscious state of mind, where your brain produces more alpha waves. Your thoughts wander back and forth, sorting through information, comparing one thing to another. In this state of attention you are:

- Trying to understand.
- Digesting information or experiences.
- Thinking through confusion.
- Weighing multiple choices.

3. OPEN ATTENTION

This is an unconscious state of mind, where your brain is producing more theta waves. Your thoughts are very wide and internal, as in a daydream. In this state of mind you are:

- Imagining possibilities, new ways to approach old problems.
- Exploring different options by seeing things in a new way.
- Associating to past experiences, stories, and people: "Oh, that reminds me of this."

Our minds are constantly shifting quickly between these three states of attention—from focused to sorting to open, and from open to sorting to focused, often without our awareness. You

A DAILY PRACTICE TO RECLAIM YOUR ATTENTION

When I ask people what is their favorite way of connecting to them-selves, most have no idea what I'm talking about. The following tool is an exquisitely simple and elegant way of taking charge of your attention. It helps you find sanity in the crazy moments of life.

- *Choose any sense—what you feel in your body, hear, or see around you—and write or describe out loud what you are experiencing for one minute.*
- *Describe just the information your senses give you, with-out thoughts, comparisons, or opinions.*
- *Shift to another sense and describe it for one full minute.*
- *Shift to a third sense and describe it for one full minute.*

For example: "Right now I am seeing the birch trees outside my window move slightly in the wind. I see pollen and new fuzzy buds on the tips of branches. I see a red bird land on the grass and turn its head. Then I feel my fingers type and each of the keys springs back. I feel my butt pressing into the seat of the chair. I feel my neck tensing as I tilt my head back. I feel thirsty. I hear creaks in the walls of this old house. I hear the inhale of my breath. I hear the clicking of my keys. I hear music down the hall."

You can set a timer and do it for any amount of time. One man I worked with did it for forty minutes and told me it was better than any drug he had tried (and he'd tried many of them). We think of it as increasing circulation to all your senses and refreshing your mind. The results are remarkable. It slows you down and puts your mind into neutral. It brings you back to center, back into your body and the present moment.

might have experienced this when, driving on the interstate at night, you passed by exit 15 and then suddenly found yourself at exit 18. You were unaware of passing exits 16 and 17. Your atten-tion shifted from the cars around you, to a song on the radio, to your own internal thoughts. What happened, in fact, is that your "thought" was changing form, shifting from focused to sorting to open attention. Your mind became like a loom, weaving different ideas in a new way, or making associative leaps between past and present. We call this way of thinking "relational logic," because your mind is creating new connections between thoughts.

We shift between these three states all the time. Each one is a stage of "mental metabolism," where your mind is taking in information, organizing it, digesting it, evaluating it, eliminating it, arranging it into new patterns and ideas, storing it, and then sorting it again to decide how to express it.

WHY DON'T WE VALUE ALL THREE STATES OF ATTENTION?

When somebody does not respond to us verbally, when he stares out the window, jiggles, or paces, we often assume he is not "paying attention." This is not necessarily true. These may be indicators of different states of thinking and different ways of paying attention. Exploring, wondering, imagining, reflecting, sorting, are all different stages of effective thinking. They are all natural aspects of paying attention—each useful for different things.

However, most of us have been taught to consider only a focused state of attention as being valuable, and we assume that sorting and open attention are a waste of time.

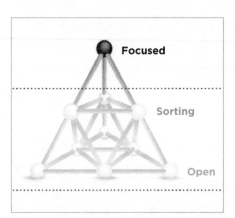

We refer to these states negatively as being confused, being distracted, or spacing out. When most of us sense our thoughts wandering, we jolt ourselves awake, grasping for the old habit of finding a quick answer or the next action step. We have been taught to analyze our way out of any problem as quickly as possible. Thus, when our minds are confused and sorting information, we panic and reflexively attempt to use logic to "get to the point," to focus.

In Western cultures, when someone looks pensive or lost in thought, we think of it as a perfect opportunity to interrupt them. When someone is working through confusion, we jump in to help, as if confusion is something to be quickly cured. We are habituated to giving answers, taking swift action, and deciding something *now*. However, unless we are willing to spend time not knowing, with our minds wide open in wonder, we won't generate the kind of innovative thinking we so desperately need.

In the recent past, numerous cognitive neuroscientists have conducted studies that reveal that, like the tip of an iceberg, only a very small percentage of our cognitive activities (decisions, emotions, actions, behavior) involve conscious attention. The vast majority of remaining mental activity is beneath the surface of our awareness, where our minds explore relationships and make unconscious connections. You may not think of this as "work," but your mind *is* in fact working in this state of open, relational thinking.

It may be, in fact, that the challenges you face have a greater chance of being resolved when you are in an open state of attention without interference. This is where ingenuity can arise, grand symphonies and great inventions can be imagined, ruptured relationships can be repaired, and solutions to sweeping systemic issues, such as climate change, can emerge.

Being able to recognize the different forms and know how to shift from focused through sorting into open attention will result in your being able to:

- Identify new connections between things so you can find meaning.
- Synthesize ideas, objects, or things that seem to be in opposition or unrelated.
- Increase the frequency of "eureka" moments, where something new is born.

- Have and express insights.
- Intuit possibilities.

Now that the value of the three states of attention is more obvious, the natural next step is to learn how you can shift from one to the other more easily by recognizing the "language of thought."

THE THREE LANGUAGES OF THOUGHT:
WHAT TRIGGERS YOUR ATTENTION TO SHIFT?

Most of us are not aware of it, but the languages of thought are a combination of perceptual elements: kinesthetic, auditory, and visual.

For example, bring a lemon to mind. You might think about the lemon visually—oval, yellow, dimpled, with green leaves—or you might envision the printed word: "l-e-m-o-n." You might think about it auditorily by describing it with specific words— "tart," "Meyer," "fruit"—or you might hear the sound made by the juice when you squeeze it. You might think of it kinesthetically by sensing how it feels in your hand, remembering the taste, the experience of eating it, or the last time you squeezed one.

What is important about these three elements? Each of them will trigger your mind to shift attention from one state to another. Each of us has a particular preferred sequence that our brain uses to create that shift. One of these elements—auditory, visual, or kinesthetic—evokes the focused state; another evokes the sorting state; and the third evokes the open state of attention. *Every person uses all three elements to think*. It is the *sequence* of kinesthetic, auditory, and visual elements that triggers your attention to first focus (1), then sort (2), and then open (3). This 1-2-3 order determines what we call your mind pattern.

What this means is that visual information may trigger one person into *focused* thinking. She can easily see details in her "mind's eye" and absorb complex visual information in a sequential way. But if you were to give the same visual information to

3 Languages of Thought

AUDITORY THINKING		**KINESTHETIC THINKING**		**VISUAL THINKING**	
Listening • Telling		Doing • Moving • Feeling		Looking • Watching	
Discussing • Singing		Making Things		Reading • Showing	
Talking				Observing • Writing	
Receptive:	**Active:**	**Receptive:**	**Active:**	**Receptive:**	**Active:**
Listening	Storytelling	Smelling	Sports	Watching	Writing
Hearing	Lecturing	Tasting	Hands-on	Reading	Editing
	Singing	Feeling	Building	Seeing	Drawing
	Telling Jokes	Sensing	Doing	Being Shown	Photograph-
	Speaking	Experiencing	Moving		ing

another person, it might trigger him into an *open* state of attention. He'd get wide-eyed, space out, and envision possibilities. The first person would think the second wasn't "paying attention." For yet another, visual information triggers her mind into a *sorting* state of attention. For instance, Mary becomes focused by looking at emails, while Matty spaces out.

Joan might have an active kinesthetic experience, such as playing a sport or walking around a room or doing a hands-on activity, and be triggered into focused attention. She will be very alert, engaged, and organized. For Karen, however, kinesthetic movement, touch, or experiences will trigger daydreams or spacing out into open thinking.

Auditory input, the most used and abused in our culture, triggers some people into focused attention: The more they talk, the more they are alert, engaged, and organized. For others, talking triggers the mind into sorting attention. They naturally talk through both sides of a situation, as if a conversation were a verbal tennis match. For yet others, auditory input triggers them into open, "spacy" attention, where their minds are full of questions.

Recognizing your natural mind pattern can unlock vast quantities of intellectual capacity that have been lying dormant or bound up in misconceptions. You may have thought of yourself as inarticulate, emotionally volatile, verbally aggressive, shy, introverted, or extroverted. *In fact, we are all introverted when our attention is open, and we're extroverted when our attention is focused.* Reconsider yourself for a moment: Are you most introverted kinesthetically, auditorily, or visually? Where are you most extroverted?

WHAT IS *YOUR* MIND PATTERN?

> *Language does not seem to play any role in my mechanism of thought . . . in my case the elements are of visual and muscular type.*
>
> —Albert Einstein

How does your mind work? How does it naturally shift states of attention and process information most effectively? The following four-step maze will help you explore this. You'll be engaging in what author and leading neuroscientist Daniel Siegel, M.D., calls "mindsight," or "metacognition," using the inherent capacity of the mind to notice itself and how it works. The self-evaluation will lead you to one of six possible mind patterns.

Unlike most assessments, which pigeonhole you into one category or another, this one is designed to increase your awareness of how the three perceptual elements or languages of thought—kinesthetic, visual, and auditory, or "KVA"—trigger you into different states of attention. This information is meant to increase your awareness of the conditions that maximize how you think, learn, and communicate. It does *not* describe personality. However, identifying the particular sequence your mind uses to shift attention will likewise enable you to notice its movement.

Go through the following maze as if it's the game Hotter/Colder, which you probably played as a child. As you read the different descriptions, please be aware that any single characteristic may not be 100 percent true for you—what is significant is your *overall description of the pattern.* If, over time, the mind pattern that you selected does not seem to fit, read through the other patterns and see if another is more accurate. On page 42 there is a comparative chart of all six mind patterns. Some people recognize their pattern immediately. Others need to observe themselves in this new way over time, until they find an accurate fit. What is most important is that you become more curious about the unique and amazing way that your mind works.

STEP 1

Choose one of the cards below that seems most true for you, then proceed to the next step.

MIND PATTERNS

 A1 AUDITORY

I'm comfortable talking to large groups of people, even without advance preparation.

I prefer to give verbal reports rather than do a visual presentation or make a model.

I naturally remember what's said in a conversation.

I speak without pause (no "um"s) and use precise language.

Words flow out easily in logical order without thinking about it.

I can multitask auditorily: I can talk with one person and listen to somone else in the background at the same time.

I tend to be critical of how things are said.

MIND PATTERNS

 V1 VISUAL

The first thing I recall of a person or place is the way something or someone looked.

I'd prefer to write a report rather than do an oral presentation or make a model.

The best way for me to organize is to make a list.

I like to make direct and steady eye contact with the person I'm talking to.

I'm highly aware of the way I look to other people.

I can multitask visually: I can read and watch TV at the same time.

I tend to be critical of how things look.

MIND PATTERNS

 K1 KINESTHETIC

I prefer to be on my feet or moving around. A stand-up desk would really help me.

I prefer to share an experience or make a model as a presentation.

The best way for me to organize is by making piles.

I can easily recall what I did and the physical sensations of an experience.

My natural preference is to start hands-on and experiment by doing.

I can multitask kinesthetically: I can do two or three things at the same time.

I tend to be critical of how things are done.

STEP 2

Choose which of the following two cards is most true for you.

MIND PATTERNS

 K2 KINESTHETIC

I know what I am feeling in my body with my eyes open.

I have lots of pent-up energy right below the surface.

If you choose this card, read V3.

OR

MIND PATTERNS

 A2 AUDITORY

To make a decision, I prefer to talk both sides through with someone else.

I frequently use metaphors when I speak and prefer to share the entire story of an experience.

If you choose this card, read K3.

OR

MIND PATTERNS

 V2 VISUAL

I can easily see three-dimensional images in my mind with my eyes open and view these from various angles— above, behind, and sideways.

I prefer to look at the person I am talking to and then look around.

If you choose this card, read A3.

OR

STEP 3

Read the card that your choice indicated in Step 2.

MIND PATTERNS

V2
VISUAL

I can easily see three-dimensional images in my mind with my eyes open and view these from various angles—above, behind, and sideways.

I prefer to look at the person I am talking to and then look around.

If you choose this card, read K3.

MIND PATTERNS

V3
VISUAL

I prefer a low amount of visual information—e.g., bullet points rather than long paragraphs.

I get overwhelmed with too much visual detail.

I've had to train myself to make ongoing eye contact.

The way someone looks at me can have a very long-lasting effect.

I don't like people telling me what to look at.

MIND PATTERNS

K2
KINESTHETIC

I know what I am feeling in my body with my eyes open.

I have lots of pent-up energy right below the surface.

If you choose this card, read A3.

MIND PATTERNS

K3
KINESTHETIC

I can naturally sit still for long periods of time.

It's challenging for me to do a physical activity in a sequential or regimented way.

When doing something physical, I prefer to go at my own speed (whether fast or slow).

I don't like casual physical touch.

I'm very sensitive to touch, and it can have a very long-lasting effect.

MIND PATTERNS

A2
AUDITORY

To make a decision, I prefer to talk both sides through with someone else.

I frequently use metaphors when I speak and prefer to share the entire story of an experience.

If you choose this card, read V3.

MIND PATTERNS

A3
AUDITORY

I naturally like quiet or music I choose and am very sensitive to sound.

I prefer to take more time to think about what I'm going to say.

Words and tone of voice can be profound and have a long-lasting effect.

I have a fear of interruption and will avoid verbal confrontation.

I prefer not to be told what to say or have my words filled in for me.

STEP 4

In the graphics below, find the mind pattern that you chose and proceed to the indicated page for a more detailed description.

If this description does not seem like you, revisit your previous choices or refer to the mind-pattern chart on page 53, and see if there is a mind pattern that fits you better. Often it is helpful to read through the chart and then observe yourself over the next couple of days with this context in mind. You may have insight into what sequence supports your mind to focus, sort, and open most effectively.

Visual, Auditory, and Kinesthetic
VAK PATTERN

V1		FOCUSED THINKING	To Trigger Concentration: VISUAL
A2		SORTING THINKING	To Trigger Sorting: AUDITORY
K3		OPEN THINKING	To Trigger Imagination: KINESTHETIC

PROCEED TO PAGE 43 ➤

Visual, Kinesthetic, and Auditory
VKA PATTERN

V1		FOCUSED THINKING	To Trigger Concentration: VISUAL
K2		SORTING THINKING	To Trigger Sorting: KINESTHETIC
A3		OPEN THINKING	To Trigger Imagination: AUDITORY

PROCEED TO PAGE 44 ➤

Kinesthetic, Auditory, and Visual
KAV PATTERN

K1		FOCUSED THINKING	To Trigger Concentration: KINESTHETIC
A2		SORTING THINKING	To Trigger Sorting: AUDITORY
V3		OPEN THINKING	To Trigger Imagination: VISUAL

PROCEED TO PAGE 46 ➤

Kinesthetic, Visual, and Auditory
KVA PATTERN

K1		FOCUSED THINKING	To Trigger Concentration: KINESTHETIC
V2		SORTING THINKING	To Trigger Sorting: VISUAL
A3		OPEN THINKING	To Trigger Imagination: AUDITORY

PROCEED TO PAGE 48 ➤

Auditory, Visual, and Kinesthetic
AVK PATTERN

A1		FOCUSED THINKING	To Trigger Concentration: AUDITORY
V2		SORTING THINKING	To Trigger Sorting: VISUAL
K3		OPEN THINKING	To Trigger Imagination: KINESTHETIC

PROCEED TO PAGE 50 ➤

Auditory, Kinesthetic, and Visual
AKV PATTERN

A1		FOCUSED THINKING	To Trigger Concentration: AUDITORY
K2		SORTING THINKING	To Trigger Sorting: KINESTHETIC
V3		OPEN THINKING	To Trigger Imagination: VISUAL

PROCEED TO PAGE 51 ➤

Characteristics of the VAK Pattern

Visual, Auditory, and Kinesthetic		
VAK PATTERN		
V1	FOCUSED THINKING	To Trigger Concentration: VISUAL
A2	SORTING THINKING	To Trigger Sorting: AUDITORY
K3	OPEN THINKING	To Trigger Imagination: KINESTHETIC

You naturally "show and tell." You enjoy looking at possibilities—flipping through catalogs, going window-shopping or people-watching—and talking to yourself or someone else about what you see. You make steady eye contact and create a visual impression with the clothes you wear, which are usually quite colorful and well coordinated. You habitually are attracted to anything in print—novels, billboards, even cereal boxes. You can keep masses of visual details stored in your mind and remember them easily. Your feelings are written all over your face. In fact, by looking at your face, others may know how you feel before you are even aware of it.

Your words express a lot of energy and are often very persuasive, selling or building a case for something. You characteristically teach by telling stories in great detail and using many metaphors to paint pictures for your listener, with your hands emphasizing important points you have just made. When you speak, you use visual vocabulary—words such as "see," "look," "colorful," "show," and "bright," and phrases such as "I can see your point" and "see you later." You often use fillers, such as "um," "like," or "you know," between thoughts.

Your Natural Gifts and Strengths
- Whatever you do, underneath it, you are teaching or selling.
- You illustrate ideas with stories.
- You write things logically.
- You have excellent visual recall—for faces, what someone was wearing, what something looked like.
- You can work at visual tasks for long periods of time.
- You're good at weaving stories that are inspiring or motivating to others.
- You can hear the whole meaning as well as details in a conversation.

Your Challenges
- You may be numb to the sensations in your body and have a diminished felt sense of aliveness—i.e., you live "in your head."
- You have to do a physical action over and over in order to learn it.
- Touch is not casual for you.
- You can become numb to how you are feeling if you are visually engaged for a long period of time.

Characteristics of the VKA Pattern

Visual, Kinesthetic, and Auditory VKA PATTERN			
V1		FOCUSED THINKING	To Trigger Concentration: VISUAL
K2		SORTING THINKING	To Trigger Sorting: KINESTHETIC
A3		OPEN THINKING	To Trigger Imagination: AUDITORY

People are often struck right away by your visual meticulousness. By nature, you are someone who can immediately spot the single typo in the hundred-page report. How you look is extremely important to you; you want your clothes, body, possessions, and surroundings to match an inner image you are trying to create. You connect with others most easily by making eye contact. You can maintain it steadily but may have to close your eyes or move to listen in depth. You instinctively feel what you see.

You usually have pent-up energy right beneath the surface and so physical activity tends to be an important emotional outlet for you. You may be a voracious reader, unless you were taught to read phonetically, in which case you might stick to magazines or newspapers. You may like to take copious notes in meetings to stay engaged.

In large groups, you can be rather quiet. With one or two peers or in small groups, however, you can be very talkative, jumping from topic to topic. It is typical for you to ask a lot of questions. People may often tell you to "get to the point," because you may make connections in your speech that may not be understandable to the listener. Gesturing, moving, or touching is essential to help you find your words.

You use lots of visual vocabulary—words that paint images and phrases that include "look," "see," "show," "imagine," "I can picture that," or "see you soon."

Your Natural Gifts and Strengths
- You have excellent eye-hand and eye-body coordination.
- You remember easily what you have seen or read.
- You can recall faces but not necessarily names.
- You are easily aware of your feelings and the sensations in your body.
- You pick up the feelings and sensations that are being experienced by others around you.
- You might be physically active.

- You have legible handwriting, good spelling, and proofreading ability.
- You may like to draw and design things in detail.
- It is easy to write almost word for word what you hear.
- You prefer working in groups or on teams rather than independently.
- You hear the whole meaning of something rather than specifics.

Your Challenges

- You don't like to speak spontaneously to large groups of people.
- Words can take a long time to access.
- You dislike having words filled in by others.
- You may find it difficult to concentrate when required to listen for long periods or when asked questions about the details of what you've heard.

Characteristics of the KAV Pattern

Kinesthetic, Auditory, and Visual KAV PATTERN			
K1		FOCUSED THINKING	To Trigger Concentration: KINESTHETIC
A2		SORTING THINKING	To Trigger Sorting: AUDITORY
V3		OPEN THINKING	To Trigger Imagination: VISUAL

You are very active in your body and may have shy, sensitive eyes. When given a chance, you most likely prefer to be in constant motion. Even when sitting, you are rarely still. Your preference is to relate to the world first in some tangible way—through action or touch. You may be a well-coordinated "natural" athlete, who seems to have an endless supply of physical energy.

Physical comfort is quite important to you. You may go to great lengths to choose the clothes that feel just right, as opposed to how they look. Touch comes easily; it is a casual but important way for you to connect. Your facial expression doesn't typically show how you feel; rather, your body speaks by how you stand, move, or touch.

You may use a lot of kinesthetic vocabulary—words and phrases that describe action or feeling, such as "getting a feel for," "how does that grab you?" or "I can't get a handle on it." You might end a conversation with "catch you later" or "let's get together soon," and you frequently use kinesthetic metaphors when you speak: "Let's go for the whole enchilada."

Your Natural Gifts and Strengths
- You have physical stamina.
- You are a competent hands-on "doer," who prefers to be on your feet and in action.
- You do things in a logical and systematic manner. Movements are strong, steady, direct, and precise.
- You enjoy telling stories of what you've done, how you did it, and how it felt to do it.
- You see the whole of something.
- You're able to access and verbalize body sensations in a specific, organized way. You can tell exactly where your head hurts or which muscle in your leg is pulled.
- You like to work with your hands—for example, tinkering with cars, working with wood or crafts.
- You are skilled at teaching people how to do things, since translating action into words is easy.
- You may be keenly interested in how things work, from complex machines to the human body.

Your Challenges

- You're overwhelmed by too much eye contact or visuals, such as detailed visual diagrams or instructions.
- You need to move and jiggle; you may have trouble sitting still for long periods of time.
- Casual touch, which comes naturally to you, may be offensive to others.
- "Nasty" looks—glances that indicate judgment or criticism—can be more painful than physical or verbal punishments.

Characteristics of the KVA Pattern

Kinesthetic, Visual, and Auditory KVA PATTERN			
K1		**FOCUSED THINKING**	To Trigger Concentration: KINESTHETIC
V2		**SORTING THINKING**	To Trigger Sorting: VISUAL
A3		**OPEN THINKING**	To Trigger Imagination: AUDITORY

You are soft-spoken and private, with a grounded physical presence. You may be interested in seemingly diverse things: football and art, for instance, or sewing and chemistry. You instinctively search for how things come together or can be integrated.

It's easy for you to be aware of the specific sensations in your body. You know very clearly, for instance, if a shirt tag is rubbing your neck. You tend to choose clothes that are comfortable and allow freedom of movement. If you are in a group, you will often look for a quiet place to sit back, watch, and listen. Commonly labeled "shy," you enjoy working or playing alone or with one close friend and many times find it easier to relate to animals or nature than to people. Your eyes glaze over if you listen to too many words, and your facial expression usually goes flat when you speak. You frequently use kinesthetic vocabulary, words that convey action or feelings, like "trying to get a feel for this" or "need to get a handle on it" or "I'll be in touch soon."

Your Natural Gifts and Strengths

- You're a deep listener and ask large questions to evoke the whole of what is being said.
- You do things logically and systematically.
- You can visualize a three-dimensional image with your eyes open, such as imagining a giraffe from any angle.
- You are able to see things from many perspectives, including the validity of many sides of an issue.
- You can see the whole of something as well as its details.
- You hear the whole of something, such as harmonies.
- You can spend long periods being physically active.
- You may have good eye-hand coordination and like working with your hands and creating in three dimensions. You're easily able to put things together, sometimes in very creative ways.
- You can acquire new physical skills with ease.

Your Challenges

- You don't speak comfortably in a detailed way to large groups of people.
- Words may take a long time to access; you dislike having your words filled in by others.
- You can get overwhelmed by too much conversation.
- You're very sensitive to tones of voice.

Characteristics of the AVK Pattern

Auditory, Visual, and Kinesthetic AVK PATTERN		
A1	FOCUSED THINKING	To Trigger Concentration: AUDITORY
V2	SORTING THINKING	To Trigger Sorting: VISUAL
K3	OPEN THINKING	To Trigger Imagination: KINESTHETIC

You are often considered "smart" because you can easily verbalize what you think and keep up with the pace of any conversation. Your words naturally pour out in logical order without hesitation. You tend to speak in statements rather than questions. The content of your speech is detailed and specific. Saying something precisely is very important to you. You may love verbal humor, are fascinated with language, and can often learn to speak other languages with ease. Most likely you enjoy explaining, debating, discussing, and arguing about almost anything. You may frequently use words and phrases such as "hear," "say," "sounds like," "understand," "that rings a bell," "let's play it by ear," and "talk to you soon."

Your Natural Gifts and Strengths
- You can explain ideas verbally.
- You're good at giving speeches, verbal reports, or participating in discussions of all sorts.
- You see the big picture and the details of a project at the same time.
- You remember precisely what was said.

Your Challenges
- You're often shy about expressing feelings or being touched.
- You dislike physical humor, such as tickling or pranks.
- You can have trouble doing hands-on, technical skills.
- You may have a tendency to interrupt others in meetings and monopolize conversations.

Characteristics of the AKV Pattern

Auditory, Kinesthetic, and Visual AKV PATTERN		
A1	FOCUSED THINKING	To Trigger Concentration: AUDITORY
K2	SORTING THINKING	To Trigger Sorting: KINESTHETIC
V3	OPEN THINKING	To Trigger Imagination: VISUAL

You are articulate and have a high degree of physical energy right beneath the surface. You naturally love to take charge and tell everyone else what to do. Your habit is to discuss, argue, or debate anything, tell jokes, and make plays on words. You understand and make verbal inferences easily and respond quickly to questions. You may have a distinctive, one-of-a-kind voice and speak clearly, precisely, and with a lot of energy, feeling, and rhythm. You frequently use words and phrases such as "hear," "say," "sounds like," "that rings a bell," "let's play it by ear," and "talk to you soon."

You perhaps are able to repeat what you've heard word-for-word, in tape-recorder fashion. This includes poetry, song lyrics, rhymes, and jokes. You can have strong feelings and opinions, which you readily express verbally.

You seem to have an endless supply of physical energy. You easily learn physical movement, even if given only verbal instructions. You can be very particular about the visual images you choose—movies, television shows, and room decorations—since you are deeply influenced by what you see.

Your Natural Gifts and Strengths

- You are a natural leader and coach and love to tell others what to do.
- You see the whole of something.
- You may be a great visionary thinker.
- You're great at giving speeches, verbal reports, or participating in discussions of all sorts.
- You can easily teach someone else what to do, without hesitation.

Your Challenges

- You might have trouble listening and may interrupt others, especially if you are feeling a lot of excitement.
- You can come across as sarcastic.
- You prefer a low amount of visual input and dislike detailed writing, diagrams, or instructions.
- You may have a great deal of pent-up energy right beneath the surface.

CHART OF THE SIX MIND PATTERNS

VAK

1. Focused	**FOCUSED THINKING** *To Trigger Concentration:* VISUAL
2. Sorting	**SORTING THINKING** *To Trigger Sorting:* AUDITORY
3. Open	**OPEN THINKING** *To Trigger Imagination:* KINESTHETIC
Easiest Way to Learn	**1.** See **2.** Hear **3.** Experience
Easiest Way to Express	**1.** Show **2.** Say **3.** Do
Language Attributes	• To make a decision, I prefer to talk both sides through with someone else. • I frequently use metaphors when I speak and prefer to share the entire story of an experience.
Visual Attributes	• The first thing I recall of a person or place is the way something or someone looked. • I'd prefer to write a report rather than do an oral presentation or make a model. • The best way for me to organize is to make a list. • I like to make direct and steady eye contact with the person I'm talking to. • I'm highly aware of the way I look to other people. • I can multitask visually: I can read and watch TV at the same time. • I tend to be critical of how things look.
Physical Attributes	• I can naturally sit still for long periods of time. • It's challenging for me to do a physical activity in a sequential or regimented way. • When doing something physical, I prefer to go at my own speed (whether fast or slow). • I don't like casual physical touch. • I'm very sensitive to touch, and it can have a very long-lasting effect.
Natural Traits	Underneath whatever I am doing, I am teaching or selling.
Frustrations	I may have difficulty doing things in a sequential order.
"Spaces Out"	With touch.

VKA

1. Focused	**FOCUSED THINKING** *To Trigger Concentration:* VISUAL
2. Sorting	**SORTING THINKING** *To Trigger Sorting:* KINESTHETIC
3. Open	**OPEN THINKING** *To Trigger Imagination:* AUDITORY
Easiest Way to Learn	1. See **2.** Experience **3.** Hear
Easiest Way to Express	1. Show **2.** Do **3.** Say
Language Attributes	• I naturally like quiet or music I choose and am very sensitive to sounds. • I prefer to take more time to think about what I am going to say. • Words and tone of voice can be profound and have a long-lasting effect. • I have a fear of interruption and will avoid verbal confrontation. • I prefer not to be told what to say or have my words filled in for me.
Visual Attributes	• The first thing I recall of a person or place is the way something or someone looked. • I'd prefer to write a report rather than do an oral presentation or make a model. • The best way for me to organize is to make a list. • I like to make direct and steady eye contact with the person I'm talking to. • I'm highly aware of the way I look to other people. • I can multitask visually: I can read and watch TV at the same time. • I tend to be critical of how things look.
Physical Attributes	• I know what I am feeling in my body with my eyes open. • I have lots of pent-up energy right below the surface.
Natural Traits	I create networks between people.
Frustrations	I may have difficulty knowing what I feel and want.
"Spaces Out"	With long verbal explanations.

KAV

1. Focused	**FOCUSED THINKING** *To Trigger Concentration:* KINESTHETIC
2. Sorting	**SORTING THINKING** *To Trigger Sorting:* AUDITORY
3. Open	**OPEN THINKING** *To Trigger Imagination:* VISUAL
Easiest Way to Learn	1. Experience 2. Hear 3. See
Easiest Way to Express	1. Do 2. Say 3. Show
Language Attributes	• To make a decision, I prefer to talk both sides through with someone else. • I frequently use metaphors when I speak and prefer to share the entire story of an experience.
Visual Attributes	• I prefer a low amount of visual information—e.g., bullet points rather than long paragraphs. • I get overwhelmed with too much visual detail. • I've had to train myself to make ongoing eye contact. • The way someone looks at me can have a very long-lasting effect. • I don't like people telling me what to look at.
Physical Attributes	• I prefer to be on my feet or moving around. A stand-up desk would really help me. • I prefer to share an experience or make a model as a presentation. • The best way for me to organize is by making piles. • I can easily recall what I did and the physical sensations of an experience. • My natural preference is to start hands-on and experiment by doing. • I can multitask kinesthetically: I can do two or three things at the same time. • I tend to be critical of how things are done.
Natural Traits	Being hands-on is natural to me.
Frustrations	I can have difficulty sitting still and looking at complex information.
"Spaces Out"	When looking at detailed information.

KVA

1. Focused		**FOCUSED THINKING** *To Trigger Concentration:* KINESTHETIC
2. Sorting		**SORTING THINKING** *To Trigger Sorting:* VISUAL
3. Open		**OPEN THINKING** *To Trigger Imagination:* AUDITORY
Easiest Way to Learn	**1.** Experience **2.** See **3.** Hear	
Easiest Way to Express	**1.** Do **2.** Show **3.** Say	
Language Attributes	• I naturally like quiet or music I choose and am very sensitive to sounds. • I prefer to take more time to think about what I am going to say. • Words and tone of voice can be profound and have a long-lasting effect. • I have a fear of interruption and will avoid verbal confrontation. • I prefer not to be told what to say or have my words filled in for me.	
Visual Attributes	• I can easily see three-dimensional images in my mind with my eyes open and view these from various angles—above, behind, and sideways. • I prefer to look at the person I am talking to and then look around.	
Physical Attributes	• I prefer to be on my feet or moving around. A stand-up desk would really help me. • I prefer to share an experience or make a model as a presentation. • The best way for me to organize is by making piles. • I can easily recall what I did and the physical sensations of an experience. • My natural preference is to start hands-on and experiment by doing. • I can multitask kinesthetically: I can do two or three things at the same time. • I tend to be critical of how things are done.	
Natural Traits	Is a great lover of nature, especially animals. Has many dissimilar interests (e.g., drawing and ice hockey). Wants to unite dissimilar elements.	
Frustrations	May have difficulty expressing feelings in words.	
"Spaces Out"	With long verbal explanations.	

AVK

1. Focused	FOCUSED THINKING *To Trigger Concentration:* AUDITORY
2. Sorting	SORTING THINKING *To Trigger Sorting:* VISUAL
3. Open	OPEN THINKING *To Trigger Imagination:* KINESTHETIC
Easiest Way to Learn	1. Hear 2. See 3. Experience
Easiest Way to Express	1. Say 2. Show 3. Do
Language Attributes	• I'm comfortable with talking to large groups of people even without advance preparation. • I prefer to give verbal reports rather than do a visual presentation or make a model. • I naturally remember what's said in a conversation. • I speak without pause (no "um"s) and use precise language. • Words flow out easily in logical order without thinking about it. • I can multitask auditorily: I can talk with one person and listen to someone else in the background at the same time. • I tend to be critical of how things are said.
Visual Attributes	• I can easily see three-dimensional images in my mind with my eyes open and view these from various angles—above, behind, and sideways. • I prefer to look at the person I am talking to and then look around.
Physical Attributes	• I can naturally sit still for long periods of time. • It's challenging for me to do a physical activity in a sequential or regimented way. • When doing something physical, I prefer to go at my own speed (whether fast or slow). • I don't like casual physical touch. • I'm very sensitive to touch, and it can have a very long-lasting effect.
Natural Traits	I am naturally good at lecturing, debating, and articulating ideas in a logical way.
Frustrations	I may have difficulty with sequential hands-on tasks or movement.
"Spaces Out"	With touch.

AKV

1. Focused	**FOCUSED THINKING** *To Trigger Concentration:* AUDITORY
2. Sorting	**SORTING THINKING** *To Trigger Sorting:* KINESTHETIC
3. Open	**OPEN THINKING** *To Trigger Imagination:* VISUAL
Easiest Way to Learn	1. Hear 2. Experience 3. See
Easiest Way to Express	1. Say 2. Do 3. Show
Language Attributes	• I'm comfortable talking to large groups of people even without advance preparation. • I prefer to give verbal reports rather than do a visual presentation or make a model. • I naturally remember what's said in a conversation. • I speak without pause (no "um"s) and use precise language. • Words flow out easily in logical order without thinking about it. • I can multitask auditorily: I can talk with one person and listen to someone else in the background at the same time. • I tend to be critical of how things are said.
Visual Attributes	• I prefer a low amount of visual information—e.g., bullet points rather than long paragraphs. • I get overwhelmed with too much visual detail. • I've had to train myself to make ongoing eye contact. • The way someone looks at me can have a very long-lasting effect. • I don't like people telling me what to look at.
Physical Attributes	• I know what I am feeling in my body with my eyes open. • I have lots of pent-up energy right below the surface.
Natural Traits	I naturally give direction and motivate people by speeches.
Frustrations	I get frustrated when I listen without talking and read a lot of visuals.
"Spaces Out"	With too many things to look at.

WHY DO MIND PATTERNS MATTER?

The text pinged on my phone at 2:30 A.M., while I was captured in the bubble of writing this book. "I'm desperate! This is the only time I have to think by myself! Will you help me?" It was from Maria, a famous country-and-western singer married to an equally famous record producer. They had three kids between them, ranging in age from three to twenty-three, and she had recently founded a global education foundation. She had been referred to me by another client, who described her as "a hungry mind who had a frantic heart and a disorganized life." It was the first time she had reached out to me directly, so I decided to respond. We texted back and forth for over an hour. She wrote that her time was so filled with other people telling her what they needed and what she should do that she wasn't sure she had an opinion or identity of her own anymore. I was both captivated by her need to own her life and curious about why she was more comfortable writing than speaking on the phone.

We decided to meet at her home outside Nashville a few weeks later. When I arrived at the sprawling Tudor estate, I was introduced to Maria's two assistants, three nannies, a "manny," a cook, a sister, and a bodyguard. The kids, two barking dogs, and a hissing cat were running in and out of the huge kitchen. One assistant closed the door to Maria's office behind me. I wandered around, searching for prompts to Maria's mind pattern. The first things that stood out were floor-to-ceiling columns of well-worn nonfiction books, arranged neatly by color. Being in someone's office is often very much like being inside his or her brain.

The first thing I noticed when Maria entered was how impeccably she was dressed. She put a hand on each of my shoulders and stared directly into my eyes, then enfolded me in the elegance of her long thin arms without saying a word. As we sat down at a large white lacquered conference table, she didn't take her eyes off me, even when she sipped tea from a delicate gold-rimmed porcelain cup. Her blue eyes were like the headlights of a car, leading her attention. It wasn't too much of a stretch to guess that her mind was very strong visually: the neatness of everything, the way she used color to organize her world, her laserlike eye contact.

She spoke in a chaotic web of questions, jumping from her children, to her husband, to a gown she had to wear to a gala, then back to the children. None of it was sequential or organized. All of it was inspirational. When she listened to me respond to one of her questions, her pupils dilated, her facial muscles flattened, and she spaced out.

I only partially attended to the content of what she was saying. Mostly I let my own mind go wide enough to notice the clues she was giving when her mind was focused and when it opened. I began to play with the idea that she was visually focused and auditorily open.

I then looked for the effect kinesthetic input had on her thinking. As she spoke about the complexity of her life, her hands led her words, like those of an orchestra conductor. When they stopped moving or touching something, she stopped talking. She grabbed objects and played with them, her words swinging from one question to another. These cues led me to infer that her mind used the VKA pattern of processing information.

"Can you help?" Maria pleaded. "My life is driving *me*! What should I do?"

I exhaled slowly, audibly, to slow both of us down; then I explained that I could not tell her what to do but I would help her discover how to shift the gears of her own mind so she could feel in charge of her life and navigate in the direction she truly wanted to go. I explained how learning to operate one's mind was exactly like learning to drive a finely tuned sports car. Most people were used to driving a car that shifted automatically, but learning how to change the gears of your attention gave you access to its true capacity.

Maria threw her head back, laughing, and explained that she actually loved racing cars and had a silver Porsche in the garage. I suggested we continue to think together while she drove. It wasn't only that I wanted the thrill of riding in the luxurious 911. I needed to verify my assumptions about her mind pattern. I also wanted to notice what effect focusing on the road instead of on other people had on her.

As we walked to the car, I explained that learning to drive your own mind involved learning the component skills first: using the clutch, monitoring the tachometer before shifting, et cetera. Eventually it would all come together in an understanding of how to drive her own life. Once she could do that, she'd also learn to read others and develop rapport with them, just as she was able to navigate smoothly between and around other cars on a racetrack.

Maria became more alive behind the wheel. Her eyes flashed and the engine growled as the Porsche clung to the curves of the open, winding road. "This is where I can *really* think," she shouted. I asked her what it was about driving like this that made thinking possible. Without hesitation, she explained that when she was in motion, her eyes on the road, with no one "yammering" at her, she felt as if she was living from the inside out. "Songs just pop into my mind and I'm totally relaxed." We were quiet for a few minutes, and then she began to sing a song. The chorus ended with the words "My life is for me. My life *is* for me!" Her cheeks were wet with tears.

Back in the office, I explained the pattern her mind used to metabolize information: visual first—seeing clearly where she was as well as where she wanted to go; kinesthetic second—turning the steering wheel while choosing the speed so she could move at her own pace; and auditory third—listening to the white noise of the engine, which enabled her to hear her inner voice (VKA).

She confided how difficult it was for her to sit still in meetings; how challenging it was to organize her days around the things that really mattered to her; how shy she felt when she had to give a speech; how hard it was for her to trust that people weren't taking advantage of her. She asked me if I really thought she could learn to shift the gears of her attention and drive her mind the way she did her Porsche. I put an arm around her shoulders and said,

"Buckle your seat belt, darlin'. This is going to be a very interesting ride!"

In the sessions that followed, I helped Maria create an operating manual for herself, based on her mind pattern, so she could impose coherence and order on her life. She used this to balance her career, her complex family-juggling act, and her philanthropic work. The events of her life didn't change, only how she responded to them.

Before

As soon as Maria checks her email at the office, she is faced with urgent messages about three critical projects, each saying that strategic decisions have to be made before the end of the day. A quick look at her calendar shows a completely full schedule, and she realizes that she will need to stay until midnight if she wants to get it all done, which leaves no time for her kids or an important event with her husband.

The business manager comes into her office and sits down before she's had a chance to respond to any emails. He slaps down next year's financials for her to evaluate and starts asking questions about bookings, insisting loudly that he needs her help. After an hour with him, trying to make critical decisions while he pelts her with questions, Maria slams the door shut and thinks to herself that she needs to replace him with someone who can work more independently. But she doesn't have time to think about that now. Her assistant tells her that the next meeting starts in five minutes. Maria realizes she hasn't looked over her PowerPoint presentation to prepare for the meeting. It's only ten-thirty in the morning, but she's already exhausted and overwhelmed.

After

Maria arrives at the office, closes the door, and puts up a large red sign that reads: PLEASE DO NOT ENTER. She sets the hands on the sign's cardboard clock for forty-five minutes. She sits down in a swivel chair and writes down in a small leather notebook the things that are most important to her (visual-1). She walks over to her stand-up desk and neatly makes three piles of paper, sorting the projects that await her attention (kinesthetic-2). She decides to review the PowerPoint presentation for a half hour but first calls her assistant and asks her to scan emails for anything urgent. She puts on headphones to listen to music that will help her generate new ideas (auditory-3), closes her eyes, and imagines the meeting she'll have at ten-thirty, running through it in her mind. When an idea comes to her, she scribbles it on a whiteboard (visual-1, kinesthetic-2). After ten minutes, she opens the PowerPoint to review it and add the new ideas (visual-1).

When her door opens at the appointed time and her manager comes in and slaps down the budget, Maria stands and paces to dispel stress (kinesthetic-2). She tells him to meet her in the cafeteria in a half hour to review the budget together after he has independently highlighted the key decision points for her (visual-1). She has suggested this because she knows a change in location to where they can sit side by side (kinesthetic-2), will help her both listen and ask questions (auditory-3). After he leaves, she shifts her mind into neutral for several minutes by staring out the window (visual-1), noticing her breath (kinesthetic-2), and absorbing the silence (auditory-3), so she can relax and open her mind to prepare for what comes next.

By noticing what she needed to help her attention focus (looking and writing), sort (moving, feeling her body and breath), and open (listening and talking, playing music, or singing to herself), Maria drove through her days with a minimum of interference and a maximum of inspiration and influence.

This might sound as complex as hearing someone describe which muscles they use to stand up, but let's personalize it so it will begin to become a global skill for you. Below are guidelines for using your mind pattern to shift your state of attention, in order to better confront a challenge or situation you're faced with.

Each state of attention is effective for different types of thinking. Here are some examples of situations where knowing when to shift from one to the other can increase your effectiveness immensely.

Shift to focused attention when you:
- Are at a meeting and need to concentrate on specifics.
- Have to do an important task that requires detailed thinking.
- Are making a presentation and really want to get your point across.
- Have a tight deadline and need to plow through a task.
- Are organizing or sequencing tasks or events.

Shift to sorting attention when you:
- Need to make an important decision.
- Find your thinking stuck and recognize you are going around and around with a problem.
- Want to be open and receptive to someone else's input.
- Notice that your thinking is getting too rigid or righteous.
- Feel that you are losing someone else's attention.

Shift to open attention when you:
- Are trying to come up with a new creative approach, idea, or product.
- Want to get in touch with what's really important to you.
- Want to access your intuition and insights.
- Need an "aha!" moment.
- Feel stressed, need to relax, or need a time-out.
- Wish to gain a wider perspective. Notice the forest instead of the trees.
- Are trying to remember something.
- Need to rely on your wisdom.
- Find yourself shutting down.

Here is how knowing your mind pattern will help you make these shifts.

Shifting from Focused to Open

In general, when you want to generate new and creative ideas, connect with other people, figure out what's important to you, or just relax, follow the 1-2-3 sequence of your mind pattern.

Visual, Auditory, and Kinesthetic VAK PATTERN		
V1	FOCUSED THINKING	To Trigger Concentration: VISUAL
A2	SORTING THINKING	To Trigger Sorting: AUDITORY
K3	OPEN THINKING	To Trigger Imagination: KINESTHETIC

If your mind uses the VAK pattern: First notice visual details, then listen to sounds around you, and then feel the overall sensations in your body.

Visual, Kinesthetic, and Auditory VKA PATTERN		
V1	FOCUSED THINKING	To Trigger Concentration: VISUAL
K2	SORTING THINKING	To Trigger Sorting: KINESTHETIC
A3	OPEN THINKING	To Trigger Imagination: AUDITORY

If your mind uses the VKA pattern: First notice visual details, then move slowly or touch something, and then listen to soothing sounds around you.

Kinesthetic, Auditory, and Visual KAV PATTERN		
K1	FOCUSED THINKING	To Trigger Concentration: KINESTHETIC
A2	SORTING THINKING	To Trigger Sorting: AUDITORY
V3	OPEN THINKING	To Trigger Imagination: VISUAL

If your mind uses the KAV pattern: First move or play with something interesting in your hand, then listen to sounds around you, and then gaze openly into space.

Kinesthetic, Visual, and Auditory KVA PATTERN		
K1	FOCUSED THINKING	To Trigger Concentration: KINESTHETIC
V2	SORTING THINKING	To Trigger Sorting: VISUAL
A3	OPEN THINKING	To Trigger Imagination: AUDITORY

If your mind uses the KVA pattern: First move or touch something, then look around, and then listen to soothing sounds or silence.

Auditory, Visual, and Kinesthetic AVK PATTERN		
A1	FOCUSED THINKING	To Trigger Concentration: AUDITORY
V2	SORTING THINKING	To Trigger Sorting: VISUAL
K3	OPEN THINKING	To Trigger Imagination: KINESTHETIC

If your mind uses the AVK pattern: First listen to sounds or to your breathing, then look around, and then notice the overall sensations of your body or something you are holding.

Auditory, Kinesthetic, and Visual AKV PATTERN		
A1	FOCUSED THINKING	To Trigger Concentration: AUDITORY
K2	SORTING THINKING	To Trigger Sorting: KINESTHETIC
V3	OPEN THINKING	To Trigger Imagination: VISUAL

If your mind uses the AKV pattern: First listen to sounds or to your breathing, then move or touch something, and then gaze openly into space.

Shifting from Open to Focused

When you want to organize your thoughts and become more sharp and alert to complete a task, follow the sequence 3-2-1 to shift your state of attention from open to focused.

Visual, Auditory, and Kinesthetic VAK PATTERN		
V1	FOCUSED THINKING	To Trigger Concentration: VISUAL
A2	SORTING THINKING	To Trigger Sorting: AUDITORY
K3	OPEN THINKING	To Trigger Imagination: KINESTHETIC

If your mind uses the VAK pattern: First move your body, then talk, and then bring your attention to visual details or write something.

Visual, Kinesthetic, and Auditory VKA PATTERN		
V1	FOCUSED THINKING	To Trigger Concentration: VISUAL
K2	SORTING THINKING	To Trigger Sorting: KINESTHETIC
A3	OPEN THINKING	To Trigger Imagination: AUDITORY

If your mind uses the VKA pattern: First talk or sing, to yourself or aloud, then adjust your physical position or walk around, and then write or doodle something.

Kinesthetic, Auditory, and Visual KAV PATTERN		
K1	FOCUSED THINKING	To Trigger Concentration: KINESTHETIC
A2	SORTING THINKING	To Trigger Sorting: AUDITORY
V3	OPEN THINKING	To Trigger Imagination: VISUAL

If your mind uses the KAV pattern: First look around, then talk or sing or whistle, and then take action.

Kinesthetic, Visual, and Auditory **KVA PATTERN**		
K1	FOCUSED THINKING	To Trigger Concentration: KINESTHETIC
V2	SORTING THINKING	To Trigger Sorting: VISUAL
A3	OPEN THINKING	To Trigger Imagination: AUDITORY

If your mind uses the KVA pattern: First ask yourself a question or sing to yourself, then look around, and then take action.

Auditory, Visual, and Kinesthetic **AVK PATTERN**		
A1	FOCUSED THINKING	To Trigger Concentration: AUDITORY
V2	SORTING THINKING	To Trigger Sorting: VISUAL
K3	OPEN THINKING	To Trigger Imagination: KINESTHETIC

If your mind uses the AVK pattern: First move or touch something, then look around or write something, and then talk or sing out loud.

Auditory, Kinesthetic, and Visual **AKV PATTERN**		
A1	FOCUSED THINKING	To Trigger Concentration: AUDITORY
K2	SORTING THINKING	To Trigger Sorting: KINESTHETIC
V3	OPEN THINKING	To Trigger Imagination: VISUAL

If your mind uses the AKV pattern: First look around, then move or adjust position, and then talk or sing aloud.

BREAKTHROUGH PRACTICE: SHIFTING FROM STUCK TO THINKING FREE

Imagine that you are in the midst of walking from one meeting to the next, your mind filled with commitments, to-do's, and decisions to be made. You haven't yet processed all that came out of the last meeting, let alone prepared for the next. Suddenly someone comes behind you and clutches your wrist. Where does your attention go?

Most people immediately redirect their attention to where they are being grabbed. They try to pull away. The harder they are grabbed, the harder they resist. What if, in that startling moment, you were to ask yourself a question: "What percentage of my body is actually stuck right now?" You most likely will calculate that it is about two percent. Now ask yourself a second question: "What percentage of my body is free?" At this point, you'll realize that 98 percent of your body is free. By shifting your attention to notice that 98 percent, you will expand your awareness to the many options that are available to you: You can move your other hand, move your feet, rotate your torso, bend at the waist, et cetera. By simply asking yourself, "Where am I free?" rather than focusing on where you are stuck, you shift your attention from stuck to free, from closed to open.

If you are stuck in your thinking, opening the visual, auditory, and kinesthetic elements will shift your attention to where there are more possibilities, as Maria did in the story above. This expanded state will enable you to create new connections between ideas and people that were hidden just seconds before.

Recognizing your mind pattern also liberates you from old stories that have limited you: "I'm not smart enough," "I'm a terrible speaker," "I'm shy," "I'm an introvert," or "I'm a klutz." Take a moment to reconsider the assumptions you have made about yourself. What could be different, what could set you free if you opened your attention? In the story that follows, Angie describes how recognizing her KVA mind pattern dissolved many of her self-limiting beliefs and liberated a huge amount of innate ability:

I graduated from one of Canada's Ivy League universities, clutching a diploma that had taken every ounce of determination for me to attain. I despised memorization. School had seemed irrelevant, boring, and too structured. What I wanted was adventure, so I could finally feel free. I wanted to follow what interested me.

I packed my bags and went to the war zone in Saudi Arabia in search of adventure. I supported myself by teaching English to Saudi women, photographing diseases for doctors' records, and processing endless procurement forms at the U.S. Army base. I spent my weekends giving swimming lessons and selling my desert photographs to soldiers. At night, as Operation Desert Storm lingered on, I sat holding my embassy-issued gas mask while listening to the voices on TV droning, "This is a Scud missile alert . . . this is a Scud missile alert." I remember thinking: Is this really where I want to be? Is this the best I can do? I wasn't scared for my life; rather, I was shaken to the core that this was the life I had chosen to live.

Soon after, I decided any change was better than being stuck in a war zone. I left and spent the next two years roaming the United States and Canada, finally landing in a Utah mountain town, selling real estate. There I met the love of my life—Dave. One of the unusual things about him was that he bragged about his mother on our first date. A few weeks later he asked me to go with him to San Francisco to meet her. As I reached out to shake her hand for the first time, in a crowded restaurant, she responded with a warm embrace. She then stood beside me and out of nowhere asked, "What's inspiring you in your life right now, Angie?" I was taken off guard and recognized this was not an ordinary woman with whom I was going to have an ordinary relationship.

I hemmed and hawed but later that evening responded to her question by pulling out my portfolio of photographs. I showed her all the portraits I had taken in the Middle East. I slowly found my voice as I shared the experiences that surrounded each image. By the end, I overcame my shyness and felt fully engaged and alive. Dawna responded by inviting me to attend a program she was facilitating for the leaders of a dozen companies, at the Royal Dutch Shell Learning Center in Houston. She asked that while she presented the keynote speech, I simultaneously draw images of the central themes and capture key phrases on a wall that was covered in blank newsprint.

At the end of her ninety-minute talk, I looked at the twenty-foot web of images and words that storyboarded what she had presented. To my amazement, throngs of people gathered around it during the break, excitedly discussing ideas. I was shocked to discover that I could recall every word she had said.

Working with Dawna over the past years and teaching intellectual diversity has led me to understand why I had such trouble paying attention at school. Because my mind uses the KVA pattern, auditory information alone spaces me out—it is difficult to focus when I am just listening. Too much auditory input causes me to daydream in images. Since kinesthetic input triggers focused attention for me, standing and moving instead of sitting still keeps me alert. Drawing frees me to connect with the words I hear.

As I write these words, I realize the most rewarding adventure I have been on is discovering how my mind works and enabling others to do the same.

Using the strategy of mind patterns makes what is silent heard and what is hidden apparent. It helps your mind grasp how to "bend the rope" that we described in the introduction and how to shift attention from where you are stuck to where you are free in order to collaborate with the intelligence of others.

CHAPTER SUMMARY

KEY CONCEPTS OF THIS CHAPTER	GUIDELINES
Mind patterns are important for recognizing the diversity of how people think, learn, and communicate.	Consider how you can make adjustments based on your unique mind pattern.
There are three different states of attention that are relevant to how we process information.	Focused attention: Helps you accomplish tasks, attend to details and timelines. Sorting attention: Helps you digest information and think through confusion. Open attention: Helps you imagine possibilities and innovate.
As a culture we tend to overvalue focused attention and devalue the other two states.	To generate more insights and connections, allow your attention to open. To work through confusion and the advantages and disadvantages of multiple options, allow your mind to sort.
There are three languages of thought: visual, kinesthetic (hands-on), and auditory.	These languages of thought cause each of us to shift to a different state of attention.
There are six unique mind patterns, each determined by how the languages of thought shift our attention.	Notice what triggers your mind to shift from focused, to sorting, to open states of attention.
When you know your mind pattern, you can consciously shift your attention state to achieve different desired outcomes.	To shift your attention from focused to open, follow the 1-2-3 sequence of your mind pattern. To shift your attention from open to focused, follow the 3-2-1 sequence of your mind pattern.

RECOGNIZING HOW OTHERS' MINDS WORK

A leader who loses his connection to his people soon loses the ability to lead them.

—Robert Ley

In my fifty years of thinking with people about relationship issues—be they minor misunderstandings or large-scale cultural clashes—I've discovered that one factor rarely if ever considered is the difference in the way the people process information.

There's the engineer who remained silent even though his idea would have averted a multi-million-dollar mistake, because he "couldn't get a word in edgewise" and had been shunned for not "going with the flow" of the majority. There are people whose minds naturally ask big questions—people whom others describe as "wishy-washy." There are those who need to move in order to think, who are dismissed as "jittery and ADHD." And there are those who need to look away in order to see the big picture; others describe them as "shifty and dishonest."

I saw an entire corporate culture shape its communication habits around a "thoughtful and scientific" leader who used the KVA pattern. Every decision was questioned deeply and made in silence or by email. That company eventually merged with another that had shaped its communication habits around *its* powerful and articulate leader, who used the opposite AVK pattern. He insisted that everything be discussed and argued about until there was spoken agreement. The merger, as you can imagine, was a multibillion-dollar disaster that failed very quickly. The analysts' mistaken assumption was that mergers rarely work.

These misunderstandings were because of false assumptions about how different people think, learn, and communicate. In this connected world, we need teams to be smarter, quicker, and more innovative than ever before. Yet when we get stuck while thinking or communicating with someone else, we attribute the difficulty to a lack of capacity, a mental deficit, or a personality trait.

Have you spent time and energy trying to get through to a colleague but instead found yourself frustrated, annoyed, and out of ideas about how to avoid the same negative patterns with them? Can you imagine how much collaborative potential could be released if you eliminated the friction caused by not understanding intellectual diversity?

In this chapter, we shed light on how to start collaborating with those who have different mind patterns. We offer you a tool we have developed that we call the "CQ playbook." It will help you bridge differences and turn the light on, so to speak, when you need to "read" another person or an entire group. As with a football playbook or a musical score, the more you use it, the more instinctual your capacity to create intentional connection will become.

THE CQ PLAYBOOK

Step 1: How Do *You* Think?

Review what you know about your own mind pattern: Consider what you need to focus, sort, and open your thinking. Review what conditions trigger effectiveness and success for you. Use the description of your pattern as your guide.

Step 2: What Has Worked in the Past?

If you will be meeting with a person you know: Identify what has already been successful with him or her. Many clues lie in the language people choose. To identify someone else's mind pattern, begin to notice if he or she frequently uses words like "see," "feel," or "hear." Notice whether she tends to describe the visuals of a scene, the words spoken, or the actions taken and feelings experienced. These are keys to what triggers her focused thinking. How does she respond to detailed visuals or big-picture overviews? Is there a lag before she speaks or an immediate verbal response? How is she affected when you sit next to her versus across from her, when you stand still together at a whiteboard, or if you walk while talking?

If you haven't met with this person before: Begin by presuming collaboration will be possible. Make a crib sheet of things you want to notice. When you first get together, ask the person to tell you about a meeting in the past that was extremely successful, and listen carefully for the conditions that contributed to that success. If you are on the phone, you can say, "I want to make sure this call is worth your while. Before we begin, tell me about a time when a similar call was really effective. What were the conditions that made that possible?" Listen to the responses for clues that you can replicate.

This kind of curiosity will replace the habit of continually concentrating on what the other person's opinion of you might be or what impression *you* are making on him. Instead, your attention will naturally expand.

The following checklist is a quick guide of things to notice about the person you are meeting with:

CQ CHECKLIST

KINESTHETIC (HANDS-ON) FOCUSED	
Prefers to do things with people rather than talk	
Likes to make physical contact—handshake, pat on back, sit close	
Well coordinated in his/her body	
Uses kinesthetic language: "Let's do it," "Hard to grasp," "Get a handle"	
Prefers to be in motion, standing, jiggling, playing with an object	
Recalls action and physical environments easily	
Organizes by piles	
AUDITORY FOCUSED	
Speaks confidently and has extensive vocabulary	
Likes precision in language	
Great verbal recall, little note-taking	
Connects first with words	
Uses auditory phrases: "Talk to you later," "Let's hear the points!"	
VISUALLY FOCUSED	
Steady eye contact	
Likes visual order, lists, and color-coding; visual precision	

Lots of note-taking	
Color-coordinated and well dressed	
Uses the phrases: "See you later," "Looks good," "Show me"	
Gives visual descriptions of experiences	
KINESTHETIC OPEN	
Can sit easily for long periods of time	
Shy about touch	
Rarely talks about action	
Physically still	
Can be awkward physically	
Private about feelings	
AUDITORY OPEN	
May take longer to speak, pauses between thoughts	
Prefers to listen, then asks questions to engage everyone	
May talk in circles or use creative words	
Easily distracted by extraneous noises	
Can space out listening to long verbal explanations	
VISUALLY OPEN	
Looks away frequently, can be eye-shy	
Little or no note-taking	
May not respond to emails, or responds with just a few words	
Dresses for comfort rather than appearance	
Prefers talking or doing to writing	
Can space out if looking at lots of visual details or long emails	

Step 3: What's Your Game Plan?

Once you have used the CQ checklist above to gather this information about the person you want to collaborate with, you will be able to modify your own approach to suit that individual's preferences. It's not necessary to figure out the exact mind pattern of the other person, just to discover as much as you can about what works and what doesn't.

Step 4: What Effect Are You Having?

The most important principle when using this strategy is to *notice the effect you are having in the moment*. This can be challenging, because when we sense a disconnection or a lack of attention from someone else, we tend to assume that it is either because we are "boring" or that the other person is to blame. This narrows our attention and limits what we notice. In fact, it is most likely *how* we are delivering the content that is not working. Step back and consider other ways you could communicate the information to make a connection.

HOW ARE YOU COMMUNICATING?	THEIR RESPONSE	
	Positive	Negative or None
AUDITORY Choice of words Questions asked Tone of voice		
VISUAL Clear visuals Pictures Diagrams		
KINESTHETIC Experience Actions Body language		

Step 5: What Adjustments Can You Make?

This strategy will enable you to become very flexible. Let's take the metaphor of singing in a choir. As soon as you notice that you are slightly off-key in developing resonance, you adjust. In fact, singing with others requires a continual series of micro-adjustments, as does playing on a sports team. You achieve collaborative harmony when you notice the effect of your communications and know ways to adjust accordingly.

The following chart is a guide for transforming a potential breakdown into the possibility of a breakthrough. The first column describes a common impasse that you may encounter with another person. The second column indicates what this breakdown may tell you about the other's mind pattern. The third column suggests adjustments that might bring about more-effective collaboration:

COMMON BREAKDOWN	MIND-PATTERN ANALYSIS	ADJUSTMENT POSSIBILITIES
Talks too much, and mostly over others.	Auditory is strong, and this helps them focus.	Invite them to move in order to open their minds. Write down what they are saying so they will feel heard.
Misses content in email and/or does not bother to re-spond.	Visual triggers open attention, and they become agitated with long emails or too many details.	Make sure the subject line is an action such as "Please re-spond by 3:00 P.M." Offer to follow up with a call to dis-cuss. Keep emails as short as possible. Highlight requested actions.
Doesn't recall what you said.	Auditory triggers open attention.	Make sure you give them time to write what you are saying; send a quick email recapping the conversation.
You feel they are not listening.	Auditory triggers open attention.	Encourage people to stand up in the back during a meet-ing, and ask someone to track the group conversation on a whiteboard.
Talks in circles or stream of consciousness.	Auditory triggers open attention.	Ask them to sketch out what they are saying, or you write it so they can see it and be-come more focused.
Needs to talk to both sides of a situation and seems to vacil-late.	Auditory triggers sorting attention.	Make two columns; ask them to write down the pros and cons.
Visually overloads people with emails, texts, or written infor-mation.	Visual triggers fo-cused attention.	Ask for summary in bullet points, or request visual to be put into two pages—one high level, and one with details.
Seems jittery and anxious to move. They may fiddle a lot while you are talking or showing them something.	Kinesthetic triggers focused attention.	Suggest they get on their feet while you talk, or use flip charts where they can stand and write as the group thinks.
Seems disengaged or spaced out after sev-eral minutes of sitting still.	Kinesthetic triggers focused attention.	Have tactile objects for peo-ple to "play" with during the meeting. Encourage people to move.

Collaborative intelligence requires you to let go of the comfortable and habitual ways you have of thinking with others and allow your mind to open and get curious about how to reconfigure your approach.

PUTTING THE CQ PLAYBOOK INTO USE

Seth was desperately honest with me. "Please fix my two bosses, because the rest of us can't go on like this much longer . . . but we're afraid we'll lose our jobs if we dare say something." I don't know how to "fix" people. Fixing implies that something is broken, and I think of people as unfinished works of art rather than broken machines—but I was intrigued enough to do a little CQ detective work.

I discovered that his bosses, Steve and Joseph, were both brilliant architects, dedicated to the highest level of excellence. They had worked seamlessly together and prospered for ten years, one picking up where the other left off. Steve was a volatile designer who acquired high-profile jobs. Joseph was his total opposite: steady and reliable, a trustworthy leader who knew how to get things done, produced stability, and got dependable results.

It seemed like a perfect combination. So why was Seth suggesting they needed a relational renovation? Their company had been bought two years earlier by one of the world's largest development firms, and that was when the problems began. Seth set up a lunch for me with Joseph and then excused himself halfway through the meal so the two of us could think together privately.

As Joseph spoke, I noticed cues that revealed how he was thinking. The polite, articulate middle-aged man sitting across from me was consistently still in his body, using hand gestures sparingly, only to accentuate what he was saying. He was dressed colorfully and described intricate visual details in the stories he told of the company's history. His face lit up when talking about the rational aspects of their business. There were many "um"s interspersing his words, but he was highly energized as he spoke.

Over coffee, he told me story after story about how erratic Steve had become, how he lashed out verbally and paced during client meetings. Sometimes he didn't show up at all. And his work habits were lazy. "It really makes me nervous," Joseph said, sounding angry rather than anxious as he shared how he had to pick up the slack and carry more than his fair share. When I asked him if he resented this, his jaw tightened and he said he felt overloaded. He confessed that he had lost his sense of partnership with Steve. He attributed that to Steve's "pulling a power play."

I began to doodle on the paper tablecloth and asked Joseph to draw the way he saw the relationship now and the way he wanted it to be in the future. He took the pen and immediately drew two tightly clenched fists, one pointing straight ahead, the other hanging down. Joseph's voice was metallic as he explained that he really wanted to help Steve but he believed that the fracture in their partnership was seeping into every aspect of the business and he was going to have to take over.

I needed to know how open Joseph was to changing his mind about Steve. I asked what behavior told him that Steve was lazy. Joseph grew visibly agitated as he told me that Steve often missed deadlines, and he responded slowly to clients' and the team's emails. "He does call people back," he admitted, "but in our business, no one has time to talk on the phone." When I asked why he thought Steve was so volatile now, Joseph described his restlessness and pacing in team meetings or staring out the windows, barely looking at clients or PowerPoint presentations. "He just doesn't give a damn anymore about what other people think. What can you do to fix this?"

His tone of voice was as much a challenge as a request. It said, "I dare you to answer this!" I didn't think responding verbally would be effective. It would be like trying to place a flower in a fist. I was curious whether using a kinesthetic trigger would open his mind to a new possibility or not. I reached for the wilted orchid plant that sat in the middle of the table and put it into his hands. As he looked down, I said to him, "If this contained the solution to your problem, what would it say about the changes that are needed?"

Joseph got very quiet and shrugged. He just kept turning the pot around and around, looking at it from different angles as if it were a riddle. Then, in an almost tender tone of voice that took me by surprise, he said, "I guess there's still too much life in this to throw it out now."

I summoned all the curiosity I felt at that moment and asked, "Are you willing to let go of your assumptions that something's broken between you and Steve so you can see if it's possible to foster the vitality you once had? Don't answer me too quickly, because this might mean you have to do something very challenging."

"I guess I'm willing, but what will I have to do?" he replied.

"You'll have to change your mind. Are you up for that?" I paused as he smiled and then nodded.

In the silence that followed my question, I felt as if his mind backed up from the cliff it had been ready to drive over, did a U-turn, and slowly began to move forward. That was all we needed to begin using the CQ playbook.

Step 1: How Do You Think? We began by exploring Joseph's mind pattern. Joseph recognized that his mind used visual to focus (V-1), then auditory to sort things out (A-2). He never discussed kinesthetic experiences, because those were unconscious to him, but he did realize how sensitive he was to touch and how rarely he moved, because it "distracted him" when he worked. He preferred to "show and tell." Thus his mind used the VAK pattern to process information.

Step 2: What Has Worked Before? I asked Joseph to think back to the years he and Steve had been in a successful partnership. Interestingly, he picked up the pen and sketched the layout of their previous offices, drawing with great concentration. He said that Steve had designed two desks near each other by the windows and a large conference table in the center, which was filled with architectural models of the projects they were working on. Joseph told me that they used to begin every day standing around them, Steve pacing as Joseph took notes from their energized conversations. This was very different from their current layout, where they had offices on opposite sides of the floor. Joseph could no longer see his partner, and it was now an ordeal to schedule a meeting. The architectural models were in a completely different location, and there was no easy opportunity for them to get together and exchange ideas. Joseph agreed the previous offices had allowed for much more natural communication between them.

Next we explored the pattern Steve's mind used when he was at the height of his effectiveness. I asked Joseph to describe those client meetings. "They'd always take place on-site, and Steve would walk next to prospective clients, sharing his vision of what was possible. It was that inspiring vision that closed our deals." He kept drawing boxes around the fists he had sketched earlier as he continued. "But things changed when we were bought out. Now most client interaction is done electronically. Steve hates it. He's slow to respond, revises what he writes constantly, and just seems awkward, flat-footed, and generally pissed off."

We began to explore what all of this implied. It seemed that kinesthetic input helped Steve's mind focus (K-1), auditory helped it to sort (A-2), and visual triggered him into open attention (V-3). Thus, all of his behavior led us to suppose that he used the KAV pattern. Someone who is visually sensitive literally sees the big picture in his or her mind in a very creative way, as did Picasso or van Gogh. Walking and talking helps them communicate that vision in an influential way. Having to communicate visually on a computer is like trying to paint by numbers. The person's visual channel gets depleted without the opportunity to move and connect with others, which was why walking the site helped Steve to pitch most naturally.

This is exactly the opposite of Joseph's VAK mind pattern. Evidently the problem in their partnership was caused not by power plays or personality differences but by *thinking* differences: What closed Steve's mind opened Joseph's, and vice versa. Their old office setup and way of collaborating had bridged those differences and maximized the value each brought.

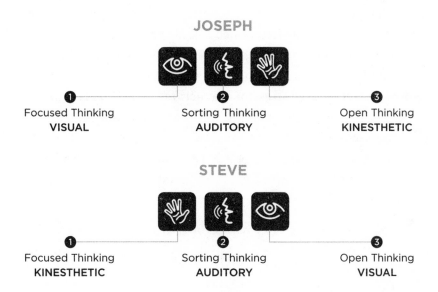

Step 3: Create a Game Plan. It was now time to think through some action steps. Joseph decided to begin every day by going on a fifteen-minute walk-and-talk with Steve. This opened his own mind so he could become receptive enough to connect, and it would help Steve focus on the priorities at hand. It also became obvious to Joseph how important it was to hire a new assistant for his partner, someone whose mind could visually organize emails and PowerPoints instead of someone who "felt" comfortable to Steve. The last suggestion I made was that before every important meeting, Joseph and Steve should walk up and down the halls together so they could articulate their joint priorities.

Step 4: What Effect Are You Having? When we met again a month later, Joseph reported that the partnership was back on track. When he and Steve walked in synch with each other and talked before meetings, Joseph noticed that the old feeling of "being on the same side" returned. In movement, Joseph's mind relaxed and opened so that insights began to emerge regularly. Likewise, when

Steve could look wherever he wanted, the full range of his innovative brilliance returned.

Step 5: What Adjustments Can You Make? These small but significant changes made it easier for both Joseph and Steve to move forward together. They functioned like a right and left hand again. It became obvious that Steve should do on-site design and inspiration, and he readily passed over all written client contacts to Joseph. They recognized stressful interactions as a signal to call each other for advice. Both leaders were clear about the contribution they were making. They sent me a card several months later with a drawing they had jointly done of two hands folded with fingers interlaced, entitled: "Partnering Non-Habitually."

COPING WITH CHALLENGES

PRESENTATIONS
VAK
Look through the audience, find one friendly face, and talk from your passion. Use your gift of story to connect to the audience's experience. Use evocative visuals. Stand still so your words stay focused.
VKA
Walk around and begin by asking a series of questions about what matters to the audience. Have a visual outline you can follow and use a model if possible.
KAV
Prepare by asking yourself what is a desired outcome that you are passionate about. Allow yourself to move during the presentation and use images rather than detailed visuals.
KVA
Be on your feet, moving; use images that prompt you what to say. Connect with the audience by asking them questions about what matters to them. Use action-based language.
AVK
Find out about your audience ahead of time, so you can walk in their shoes, and speak to what matters to them. Stand still or sit. Avoid holding anything in your hands.

AKV

Make sure your presentation uses visuals. Remember to ask questions of the audience. Notice what you are feeling in your body to slow you down, and talk *with* people—not *to* them.

PERFORMANCE REVIEWS

VAK

Focus on seeing visual details rather than making up stories about how you are seen. To remain open, feel your feet on the ground.

VKA

Hold something in your hand that represents what really matters to you, or take notes on what the other person is saying.

KAV

Go for a walk with the other person if possible. Allow your eyes to wander, and tell the other person it helps you listen more effectively. Ask for specific actions you can take.

KVA

Request that you can remain on your feet if possible. Take notes by mind-mapping. Write down the questions that come up for you, and then ask them when it's appropriate.

AVK

Avoid interrupting or arguing; instead, ask to discuss your thoughts on significant issues when the other person is open to listening.

AKV

Avoid talking over the other person or building a case against what they are saying. Hold something in your hand and notice your breathing to keep your mind open.

MAINTAINING BALANCE WHILE IN CONFLICT

VAK

Allow yourself to move and look wherever you want to. Notice your breathing and the sensations in your body. Avoid telling yourself any stories and reflect what the other person is saying.

VKA

Look at something beautiful and keep awareness of your own heart beating, your breath, and physical sensations. Doodle on paper to keep your mind open. Inquire of the other person so you can stay connected.

KAV

Name the sensations in your body to keep your mind open. Say explicitly what you need and want. Look at your own hands and at something that reminds you of what really matters.

KVA
Move around, letting your eyes wander. Doodle as you reflect on what is being said. Feel your belly and spine to help you find your words. Call a time-out when your ears are full.
AVK
Name what's important to you as a headline and ask if the other person is willing to listen for "X" minutes. Keep your eyes focused on the other person to notice the effect of your words.
AKV
Have awareness of your own tone of voice. Stay on your feet and be aware of your breath. Allow your eyes to see your own hands as you notice your body sensations. Keep asking yourself what really matters to you.

HOW TEAMS CAN MAXIMIZE INTELLECTUAL DIVERSITY

The strategy of mind patterns draws on our inherent need to connect. In spite of astounding new technologies that appear to make communication easier, we are still not connecting in ways that support true collaboration. We are merely thinking "alone together," as social scientist Sherry Turkle said, and many people feel more frenzied and isolated than ever before. Companies like Best Buy and Yahoo are now requiring employees who work remotely to come into the office for the specific purpose of "working together." And we can only work together if we know how to think together. A mind-share mentality requires what I call "differentiated connection": thinking with people who bring different and varied talents to the table.

Many of the influential "Possibilists" we write about in this book discovered how to use differentiated connection to inspire large-scale collaborative breakthroughs. As one of my thinking partners, Al Carey, the CEO of PepsiCo Americas Beverages, says, "The next great leader will be a diverse team. People who want to operate as the hero-who-knows-everything will either change or become extinct." Leaders who understand and maximize the different ways that people process information are more prepared to inspire, empower, and meld the diverse intellectual assets within their organizations.

Jazz musician Dave Brubeck was also a great example of this. "[He] capitalized on the differences between musicians in his group to create classic music," said Ted Gioia, in the documentary *Jazz*. "They were all so different, but Brubeck made it work. He wasn't threatened by differences. They inspired him. . . . It's to his credit that he was able to hear these musicians that played very differently from him and was able to see that by taking them and getting their different sounds, he was adding, not subtracting. . . . He had an instinct for differences and how they were going to add to his music."

USING THE CQ PLAYBOOK WITH TEAMS

What follows are guidelines for how to use the CQ playbook with teams to create a collaborative environment that accommodates the needs of every mind pattern. It will enable you to transform habitual and deadlocked meetings into energetic and lively sessions that will liberate collective intelligence.

Step 1: How Do We Think?
The most effective way to understand the intellectual diversity present on a team is to create a mind-pattern team map.

Map the Team

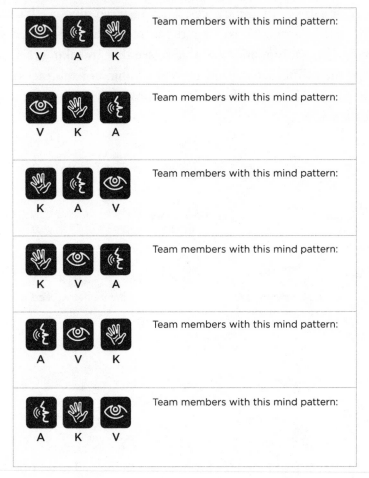

Write each team member's name next to his or her mind pattern. As you consider the team map, you can also calculate percentages of what team members need to focus, sort, and open their attention (for example: 60 percent need visual to focus). In a meeting when your team is experiencing stuck thinking, use the map to consider what may free it up.

Step 2: What Has Worked Before?

Ask people to give examples of the best meetings they have ever participated in, being as specific as possible. Capture what each person says on a flip chart.

Step 3: What Is Our Game Plan?

Using the information you have just gathered, try one or more of the suggestions from the list below to free the thinking and maximize the contribution each member of the team could make.

Consider the Environment

Kinesthetic/Physical

- Are there chairs that move? Is there room to move, the ability to sit or stand?
- Are there smaller café-style tables for small-group thinking?
- Are there balls and other objects in the room for people to fiddle with?
- Are there several flip charts or whiteboards around the room?
- Is there natural light?

Visual

- Post large sheets of paper on the walls or use several flip charts.
- If you are projecting visuals with many details, consider handing out hard copies as well, so people can see more easily.
- PowerPoint can be useful for reporting specific information but not necessarily effective for facilitating collaboration. Designate someone to draw on a flip chart while people stand around it, or ask someone who is interested to record the meeting graphically, or learn how to create a Prezi (new multi-dimensional presentation software: prezi.com), which can be projected.

- Consider preparing visual information on two levels: 1) the big picture or the high-level overview, and 2) the details, in a separate visual form, highlighting only the three or four critical things that you do not want people to miss.

Auditory
- Eliminate as many sound distractions as possible for those who are sensitive to them.
- Create silence for small periods of time during the meeting itself, so that everyone can think through his or her response to an important question or issue.

Step 4: What Effect Are We Each Having?

Save the last five minutes of each meeting to discuss what has and hasn't worked in this session. Ask people to name the effects of the different elements on them—for example: "When we clustered in small groups around flip charts, I got really engaged. When we sat not moving for twenty minutes, I spaced out completely."

Step 5: What Adjustments Can We Make?

Summarize the feedback above and ask people what they would stop, start, and continue to make their meetings more effective.

HOW DO YOU CREATE THE CONDITIONS FOR A TEAM TO OPEN ITS THINKING?

The following story illustrates how we used innovative thinking processes to help the leadership team of an agricultural company break through to find a common vision. There was a gap in trust between old members of the company, who had worked there for decades, and new members, who were eager for change. In spite of the fact that it was crunch time in the fourth quarter and everyone was overloaded with work, Mark, the CEO, scheduled a half-day retreat for the leadership team at a nearby hotel. "Can't you see that we don't have time for this soft stuff?" Jason, the new CFO, grumbled when he heard about the off-site. "We have to make our numbers. That's what you told me to focus on, so that's what I've been telling this team to do!"

I'm not sure how Mark finally convinced Jason to come to the retreat, but show up he did, along with eight old and new team members. Mark hadn't told any of them what Angie and I were planning, because I hadn't told him yet. Mark had given us four hours and charged us with unifying the leadership team in a shared vision. I knew that their thinking had been tightly focused for months. Unless they could somehow open their minds to collaborate, they would see only the bull's-eye, never the whole target.

We asked the team to do the mind-pattern assessment and learned that for 40 percent of the team, auditory input triggered focused attention; for 60 percent, auditory input triggered the opposite, open attention. We knew we could not reach resonance if we met in their habitual style—sitting around a table with the old guard on one end and the new members on the other, four of them talking and six of them checked out.

To find a common desired outcome, we decided to use a non-habitual process that encouraged movement and visual thinking. We invited all the team members to go for a twenty-minute walk around the hotel grounds and use their smartphones to take three photographs: one representing the collective vision they wanted to achieve in six months, one representing that vision realized in a year, and the last of that vision realized in five years. Our intention was for old and new members alike to face a challenge that was equally awkward for everyone but that would allow all the diverse intelligences to participate.

Angie printed their images and hung them on the walls under the appropriate label: "Six Months," "One Year," and "Five Years." Standing together and looking at the photographs, we asked each person to think about the conditions and actions that were needed to make his or her vision a reality and what each person was willing to commit to to make that happen. We requested they write their thoughts on Post-its and place them next to the photographs. By doing this, we now could all "see" the collective thinking instead of just hearing it.

Jason's mind used the AVK pattern. He was the first to volunteer. His photographs were so stunning that they magnetized everyone's attention. His voice was calmly energized as he explained what the images meant to him. The rest of the team asked questions and commented on what they saw in the photographs. Jason was truly engaged listening to each of the others as they spoke. He seemed to be having a new experience: being on the same side as everyone else. He stood next to what he wrote on his Post-it, looked at each person, and said, "I commit to asking each of you how I can be of support to make our vision a reality." The work continued, with each person building on what others said. The barriers of old and new began to dissolve into an atmosphere of flow and alliance.

As we closed the meeting, Jason said, "I'm really glad I came. I'm completely surprised and a little embarrassed to say that, as a result of being here, I finally feel part of this team. I'm glad that we took the risk so we can have one another's backs as we go forward."

In the debrief afterward, Mark wanted to know how we came up with the process that not only opened Jason's mind but also aligned the whole team around a shared vision. Angie and I explained that by looking at all of their mind patterns, we knew that walking around silently while thinking about questions and using visual images would break the habitual verbal tennis match they had been playing and would allow them to practice opening their minds together.

Mark replied with excitement, "Given how disconnected we were when we started today, I want to hang these photographs in our main office so that when we enter each day, those employees who have been with the company twenty years and those who have been here just two months will all be reminded of our common vision—and the role each of us plays in activating it."

Within a year, the leadership team turned the company around, enabling its eventual sale for a higher price than even the most optimistic valuation.

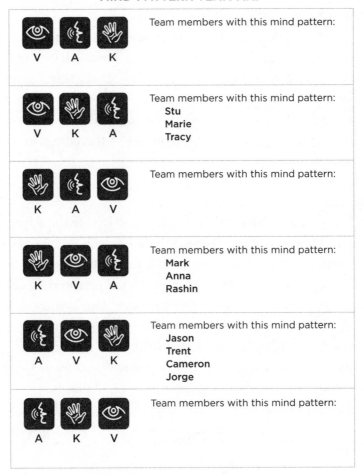

MIND-PATTERN TEAM MAP

Mind Pattern	Team members with this mind pattern:
V A K	
V K A	Stu Marie Tracy
K A V	
K V A	Mark Anna Rashin
A V K	Jason Trent Cameron Jorge
A K V	

BREAKTHROUGH PRACTICE:
USING MULTI-SENSORY TEAM PROCESSES TO GENERATE IDEAS

Musical Brainstorm

- Play classical music (or any music without lyrics) for a few minutes while team members think about a particular issue as they sit still or walk around. When the music ends, have people write as many ideas as they can on Post-its.

- Ask people to share their ideas as they post them. Host a standing conversation about the questions: "What are we all saying? What are we all asking?"

The Mural

- Ask team members to think in silence of a metaphor that describes what the team is trying to accomplish (this could be a vision, a new product, etc.). Have them stand around a long piece of paper that covers the wall like a mural. Have them speak about their metaphors as they draw them as best as they can. Have a discussion about the common themes and meaning.

The Pizza

- Cover round tables with blank paper. Divide the paper with a marker into pizza "slices," based on the number of team members. If there are more than six people, use two tables. Ask one person to be timekeeper. Each person then chooses a slice and, when the timekeeper says "Go," writes down as many ideas as possible about the topic. After two minutes, move one space to the left. In the next two minutes, read what the person before you wrote and add to it. Continue reading/writing until you have been to all places.
- Ask the group to complete the following: "What I learned was . . ." "What surprised me was . . ." "What inspired me was . . ."

The Sculpture

- Ask the group to break into teams of four and, using the materials available in the room, silently create a sculpture representing the problem or challenge.
- Step back after ten minutes, and while walking around the completed sculpture, answer the following: "One thing I didn't realize before is . . ." "One thing we still need to know is . . ." "To move us forward we need to . . ."

GROWING THE THINKING WHILE GROWING
THE ORGANIZATION: USING CQ IN A WHOLE COMPANY

Angie shares the story of how we helped all the employees of the agricultural company described above to increase their CQ and generate innovation in order to achieve extraordinary results:

The company campus was so large, we needed a golf cart to tour the property. It struck me immediately that everywhere I looked, there were thousands of tiny patented seedlings being tended with exquisite care. I wondered if the people were being equally well tended.

I asked to see the main meeting locations and was taken to a trailer where a daily briefing was being held. Every inch of space in the stifling room was filled with human bodies. The leader sat at the end of a table, reading numbers off a sheet of paper. The rest of the people sat, stood, or perched on cabinets, visibly straining to hear what he was saying. I wondered how people could think like this. Every other meeting room we saw was equally cramped.

We gathered in the office of the CEO to develop a plan to grow their people with the same care that they gave their seedlings. This meant not only improving the meeting environments but also creating the conditions that would enable people to think well together. We began by doing a collaborative-intelligence assessment of the top three hundred fifty leaders in the company.

From the assessment, we discovered that 40 percent of the people identified that kinesthetic helped them focus their attention, 40 percent identified that visual helped them focus, and 20 percent identified that auditory helped them focus. What this meant was that four out of every ten employees needed room to move around in order to think most effectively. An equal number needed to be able to write and see visuals. This meant that the meeting environments really needed to change in order to create the possibility of high-quality thinking. Some of the quick fixes we initiated were:

- Removal of all unnecessary items like file cabinets, broken chairs, etc., from meeting rooms, to allow for tables and space to move around.
- Installation of flip charts and whiteboards.
- Adding projectors so each team could stand and collectively look at spreadsheets and presentations. Since for many people visual triggered open thinking, we used large font sizes and highlighted only one or two key points on all the visuals.
- People were encouraged to stand up and move around in the back of the meeting rooms or get up and draw on a flip chart.
- Sidewalks were installed between buildings, which encouraged people to walk between them to increase communication throughout the system.

These small changes created room for effective thinking to grow. The more people learned about how to use their own minds well, the less shy they became about asking for what they needed to think effectively. It became a cultural norm to speak up when someone didn't understand something, so, instead of feeling stupid, they communicated when they needed information presented in a different way.

Next we created a mind-pattern map for each individual team within the company, which showed a composite profile of the members' mind patterns. In some teams—finance, for example—59 percent of the members needed visual information to focus. On other teams—like operations—64 percent needed kinesthetic input to focus.

For most teams, the greatest challenge came when they met with other departments. Finance, for example, used spreadsheets to communicate with one another but found they were not effective with other departments, because their spreadsheets were too visually complex. Data was being missed because people in other departments, with different mind patterns, were unable to unpack the dense information or to understand the implications of it.

Once people understood this as an issue of intellectual diversity instead of irresponsibility, we worked with each department to discover how they needed information presented. Some departments preferred spreadsheets and wanted bullet points to highlight key data. Other departments requested graphs that tracked financials over time, with color-coded bars so they could quickly compare data. The solution wasn't a change in software, management, or training procedures. What was needed was the simple awareness that what worked for some people didn't necessarily work for others. The teams started to tailor the way they presented their information, and as a result, the tension between departments was greatly reduced. They began to execute effectively against their strategic plan.

This is a perfect example of how understanding intellectual diversity can dissolve internal tensions, not only creating a better working environment for everyone involved but also directly translating to the bottom line.

MIND-PATTERN TEAM MAP EXAMPLE 1

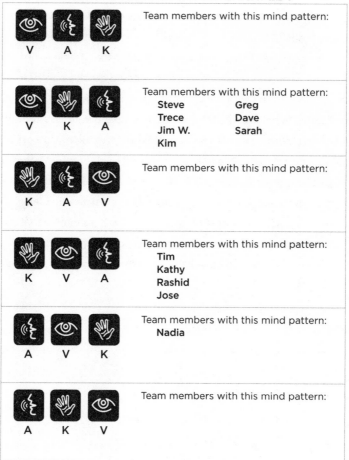

Pattern	Team members with this mind pattern:
V A K	
V K A	Steve Greg Trece Dave Jim W. Sarah Kim
K A V	
K V A	Tim Kathy Rashid Jose
A V K	Nadia
A K V	

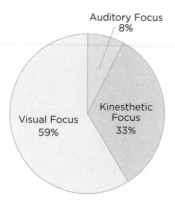

Auditory Focus
8%

Visual Focus
59%

Kinesthetic
Focus
33%

FINANCE TEAM

MIND-PATTERN TEAM MAP EXAMPLE 2

Pattern	Team members with this mind pattern:
V A K	
V K A	Matt George
K A V	Tom Meredith Monty
K V A	Marco Stu Georgia Kent
A V K	Pat Tom W.
A K V	

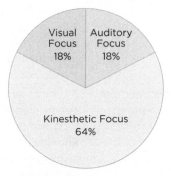

Visual Focus 18%
Auditory Focus 18%
Kinesthetic Focus 64%

OPERATIONS TEAM

CHAPTER SUMMARY

KEY CONCEPTS OF THIS CHAPTER	GUIDELINES
The CQ Playbook is a tool you can use to increase the effectiveness of your collaboration with one other person or a team on a company-wide level.	**1. Review your mind pattern** Awareness of your mind pattern will allow you to use your own mind more effectively. Discover the specific conditions that support and what limits your ability to communicate well. **2. Investigate what has been successful in the past** From the perspective of mind patterns, identify what has been successful with the other party in the past: detailed visuals, space to talk, big-picture visuals, the ability to stand up, walking while talking. **3. Come up with a game plan** Based on past success, modify your approach according to what you know about your mind pattern and what supports your best thinking as well as the other party's. Create an approach that works for both of you. **4. Notice the effect you are having** Having simple awareness of how you are affecting another can give you the necessary clues to adjust. Most often we think of the content we are communicating, not how we are communicating it. **5. Adjust** Have options ready so you can adjust if you are not producing the effect you want. Use the Common Breakdown chart to help you figure out some quick fixes.
Mapping the team's collective mind patterns will enable you to understand the intellectual diversity of your group and tailor your approach to maximize collaboration.	By using team maps, you can figure out the predominant triggers that focus and open the team's thinking. Knowing this will help you design meeting processes that are more customized and effective for that particular team.

GROWING BEYOND THE CHALLENGE

Rachel Naomi Remen, M.D., a beloved author, teacher, and healer, tells a remarkable story about the enormous potency of our mental resources. When a young male patient of hers was first diagnosed with juvenile diabetes, he became self-destructive and full of rage. After six seemingly unproductive months in therapy with Rachel, he had a most amazing dream:

> *The patient sat facing the serene, peaceful small stone statue of a Buddha. Then, without warning, a dagger was thrown from behind him and lodged itself deep in the Buddha's heart. The young man felt betrayed, outraged, and in despair, but as he sat there crying, the statue, ever so slowly, began to grow. It was just as peaceful as before, but the Buddha grew and grew until it was enormous, filling the room. The knife remained, but it now was tiny in comparison to the chest of the huge, smiling Buddha.*

The talents within us can become stronger than whatever challenges we may face. They may even free us from that which we must endure.

Rachel ends the story with these words: "Sometimes someone dreams a dream for us all."

THINKING TALENTS

The "Me" of "We"

THINK MIND PATTERNS **TALENTS** INQUIRY MIND SHARE CQ

Identifying the specific ways of thinking that energize you and others

UNCOVERING YOUR
THINKING TALENTS

Our minds are partly defined by their intersections with other minds.

—Daniel Siegel, M.D.

One very cold December afternoon, the phone in my office rang. A man's raspy voice asked if I was the woman who had written *How Your Child IS Smart* and *The Open Mind*. He introduced himself as Ned Herrmann, and within minutes we were engaged in a compelling conversation. He told me he was very excited about the concept of mind patterns. He had spent much of his life researching the expansion of human capacity, first as director of training at General Electric and then as the head of his own organization, Herrmann International.

His book *The Creative Brain* arrived a few days later, and I was humbled to discover that he was well into his seventies and an expert in the fields of human development, brain dominance, and learning. In subsequent conversations, it became clear that he and I were traveling along different banks of the same river. We had both been fascinated with finding ways to grow human capacity. I was struck by the fact that, even at this late stage of his career, he was still hungry to learn and open to considering my work as a complement to his.

Herrmann's model is based on more than 130,000 brain-dominance surveys (known as the "HBDI") and proposes that there are four different "cognitive styles"—preferred ways of knowing and approaching problems: analytic, procedural, relational, and innovative. He identified the first two as left-mode-dominant processes and the second two as right-mode dominant. In the same way that we develop preferred hand, eye, ear, and foot dominances, he said, we also develop brain dominances, which are expressed in how we think, understand, and communicate what we know.

According to Herrmann, although we are born with the capacity to use all four of these different cognitive styles, as we mature we tend to develop preferences. I think of these as our different ways of being smart. Our lives shape us the way wind shapes a tree, and we tend to develop particular cognitive preferences—and avoidances—when faced with problems. They correlate strongly with the content we choose to focus on and value in any given situation. Cognitive styles are different from mind patterns, which are the specific ways our brains process information, and they are different from skills, which we develop through education and training.

As a result of my conversations with Ned Herrmann, I came across work by the Gallup organization that investigated why some companies were more productive than others. The question that interested them the most was: Did people have the opportunity to use their strengths every day at work? They found that the more people who answered "yes" to this single question, the higher the success was of that organization. Gallup became very interested in pinpointing why this was true and what those individual strengths were. As a result of thirty years of research, they identified thirty-four of what they called "signature strengths" in their sample population. They stated that most adults have five.

My colleagues and I synthesized and adapted the work of Herrmann and Gallup, along with the latest findings in neuroscience and our own hands-on experience of working with dozens of companies. The result was a strategy that includes thirty-five of what we call "thinking talents." When combined with an understanding of mind patterns, this strategy will help you identify your unique intelligence and increase your collaborative potential.

Thinking talents are your natural ways of approaching challenges, ways that *increase* your mental energy. It is well established that the brain uses more energy than any other human organ, accounting for up to 20 percent of the body's total expenditure. Your thinking talents are so intrinsic that if they were to disappear, you would be unrecognizable. Thinking talents compose your own singular brilliance. Being aware of them will help you to maximize what you bring to the table when working with others. As on a baseball team, how the individuals' separate and specific abilities work together will determine how the team performs.

In this chapter, you will discover how to use your unique thinking talents to contribute your highest-quality thinking to others without burning out. There is also additional information in the appendix on how to activate your thinking talents, and the thinking talents of those around you, in various work situations.

WHAT ARE YOUR UNIQUE THINKING TALENTS?

Identifying your thinking talents begins with reading through each of the thirty-five talents in the "cards" represented on the following pages. *All you need to remember about thinking talents are the following three characteristics:*

- They are innate ways of thinking. That is, you've always been really good at doing them, even if you never had any specific training, and you tend to use them when faced with challenges.
- You get natural joy and energy from using your thinking talents, and you don't burn out.

• You excel in using these talents and enjoy developing capacities with them.

Understanding these aspects will help you distinguish thinking talents from skills, personality traits, or other capacities.

The thinking talent self-assessment works like a card game. You will see that each thinking-talent card has a label at the bottom that reads "ALWAYS-SOMETIMES-NEVER." As you read the cards that follow, sort them into three categories. The first is for cards that describe: "This ALWAYS gives me energy." The second is for cards that describe: "This SOMETIMES gives me energy." The third is for cards that describe: "This NEVER gives me energy." We suggest you take a piece of paper and create three columns with these labels. As you go through the cards, thinking of all areas of your life, write the talents in the appropriate columns.

Once you have sorted all the talents into these three categories, go to the "ALWAYS" group and edit it down to the five to eight strongest talents. If you have more than eight, ask yourself which ones have always been true for you and always will be true for you; eliminate those that aren't quite as strong. If you have fewer than five, go to the "SOMETIMES" group and add the strongest ones there to the "ALWAYS" group until you have five. You may have talents in your "ALWAYS" group that you think of as irrelevant to your work, but if they fit the above criteria, please consider them thinking talents anyway. The five to eight cards remaining in the "ALWAYS" group will most accurately describe what you consider to be your dominant thinking talents.

There is no way you can be wrong. As your awareness of thinking talents increases, you'll recognize things in yourself you never noticed before, so over time you might need to reconsider some of your choices. As your understanding grows, you can always change your mind.

In the future, when you have a breakthrough in your thinking, complete a task well, or have an experience that makes you feel fully alive, take a minute to reflect on what thinking talents you just used. It's also useful to notice how your talents show up for you in different domains of life: work, exercise, family, hobbies, or with different people. Through this broad spectrum of observations, you will collect insights that will be the optimal guide for using your thinking talents well.

THINKING TALENTS
Adapting

"How can I adapt to what's happening now?"

Lives in the moment and discovers the future one choice at a time; expects and enjoys detours. Flexible, adjusts easily to change.

ALWAYS   SOMETIMES   NEVER

THINKING TALENTS
Believing

"Does this mesh with my beliefs?"

High ethics guides behavior; people know where this person stands. Makes decisions based on values.

ALWAYS   SOMETIMES   NEVER

THINKING TALENTS
Collecting

"What am I interested in here?"

Collects information, things, quotations, artifacts, or facts—anything that is deemed interesting. The world is exciting because of its variety; acquiring, compiling, and filing stuff away keeps things fresh.

ALWAYS   SOMETIMES   NEVER

THINKING TALENTS
Connection

"How is this part of something larger?"

Loves to connect people and/or ideas; sees the relationship between things and/or people; perceives how one thing is part of something larger.

ALWAYS   SOMETIMES   NEVER

THINKING TALENTS
Creating Intimacy

"How can I be closer and more genuine with the people I already know?"

Comfortable with intimacy; encourages deepening of relationships; "the more that is shared together, the more that is risked together." May have a challenge meeting new people.

ALWAYS   SOMETIMES   NEVER

THINKING TALENTS
Enrolling

"How can I relate to this new person?"

Enjoys challenge of meeting new people and getting in their good graces; enjoys developing rapport, breaking the ice, making a new connection, then moving on.

ALWAYS   SOMETIMES   NEVER

THINKING TALENTS
Equalizing

"Is everyone being treated fairly?"

Needs balance and to know that people are being treated in the same way; turned off by individualism; feels a need for a consistent environment of clear rules, where people will all know what's expected.

ALWAYS   SOMETIMES   NEVER

THINKING TALENTS
Feeling for Others

"What are people feeling now?"

Senses emotions in those nearby; shares their perspective in order to understand their choices; hears the unvoiced questions; anticipates others' needs.

ALWAYS   SOMETIMES   NEVER

THINKING TALENTS

Fixing It

**"What's the solution to
this problem?"**

Energized by breakdowns;
loves to identify what's wrong and
repair it or anticipate what might go
wrong and avert it. Enjoys rescuing
and saving something.

ALWAYS   SOMETIMES   NEVER

THINKING TALENTS

Focusing

**"What's the point
here?"**

Capacity to concentrate on a goal
for a long period of time. May need
clear destination or will get
frustrated; able to filter out
distractions; keeps people on point
and off tangents.

ALWAYS   SOMETIMES   NEVER

THINKING TALENTS

Get to Action

**"What can I do
right now?"**

Impatient for action rather
than contemplation. Must make
something happen.

ALWAYS   SOMETIMES   NEVER

THINKING TALENTS

Goal-Setting

**"What can I accomplish
today?"**

Has daily drive to accomplish
something and meet a goal.
Every day starts at zero and must
achieve something tangible.
There is a perpetual whisper
of discontent.

ALWAYS   SOMETIMES   NEVER

THINKING TALENTS

Having Confidence

"What, me worry?"

Knows he or she is able to deliver. Self-assured; no one can tell this person what to think. Alone has the authority to come to conclusions.

ALWAYS   SOMETIMES   NEVER

THINKING TALENTS

Humor

"What is amusing about this?"

Enjoys seeing the humor in situations. Can lighten tense moments and puts self and others at ease with laughter.

ALWAYS   SOMETIMES   NEVER

THINKING TALENTS

Including

"How can I stretch the circle wider?"

Desires to make others part of the group so as many as possible can feel its support; no one should be on the outside looking in; accepting, nonjudgmental.

ALWAYS   SOMETIMES   NEVER

THINKING TALENTS

Innovation

"How can this be done differently?"

Loves to create new processes or products; easily bored with routine. Energized by never having done it before.

ALWAYS   SOMETIMES   NEVER

THINKING TALENTS

Love of Learning

"What can I learn next?"

Drawn always to the process more than the content of learning; energized by the journey from ignorance to competence. The outcome is less important than what is learned.

ALWAYS   SOMETIMES   NEVER

THINKING TALENTS

Loving Ideas

"What's a thrilling idea or theory to explain this?"

Searches for concepts to explain things; loves theories; derives jolt of energy from a new idea.

ALWAYS   SOMETIMES   NEVER

THINKING TALENTS

Making Order

"How can I align all these different variables?"

Enjoys managing and aligning many variables into the best configuration. Jumps into confusion and devises new options; organizes what's messy.

ALWAYS   SOMETIMES   NEVER

THINKING TALENTS

Mentoring

"What can help others grow?"

Sees potential in others; every person is a work in progress; goal is to help others achieve success; searches for signs of growth in others.

ALWAYS   SOMETIMES   NEVER

THINKING TALENTS

Optimism

"What's right about this?"

Generous with praise; always on the lookout for the positive; contagiously enthusiastic; finds a way to lighten people's spirits. The glass is always half full.

ALWAYS   SOMETIMES   NEVER

THINKING TALENTS

Particularize

"How is each of us unique?"

Intrigued by unique qualities of each person; observes each person's style and how each thinks and builds relationships; keen observer and developer of others' talents and strengths.

ALWAYS   SOMETIMES   NEVER

THINKING TALENTS

Peacemaking

"Where is the common ground?"

Looks for areas of agreement; holds conflicts to a minimum; prefers to search for consensus; will modify own direction in service of harmony.

ALWAYS   SOMETIMES   NEVER

THINKING TALENTS

Precision

"How can I order this chaos?"

The world needs to be predictable; imposes structure, sets up routines, timelines, and deadlines; needs to feel in control; dislikes surprises; impatient with errors. Control is a way of maintaining progress and productivity.

ALWAYS   SOMETIMES   NEVER

THINKING TALENTS

Reliability

"How can I do this right?"

Excuses and rationalizations are not acceptable; has to take responsibility for anything committed to; reputation for conscientiousness and dependability. Easily frustrated by what is perceived as others' irresponsibility.

ALWAYS   SOMETIMES   NEVER

THINKING TALENTS

Seeking Excellence

"How can this be excellent?"

Excellence and efficiency are the measure—doing the best with the least. Everything—people, processes, products—is judged by how to make it better.

ALWAYS   SOMETIMES   NEVER

THINKING TALENTS

Standing Out

"How can I be recognized?"

Wants to be known for making a difference and be admired for credibility, success. Highly motivated toward rewards and recognition programs.

ALWAYS   SOMETIMES   NEVER

THINKING TALENTS

Storytelling

"How can I bring these ideas to life with a story?"

Needs to explain by painting vivid pictures until others are inspired to act.

ALWAYS   SOMETIMES   NEVER

THINKING TALENTS

Strategy

"What are alternative scenarios, and what is the best route?"

Sorts through clutter; recognizes all the possible options; engages in "if this, then that" thinking.

ALWAYS   SOMETIMES   NEVER

THINKING TALENTS

Taking Charge

"How can I get others aligned with me?"

Likes to be the boss; restless unless sharing opinions. Uses confrontation if necessary and naturally directs others into action.

ALWAYS   SOMETIMES   NEVER

THINKING TALENTS

Thinking Ahead

"Wouldn't it be great if . . . ?"

Fascinated by the future. Describes a detailed future that pulls him or her forward; needs to inspire others in the dream; cherishes visions that energize and give hope.

ALWAYS   SOMETIMES   NEVER

THINKING TALENTS

Thinking Alone

"What can I think about now?"

Poses questions to self and tries to figure them out; constant mental hum; needs to be alone to think to come up with an answer; dislikes being put on the spot to respond.

ALWAYS   SOMETIMES   NEVER

THINKING TALENTS

Thinking Back

**"How is the past a blueprint
for the present?"**

Looks back to understand the
present and future; the present alone
is confusing. May have trouble getting oriented to the new, and needs
to understand the context of something in order to move forward.

ALWAYS   SOMETIMES   NEVER

THINKING TALENTS

Thinking Logically

**"Why is this true?"
"Prove it to me."**

Dispassionate;
theories must be sound,
logical, based on solid data.
Exposes clumsy thinking;
sees patterns in data.

ALWAYS   SOMETIMES   NEVER

THINKING TALENTS

Wanting to Win

**"Am I better at this than
everyone else is?"**

Compares performance to that of
others; likes measurement to
facilitate comparison;
competition is invigorating.

ALWAYS   SOMETIMES   NEVER

SHADOW ATTRIBUTES

Some people have difficulty identifying their thinking talents, because as a society we have been conditioned to focus attention on fixing our deficits rather than maximizing our strengths. Most training programs emphasize weaknesses that need to be improved. Furthermore, some cultures, religions, and family traditions consider modesty a virtue, thereby eclipsing the ability to even admit one's talents.

Therefore, we have developed an additional lens we call the "shadow attribute," to make it easier to recognize a talent. It's a way of understanding what the hidden talent is behind particular behaviors. For instance, the shadow attribute for optimism is "cheerleading." Jamie, no matter how bad things got, always cheered other people on, to the point where they rolled their eyes and said she was denying reality. The shadow attribute characteristically shows up when a talent is rough, excessive, or displayed in an unconstructive way. In fact, once Jamie recognized this as a shadow attribute of optimism, she learned the best time and way for the talent to shine. This is a very different outcome than if she had just thought of the opposite of optimism, which is pessimism. The value of recognizing the shadow attribute is that it can lead you to the hidden thinking talent that waits to be identified and developed.

In this chart, the left column lists the shadow attribute of each thinking talent. Review the chart, scanning for any attribute that stands out as very familiar. Decide if the associated thinking talent should be in the "ALWAYS" pile you created from the previous assessment.

SHADOW ATTRIBUTE	THINKING TALENT
Wishy-washy	Adapting
Righteous	Believing
Hoarding	Collecting
Enmeshed in too many ideas or people	Connection
Overly loyal	Creating Intimacy
Pitchman	Enrolling
"It's not fair!"	Equalizing
Co-dependent	Feeling for Others
Critical	Fixing It
Obsessive on one thing	Focusing
Impatient	Get to Action
Driven	Goal-Setting
Arrogant	Having Confidence
Wise-ass	Humor
Consult everyone on everything	Including
"There must be a new way!"	Innovation
Learning junkie	Love of Learning
Pie in the sky	Loving Ideas
Controlling	Making Order
Preachy	Mentoring
Cheerleading	Optimism
Nosy	Particularize
Conflict-avoidant	Peacemaking
Nitpicky	Precision
Plays by the rules	Reliability
Never satisfied	Seeking Excellence
Narcissist	Standing Out
Exaggerating	Storytelling
Scheming	Strategy
Bossy	Taking Charge
Crystal-ball gazing	Thinking Ahead
Loner	Thinking Alone
Stuck in the past	Thinking Back
Skeptical	Thinking Logically
Ruthless	Wanting to Win

Nadine, a marketing executive, also used the shadow attributes to uncover a thinking talent. She didn't recognize that "having confidence" was one of her talents until she read the shadow attribute of "arrogant." It had always worked against her. In all her reviews, she was described as bossy and conceited. How could this be a talent? Once she understood that this attribute was really the thinking talent of "having confidence" in disguise, she learned to adapt her language and style to her benefit. This resulted in her being promoted to account director—a position where having confidence magnetized clients, who felt like they were in capable hands.

In order to make sure we are using our talents well and creating excellence as a result, it's also important to look at when and where we exhibit a shadow attribute and then transform it. We are all naturally equipped with the most powerful tool to change habits—self-awareness—but we might not all have fully developed this tool. To transform a shadow attribute, you need to name it, contain it, and aim it. Name it by identifying the thinking talent that it's associated with; contain it by using it knowingly and wisely; aim it by engaging it on behalf of your goals. Repeat this practice with each of your shadow attributes—name it, contain it, and aim it until the thinking talent is readily apparent to you.

Jack is a perfect example of this. He is chief technical officer of a major film studio who has the talent of "thinking logically." He needs to reason through an idea before he will buy into it. He endlessly questioned himself about data, paralyzing every new idea by analyzing it to death. His constant questioning would come across as annoying skepticism and resistance. In his first session with Angie, Jack realized that skepticism is the shadow attribute of thinking logically. He learned to *name* this talent in conversation so people knew where he was coming from. "I tend to think logically, so I just need to ask a couple of clarifying questions. . . ." He also *contained* it, by limiting the time he devoted to thinking logically and relying on other talents to develop ideas. And he *aimed* it by asking himself how he could use his logic to extend his influence and create blockbuster movies.

WHY DO WE LOSE TOUCH WITH OUR THINKING TALENTS?

If we all have these bright gifts, why don't we always know how to use them?

One reason is our "deficit-oriented culture," which spans psychology, education, and the workplace. Another is that perhaps we were steered away from our natural talents by parental or societal influence. Many of us as children were criticized for our talents. Oprah Winfrey has said that her family described her self-assurance when she was a child as being "too full of herself." I was a born storyteller, but I was always accused of exaggerating. What about you? Are there ways of thinking you used as a child that were shut down because of what someone said about them?

I once worked with an architect who was described by the other partners in his firm as a "lost soul." People commented that he spent far more time in the hallways, cafeterias, and break rooms talking to co-workers than at his drafting table. I witnessed how he came alive in conversation with others and asked if he noticed the difference.

"I just seem to be good at listening to people tell me about their problems," he responded. I asked if he liked hearing people speak about their troubles or if it wore him down. He said that ever since he was young, he was the guy people would confide in, the shoulder to lean on. I asked if he had ever thought about going into human resources or becoming a counselor. He looked away, embarrassed, and said that his dad had always told him that was girl stuff. Instead, he acquired skills and training as an architect, but his soul *was* lost, following someone else's opinion of what he should be. Once he discovered his thinking talents, he decided to change roles and became his company's human-resources specialist.

A third reason that recognizing thinking talents can be a challenge is that they come so easily to us that they are almost invisible—we often don't realize they make us exceptional. A fifty-two-year-old accountant I met in one of our workshops uncovered his natural talent of "humor." He had always known he was able to make people laugh but never considered it a gift. The rest of us listened incredulously as he described how he had thought of his brilliant sense of humor as "that old thing." He thought of himself as a smart-ass. Others may see it in you, but you yourself have to acknowledge your gift and its value in order to develop it.

Whether we were criticized or just taught to veer away from these parts of ourselves, we have been missing the tools to develop our thinking talents. This strategy will help you recognize and activate your unique talents. In meetings and communications with others, you will feel more aware, energized, and alive instead of burned out and tired.

Synthesizing our research and experience with Ned Herrmann's work resulted in a simple and effective way for categorizing the different aspects of human capacity. In the same way that an orchestra is divided into four groups of similar instruments—string, woodwind, brass, and percussion instruments—we have arranged thinking talents into four different cognitive styles: analytic, procedural, relational, and innovative. Each of these represents a different way of thinking through a problem. Mapping your talents into these domains is a powerful process that will help you organize and utilize your thinking talents.

DISCOVERING YOUR COGNITIVE STYLE

To discover your preferred way of thinking through a challenge, simply circle the talents you have on the map that follows. You can also access this map online at CQthebook.com/map to print and use.

You will notice there are four talents in the gray center column. These are "cross-quadrant," meaning that they are not limited to any single domain.

This map can help you identify the most natural way you approach challenges and therefore the contribution you can make to

THINKING-TALENTS MAP

ANALYTIC
Concerned with data, facts, numbers, being "logical" and rational

COGNITIVE STYLE

INNOVATIVE
Concerned with the future, newness, possibilities, strategy, "big picture"

Making Order

Thinking Logically

Talents in All Quadrants

Innovation

Loving Ideas

Seeking Excellence

Collecting

Wanting to Win

Love of Learning

Thinking Ahead

Fixing It

Standing Out

Strategy

Humor

Adapting

Reliability

Thinking Back

Thinking Alone

Optimism

Including

Connection

Get to Action

Having Confidence

Creating Intimacy

Peace-making

Enrolling

Focusing

Equalizing

Goal-Setting

Storytelling

Particular-ize

Believing

Taking Charge

Precision

Mentoring

Feeling for Others

PROCEDURAL
Concerned with process, operations, logistics, tactics

COGNITIVE STYLE

RELATIONAL
Concerned with feelings, morale, teamwork, development of people

the collaborative intelligence of any group. Let's start by learning how to read it: Step back and notice where your thinking talents are clustered. Is there a predominant quadrant for you? In which quadrant (or quadrants) do you have no thinking talents represented? For instance, if a person has several in the innovative quadrant, it will be most natural for them to solve a problem by brainstorming new possibilities. Another may have several thinking talents in the procedural quadrant and approach the same problem by focusing on timeframe, logistics, and other details. Someone who is very strong in relational thinking will consider how challenges affect people. A person who is talented in analytic thinking will first consider why the challenge exists in the first place. All of these are very different yet significant perspectives on the same problem.

What happens when you have talents in different quadrants? Herrmann's findings were that 7 percent of adults have one cognitive preference; 60 percent exhibit two; 30 percent show three; and just 3 percent have equal preferences for all four styles. This helps us to understand why so many of us feel fragmented in our thinking. If, for example, a person's thinking talents are all in two quadrants, they may constantly feel pulled in two directions when faced with a challenge, because they are considering it from two perspectives at the same time. The breakthrough practice at the end of this chapter will help you integrate your thinking talents and resolve tensions between them.

DISCOVERING YOUR BLIND SPOTS

Equally important as knowing your mind's sweet spots—the talents you have, the talents that are hidden, and how they combine—is recognizing your mind's blind spots, which are the talents you lack. People worry and stress in the quadrants where they have blind spots. If you don't have "feeling for others," for example, you may worry about how people will react to you. If you don't have "making order," you worry because you have trouble organizing and prioritizing. If you don't have "focusing," you're concerned about being easily distracted. We seem to know intuitively when we are missing a natural ease and excellence of thinking in these areas, even if we fail to recognize it consciously. Conversely, you don't worry in the domains where you have the necessary thinking talents, because you innately trust your capacity.

Two common assumptions cause us to deny our blind spots. The first is the belief that we should all be competent at everything. The second is the belief that we should be able to think through and solve any issue independently. Both of these erroneous beliefs can lead to what I call "skilled mediocrity," and they point to the inescapable fact that we need one another. Blind spots reveal where collaboration is necessary so you can give and get the support you need to produce excellence.

Looking back to the thinking-talents map on page 126, notice if you have any quadrants that are devoid of thinking talents. These are your blind spots. Also notice which thinking talents are missing, because they too may be blind spots in certain situations.

WHY DO THINKING TALENTS MATTER?

Everyplace my eyes landed in Nick's office held some sports object encased in a glass box or frame. This was not a typical CEO's corporate lair; this was a gallery of greatness. Basketballs, baseballs, bats, footballs, gloves, rackets, hockey sticks, helmets, and jerseys, each autographed by a famous athlete with a note of genuine appreciation for Nick: "Value your support . . ." "To my friend . . ." "Couldn't have done it without you . . ."

Sitting in the middle of all this was a very tall man who was chewing nervously on the end of a pen as he flipped through a thick stack of papers and charts. Pushing the papers to one side, he said with some relief, "I'm glad you're here. This cost–benefit analysis is driving me crazy—the damn thing can wait!" His voice was as big as he was and came from the center of his belly. It was a voice you had to pay attention to, a voice you do *not* want to hear behind you on an airplane, a voice that came from the kind of man you want to have around when there is trouble.

I pointed to two basketballs enclosed in glass boxes on the opposite wall and asked if he would tell me the story of how he got them. I actually had no interest in the balls themselves, but I wanted to notice what energized his thinking as he described what they meant to him. As if released from a too-small cage, Nick popped up and strode across the room. Placing one hand on each, he told me how famous basketball coaches had signed them, the one on the right by John Wooden and the one on the left by Bobby Knight. Much to his chagrin, I hadn't heard of either, so Nick launched into a passionate description of the differences in leadership style of each coach. "Being a CEO and being a coach both require you to understand the different qualities of each player's potential so you can help grow and activate it. Then you need to blend all the different personalities with each other. Wooden and Bobby Knight used totally different strategies to do this. Are you with me?" I nodded enthusiastically. What he was saying matched everything I had learned and taught leaders for decades.

"The coach and players have a reciprocal need for each other if they want to achieve greatness, in the same way that a business leader and his direct reports do," he continued. "The players recognize that the coach holds the key to their future careers. Bobby Knight thought that their successes and failures reflected back on him and insisted that they follow his orders. His nickname was 'General,' and he was an expert in offense, requiring his players to be unselfish, highly disciplined, and extremely well prepared. He was known for achieving remarkable results and also for being extremely rough on his players."

Nick looked at me with a blue laser gaze. I hadn't missed a word—and I didn't dare. I was meeting the Bobby Knight in him. He continued, "John Wooden, on the other hand, had been a great player before he was a coach, in the same way I was a successful salesman before I was an executive. He never used the word 'winning.' What he wanted was for each player to be the best he could be during adversity. He used to say, 'Do not let what you cannot do interfere with what you can. Measure yourself not by what you have accomplished, but by what you could have accomplished with your ability.' "

I listened to him intently, searching for the talents that were driving his thinking. "All the coaches I've ever had in my life, as well as all the bosses in this company, have been like Bobby Knight. What's always drawn me to John Wooden is that he created teams where there was a real incentive for players to help each other improve their game. He recognized each person's potential and developed it while creating an environment of pure collaboration and excellence. That's what I want to do as the CEO of this company. That's what I want you to help me do."

The room vibrated with his passion. I leaned forward and asked, "How do you want me to help you, Nick?"

He pulled on his right ear and, in a voice that was as tender as it had been fierce only seconds before, he said, "I'm smart in a lot of operational ways, but I need to know more about how to recognize the different kinds of talent in the people who work for this company, so I can inspire them to realize their potential. There are no books about that, no training programs, but from what I've heard, it's something you know a lot about. So teach me."

I explained that he'd need to start by learning to name his own thinking talents, then claim, reframe, and aim them. Like many of us, Nick gave to everyone else what he most needed to give to himself. Later that day, I sat in on his leadership team meeting, fascinated as he went around the room naming a specific moment when he had observed each person excel. The besieged director of marketing was last: "Chandra, you pulled your team forward when they had to make that presentation for the board by matching each person with what he or she is best at and then letting them work together like fingers on a hand. You let *them* take the credit while you stood in the back of the room. That's leadership at its best."

By the time Nick's team went to work on their agenda items, the energy in the room was highly charged: Every person's particular assets were front and center in their minds, waiting to be aimed.

After the meeting was over, I pulled Nick aside and pointed out how effective that had been, with one exception. "The only person in the room who didn't have his talents recognized was you! You didn't name a 'moment of greatness' for yourself or allow anyone else to do it either. If you aren't aware specifically of the talents you bring to the game, how can you ever develop them to serve others? That's not self-promotion or selfishness. It is simply, as author Parker Palmer says, good stewardship of the gifts you were put on earth to offer."

He unconsciously pulled on that right ear again and shook his head sheepishly. "What can I say? I was raised to believe that tooting your own horn meant you were a conceited jerk. But I do understand where you are coming from. Okay, one of my thinking talents obviously is mentoring, right?"

He went on to enchant me with one compelling example after another. He had inspired the sales force to beat last year's numbers in spite of the financial downturn and proved that growing people could help grow results. He told me how he had just promoted to the position of senior district manager a man from Nigeria whom he had hired years earlier as a rookie salesman. He shared how he had sponsored a local foster child to become a champion basketball star in his community. This wasn't bragging. Nick genuinely lit up with each story.

The following day, we sat down at his big oak desk and went through the thinking-talents assessment. As we reviewed his choices, Nick leaned his chin on his right hand and covered his mouth with his fingers, actually blushing as he told me that he knew he had an ability to recognize and develop greatness in people, unlike the rest of the senior leaders in the company. He stood up, took his phone out of his pocket, and began to toss it in the air mindlessly as he launched into a long and excited story about how he also could sell anybody anything, even the toughest customers they had. It wasn't because he was slick but rather because he could fix any problem a customer had. "I guess fixing people's problems *is* another one of my thinking talents." Again, I could see him light up. I knew he could feel the energy that pulsed through him as he said those words.

I pulled out a blank piece of paper and asked him to trace his hand on it, writing "Mentoring" in the palm and "Fixing It" on top of the index finger. As he began to recognize that feeling as an indicator that he did have a particular thinking talent, he meticulously wrote "Get to Action," "Optimism," and "Storytelling" on the other three fingers.

As I stood up, ready to leave, Nick's phone buzzed and he looked at the screen. After apologizing, he furiously texted a message and waited for a reply. I assumed the stock market had tanked. He received another text and then slammed his phone on the desk. He explained it was from his seventeen-year-old son, Randy, who was supposed to notify his father whenever he used the family car. Nick picked the phone up and speed-dialed. This struck me as unusual behavior, since he had made a rule for all team meetings that phones had to be deposited in a basket outside the door.

As he spoke to his son, a shadow crossed his face. Nick pelted Randy with advice about what he should and shouldn't be doing and what terrible things would result in the future if he didn't follow these suggestions.

When the phone was back in his pocket, he paced around the desk and asked me, with great frustration, "Why does everyone at work love to listen to me but my own family ignores me? Why do I inspire everyone in the company but my family says I control them? And why, when I'm only trying to help him so he won't have to struggle like I did, does my own son tell me to just leave him alone and give him space?"

I went over and put my hand on his shoulder, explaining that the very capacities that had made him such a successful CEO were making him falter as a father and husband. He stopped dead in his tracks. I described shadow attributes and ticked off on each finger how "fixing it" made his son feel disrespected, because he wanted to learn to work through his own challenges; how "optimism" led his wife to feel that he swept family problems under the rug; how "getting to action" made the family feel stressed, because they could never just relax; and how Randy felt unloved, because he interpreted his father's "mentoring" as dissatisfaction and disrespect.

Nick took a step back, moving away from me. His right hand went up to pull his ear. "How do you know all that? Has my wife been talking to you behind my back? Besides, I thought you were on my side and believed in focusing on assets. This all sounds pretty deficit-focused to me!"

I laughed and reassured him that shadow attributes are not deficits. They are just talents that are eclipsed. When he brought them into his awareness and used them as artfully as he did at work, he would be able to support those he loved the most.

"This is really interesting, Dawna. I mean it, but what makes it hard to do that at home is that I am a champion worrier, especially about the future. I worry obsessively and excessively about all the terrible things that could happen, that will happen, to those I love and am supposed to protect."

I invited him to sit down with me and analyze his thinking-talents map, to discover what was contributing to his stress. He hovered over the desk and pointed to the obvious: There were no talents in the "innovative" domain. Because he had taken numerous training programs in strategic analysis and action planning, he had skills in this area, but skills are not talents, and they didn't prevent him from worrying. This empty quadrant was Nick's blind spot, causing him to be like a car driving in the night without high beams, veering helter-skelter in the dark, worrying endlessly about every possible negative outcome.

I asked him to draw a pie chart representing how he spent his time at work. He divided it into sections that showed the kinds of tasks he did on a typical day. Then he circled in green the tasks where he got to use his talents and in red the tasks where he had skills but no talents. We discovered that 40 percent of his time was spent in the red zone. I asked him to create a second chart and label it "Desired Future." He assigned 90 percent of his time to those tasks that maximized his thinking talents. In order to make this desired future happen, we looked at the maps of his leadership team and figured out how to form thinking partnerships with those members who excelled in the innovative domain, where he had a blind spot. Not only did this enable Nick to get support in tasks that were typically laborious for him, it also freed him up to use his relational thinking talents to mentor others. This was, and still is, unusual and courageous behavior for a CEO. It created true "connective tissue" for the other leaders, because, like the sports teams he admired, everyone knew how to be of real support to one another in achieving a common goal.

To make Nick's self-discovery relevant to you, consider these questions:

- Which thinking talents do you habitually use?
- Which of your thinking talents are hidden as shadow attributes waiting to be developed?
- What are your blind spots?
- Which quadrant is causing you the most worry?

THINKING TALENTS—WHAT LIGHTS YOU UP/WHAT BURNS YOU OUT?

TALENT	LIGHTS YOU UP	BURNS YOU OUT
Adapting	• Helping when there are many balls to juggle or plans go awry. • When there is rapid change happening.	• When others are inflexible. • Long-term plans or routine.

TALENT	LIGHTS YOU UP	BURNS YOU OUT
Believing	• When there is a strong sense of purpose. • When you can make decisions based on your values.	• People who don't know where they stand. • Having to compromise your values.
Collecting	• Acquiring, compiling, and filing away things. • Collecting data, facts, or information.	• Letting go of what is no longer needed. • Lack of organization.
Connection	• Making connections between things or ideas. • Linking people to one another.	• Thinking linearly. • Conflict.
Creating Intimacy	• Teaming with others long-term. • Consistent one-on-one connection with others.	• Meeting and greeting new people in casual settings. • Hectic schedules that don't allow for deeper connection.
Enrolling	• Meeting new people. • Looking for chances to sell or enlisting others.	• Maintaining close relationships over time. • Isolation and routine in relationships.
Equalizing	• Creating and applying rules and regulations to maximize fairness. • Making expectations explicit and consistent.	• Unfair or special treatment. • Changing guidelines.
Feeling for Others	• Demonstrating emotional care for someone. • Anticipating others' needs and feelings.	• Being around negative feelings or pessimistic people. • Too much communication (email, text) when you cannot sense the other person's emotions.
Fixing It	• Identifying or anticipating what might go wrong and fixing or averting it—people, situations, or things. • Rescuing or saving people, things, or situations.	• When you can see what's wrong and can't fix it. • When others don't want you to help—for instance, when they want to learn to do it themselves.
Focusing	• Uninterrupted freedom to concentrate on a goal with timelines. • Keeping others on point.	• Being interrupted or having to multitask. • When purpose, task, deadlines are not clearly defined or understood.

TALENT	LIGHTS YOU UP	BURNS YOU OUT
Get to Action	• Spurring others out of talk into action. • Making something happen as soon as possible; short timelines.	• Indecision or meetings without clear goals. • Contemplation and analysis rather than action.
Goal-Setting	• Defining and tracking daily concrete goals to work toward. • Big targets and challenging goals and assignments.	• Absence of specific ways to measure progress. • Time off or work that is not challenging.
Having Confidence	• Autonomy of action and decision. • Calming challenging situations with employees or customers.	• Being in a position where you have to ask for help. • Being told what to say, do, or think.
Humor	• Lightening otherwise-tense moments and putting others at ease. • Using humor in written communication or speeches.	• Using humor as a defense strategy to protect yourself from others or your own emotions. • Highly analytic situations or those where humor is seen as a challenge to authority.
Including	• Finding ways to make others feel a part of the group. • Welcoming new people.	• Firing people, sharing bad news or difficult information. • Excluding someone from a situation where they would be useful.
Innovation	• Creating new processes or products. • Figuring out all the new ways to accomplish something or keep them interesting.	• Routine and standardized ways of doing things. • Looking back at how something was done before.
Love of Learning	• Continual learning. • Sharing what you are learning.	• Leapfrogging from learning thing to thing without any depth. • Having to do routine things when no learning is involved.

TALENT	LIGHTS YOU UP	BURNS YOU OUT
Loving Ideas	• Having a new idea, concept, or theory. • Being involved at the beginning of something.	• Having no place to contribute your ideas. • Coming in at the middle or end of a project, when you have to suppress your ideas or give input on how it could be done.
Making Order	• Lining things up in a logical way. • When many things are going on at the same time and you get to create a sequence.	• When your capacity to align different variables isn't needed or valued. For example, there is already a system developed and you cannot offer input. • When you cannot make order out of chaos or confusion.
Mentoring	• Helping others grow their potential. • Guiding people through new situations.	• Trying to help a struggling employee when it's appropriate to give up. • When there is no opportunity to grow someone. For example, if the focus is only on the bottom line and not on development of people.
Optimism	• Finding ways to recognize what's right about a challenging situation. • Painting an exciting picture of possibilities.	• Being around skepticism. • Having to recognize pitfalls, problems, or give negative feedback.
Particularize	• Recognizing and sharing what is unique about someone. • Tailoring something to meet the specific needs of someone else.	• When a one-size-fits-all or standardized approach is required. • Generalizations about people.
Peace-making	• Resolving conflicts or arguments. • Finding common ground or consensus.	• Unresolved conflict. • Standing up for your own needs.

TALENT	LIGHTS YOU UP	BURNS YOU OUT
Precision	• Setting up predictable routines, timelines, and deadlines. • Maintaining progress and productivity.	• Situations that require flexibility, instinct; unpredictable changes. • Unable to question how exactly to do things.
Reliability	• Living up to commitments. • Delivering on time—every time.	• Others' excuses and rationalizations for lack of performance or not living up to commitments. • Being responsible for others and things not in your control.
Seeking Excellence	• Doing the best you can with the least. • Continual improvement to make things better.	• Inefficient processes or meetings. • Having to accept something mediocre or go with the status quo.
Standing Out	• Doing something for which you know you'll be recognized. • Performing in a way that allows you to stand out as having made a difference.	• When your contribution is not acknowledged. • Being invisible in a team or group.
Storytelling	• Bringing ideas to life through story. • Inspiring others to engage through narratives.	• Having to think with only facts and figures. • Thinking only in "why" and "how."
Strategy	• Finding alternative possibilities and options. • Anticipating future challenges and their solutions.	• Shortsightedness. • Single-mindedness, as in "My way or the highway."
Taking Charge	• Directing others into action. • Unifying engagement.	• Working alone. • Having no opportunity to lead.
Thinking Ahead	• Seeing the possible future outcomes of an action or event. • Helping others overcome fears of the future.	• People whose thinking is stuck in the past. • Others' dismal view of future possibilities.

TALENT	LIGHTS YOU UP	BURNS YOU OUT
Thinking Alone	• Time to think through situations and contemplate pros and cons. • Solitude to explore what you believe at your own rhythm.	• Being put on the spot to respond immediately, without advance notice. • No personal space or time to mull over a decision.
Thinking Back	• Setting a historical context for a present problem. • Recalling how things were done in the past.	• When others don't learn from history. • When others jump into what is new without considering what has already been done.
Thinking Logically	• Thinking about and explaining why something is the way it is. • Exposing holes in partial thinking.	• Intuitive action. • Hidden or partial logic.
Wanting to Win	• Competing against someone else. • Having specific targets to measure who wins.	• "Everyone wins" philosophy. • Having no way to prove you can be the best.

BREAKTHROUGH PRACTICE:
CREATING INTERNAL AND EXTERNAL COHERENCE

The following two practices will help grow your capacity to use the thinking-talents strategy. The first focuses on creating an *internal* coherence of your talents. The second helps you identify *external* thinking resources that you may need to complement your blind spots. They can be applied in both personal and professional contexts.

The sum of something can be greater than a total of its parts. That's certainly true of thinking talents. When they are combined, aligned, and working well together, you have a sense of internal coherence, similar to a chord in music. A chord is a harmonic set of three or more notes that is heard as a simultaneous sound. The harmony of different notes creates the magnetism.

When individual notes aren't combined well, they create noise rather than music. When your talents clash, it can feel like an internal battle: "I have a great idea, *but* I can't see the reason to change what we have been doing for years" (*"innovation"* battling *"thinking back"*). "I want to get this done, *but* I'm worried about what people might think" (*"get to action"* battling *"feeling for others"*). "I'm trying to get organized, *but* everyone else has needs that are more important" (*"making order"* battling *"adapting"*).

The static in these examples is caused by just two talents opposing each other. Imagine the cacophony when five or six are pulling you in different directions. Whether you are trying to accomplish a task, make a decision, or generate ideas, you need to bring as much of your capacity to it as possible by aligning all of your diverse talents. Creating this kind of internal coherence is a practice that requires you to understand the needs of each. We call it "consulting your inner board of directors."

BREAKTHROUGH PRACTICE PART 1:
CREATING AN INNER BOARD OF DIRECTORS

This is a practice to use when you feel inner tension or are facing an important decision. It's a way of making sure you are putting the best of your capacity to good use rather than being dominated by one or another of your talents. Here's how:

- Write each thinking talent on a card or Post-it.
- Place them in front of you.
- Go through them one by one, asking each the following question: "How can this thinking talent help me in approaching this challenge?" Write down the answer to this question.
- Looking at all of your answers, consider what new actions you could take.

BREAKTHROUGH PRACTICE PART 2:
FORMING THINKING PARTNERSHIPS

- Create a pie chart of how you spend your time at work or at home. You may choose to make a separate one for each.
- Put a mark on each task where you get to use your thinking talents and a different mark for those tasks where you don't.
- Reflect on the task you worry about the most. Notice which quadrant it falls in and the thinking talent that would be most effective to resolve it.
- Consider all the people in your world and search for the one(s) who might possess that capacity. Think also about those who might benefit most from the talents that come naturally to you.
- Form one or more thinking partnerships for a limited period of time to help each other work through challenges. Then evaluate whether you are worrying less and excelling more as a result.

Angie shares a story of how using these practices helped the CEO of a nonprofit foundation access her capacities to create career breakthroughs.

Anne had been struggling with whether to stay with the nonprofit she had built from scratch or to start something new. She was deeply invested in the organization's success but was tired of the bureaucracy that had evolved. Leaving meant increased financial risk and limiting her available resources; she'd have to start over again. Anne felt stuck between internal opposing forces. She was at a major life intersection and struggling with how to think through it. We were sitting in a café in Brazil, sipping celebratory mojitos. We had just completed a major workshop for children and educators, and Anne's mind turned to "Now what?" I pulled out my laptop and shared the thinking-talents map that she had created the previous month. I then asked her to think of each of her talents, like a wise member of an inner board of directors, and consider what advice they would each offer.

One by one, Anne consulted her talents: Standing Out told her it was time to be recognized for something original and to develop a new brand; Enrolling reminded her that she had all the people necessary to get a new venture off the ground; Feeling for Others advised her that the future happiness of the people in her existing foundation was very important; Believing said that she was still passionate about the mission of that organization; Adapting suggested that she find a way to do both; and Getting to Action insisted that she not stall or procrastinate on either option.

Then Anne leaped to her feet and said, "Why do I have to choose one or the other?" She realized she could stage her departure from the foundation, consulting with them over the next eighteen months, which would allow her to maintain some needed resources and connections while giving her the autonomy to start her own business. By drawing on the collaborative intelligence of her whole inner board of directors, she found a way to connect her past accomplishments and her future horizon. That warranted another mojito!

A month later, Anne's Chicago home-base apartment was the site of our next rendezvous. We sat next to each other on a couch covered with an Indian silk throw, surrounded by objects collected from her travels. As she began to share her current state, I noticed that her voice sounded deflated. Since our last conversation, she had plenty of time to feel the tension between where she had been and where she wanted to go.

First I asked her if she was still sure she wanted to start her own company. "Of course," she replied immediately. "I just don't have the slightest idea how to get there." I suggested we look at her thinking-talents map again, to see the internal resources she had to do that. The first thing we noticed was how strong she was in the relational quadrant. I wrote the concerns she had on Post-its and placed each next to the appropriate quadrant. We put her worry about writing a business plan into the analytic quadrant; her worry about developing an infrastructure and an action plan fell into the procedural quadrant.

We discovered that all of her concerns, in fact, fell into the analytic and procedural quadrants. Interestingly, her blind spots were where I had most of my thinking talents. I suggested we create a thinking partnership to help her strategize through the transition. Her shoulders relaxed and her face lit up as she said, "I still have no idea how I'll get there, but now I can't wait to get started!"

The strategy of thinking talents will truly light you up. It will keep you from getting stuck and burned out in habitual thinking and it will make you feel more fully alive when approaching a new challenge. Each time you use it, the world will appear more full of possibilities and your contribution to it more apparent. It will energize the innate desire you have to make a difference, and it will help you find your way around dark corners guided by someone else's brightness.

CHAPTER SUMMARY

KEY CONCEPTS OF THIS CHAPTER	GUIDELINES
Thinking talents are your innate ways of thinking. They help you understand your own potential and learn to recognize and connect with the gifts of others.	To create breakthrough thinking, consider how you can engage the most energized talent of each person in your group, including yourself. Knowing your thinking talents will give you energy, help you excel at work, and prevent burnout.
Three forces can prevent you from recognizing your thinking talents: • Deficit-oriented culture • Parental influence • They are invisible to us	Using the tools in this chapter, identify your five or six predominant thinking talents by what makes you feel energized and grows your excellence. To recognize your thinking talents: • Track what is right with you. • Notice societal and parental influences that steer you away from your natural gifts. • Consider the innate talents you may not have developed yet.
Shadow attributes are thinking talents disguised as deficits. Awareness can transform a shadow attribute into a thinking talent.	Identify shadow attributes in familiar behaviors to help you uncover and develop the thinking talents beneath them. Transform a shadow attribute into a talent by naming it, containing it, and aiming it.
Each of the thinking talents is categorized into one of four cognitive styles.	Organize your thinking talents into their cognitive styles (analytic, procedural, relational, innovative) to best leverage them.
Identify the blind spots revealed by your thinking talents to identify where you need support.	Form thinking partnerships with those whose strengths complement your blind spots.

BECOMING A THINKING PARTNER TO OTHERS

The word ubuntu *means that a person becomes human through other persons.*

—Archbishop Desmond Tutu

In the previous chapter, you identified your own thinking talents and cognitive styles. As our client Nick discovered, you first need to be aware of your own talents and blind spots and understand how they show up in different situations. Now it's time for you to learn how to recognize and utilize the thinking talents of others.

There are three specific situations where knowing someone's thinking talents is immensely helpful:

- When you want to strengthen your connection and increase your influence with someone.
- When you encounter a specific challenge or breakdown with a person and want to move beyond it.
- When you want to increase the chances that someone else will understand your ideas.

Let's start by looking at how to use thinking talents to strengthen your connection and increase your influence with someone else.

Increasing your influence does not mean forcing other people to think the way you do. Being influenced does not mean having to agree with someone else. Rather, influence involves creating permeability in *your* thinking so that collaboration can naturally emerge between you and another person. This means you are willing to stretch your mind and become more curious about that other person, rather than sealing yourself off in an isolated bubble with your own opinions.

The way you influence another person is unconscious in most situations. In the well-worn paths of habitual thinking, you either like someone or not; you decide they are with you or against you. Without realizing it, you may withhold such resources as personal connections you may have, knowledge from your own life experience, financial or moral support of a project or idea. Obviously, thinking like this does not lead to effective collaboration.

As Nick learned, you may not be able to change other people, but you can change how you perceive them and how you relate to them. Understanding thinking talents can empower you to develop rapport and deepen connections where you never thought possible.

We've developed a three-step process to increase permeability in your thinking so you can understand more clearly what drives someone else's thinking:

WALK CURIOUSLY IN ANOTHER PERSON'S SHOES

1. Ask questions that will help you discover what energizes the other person.

For example:

- "Tell me about a time in your past when you felt truly engaged. What were the conditions that allowed that to happen?"

- "In your current work situation, what energizes you and makes you want to be a part of this team?"

2. Figure out which thinking talent(s) the person was using to generate that energy.

Refer again to the thinking-talents map. Sometimes it is easier to notice which of the four cognitive styles is driving the thinking—analytic, procedural, relational, or innovative. Other times, it is easier to pick up on the specific thinking talent. Written below each talent on the map is a general characteristic that people may display if they have that particular talent.

3. Establish rapport by acknowledging the person's thinking talents.

Communicate in the language of that individual's thinking talent. The characteristics below each talent can help you do this. For instance, if you sense that "believing" is driving his or her thinking, refer to those values or talk about yours. For example: "I hear how much you believe in this and how important it is to you." Or, if "thinking logically" is influential, you may say: "I'll try to make my logic explicit, so you know where I am coming from." This is a natural way to demonstrate respect. The person will know you "get" him or her.

In the story that follows, Angie teaches a high-strung designer how to use these three steps to engage and influence others:

Jan was in high demand but complained about the continual staff turnover at her interior-design firm. She knew she had the reputation of being a "tough broad" and realized changes were needed. Training new people over and over was disruptive and aggravating, so she wanted to learn to create better rapport with her staff. To do this, I suggested that she had to become more permeable in her thinking.

DRIVERS-OF-THINKING MAP

ANALYTIC
Concerned with data, facts, numbers, being "logical" and rational

INNOVATIVE
Concerned with the future, newness, possibilities, strategy, "big picture"

Making Order
Organizing and aligning

Thinking Logically
Rational and data-focused

Talents in All Quadrants

Innovation
New and different approaches

Loving Ideas
Looking for new theories, concepts

Seeking Excellence
Making the most of everything

Collecting
Acquiring things or facts

Love of Learning
Drawn to learn something new

Thinking Ahead
Always focused on the future

Fixing It
Seeing what's wrong, solving problems

Wanting to Win
Inspired by competition

Standing Out
Desiring recognition for success

Strategy
Finding alternate scenarios, options

Adapting
Flexible, doesn't mind change

Reliability
Responsible and accountable

Thinking Back
Using the past as a benchmark

Humor
Always finding humor in situations

Optimism
Positive enthusiasm

Including
"All for one, one for all"

Connection
Networking, building bridges

Get to Action
Making something happen now

Having Confidence
Self-assured

Thinking Alone
Needing time to contemplate

Creating Intimacy
Maintaining deep relationships

Peacemaking
Seeking harmony

Enrolling
Creating new relationships

Focusing
Single-minded concentration

Equalizing
Fairness for everyone

Goal-Setting
Constantly driven to accomplish

Storytelling
Using stories to inspire

Particularize
Observing and fostering uniqueness

Believing
Ethical, high values

Taking Charge
Directing others into action

Precision
Concerned with exactness

Mentoring
Fostering growth in others

Feeling for Others
Empathetic

PROCEDURAL
Concerned with process, operations, logistics, tactics

RELATIONAL
Concerned with feelings, morale, teamwork, development of people

The first employee she introduced me to was Mike, a talented carpenter-craftsman who was down on his luck and grateful for this work, even though it was below his skill level. Jan had been thinking of letting him go because he was "slower than a snail" and needed specific directions for everything, but she agreed to use the three steps to try to connect with Mike rather than fire him.

Jan sat across from Mike as he built a piece of furniture, and she noticed how he meticulously laid out every screw, nut, and piece of hardware, like a surgical nurse prepping for a big operation. In order to find what lit him up and energized him, she said, "I've been surveying people around here, Mike, and want your opinion as well. What would be the ideal work environment for you—one that could allow you to work at your best?"

After thinking about it for a minute, he responded, "Just a lot of space. I like to keep everything organized. I am a little frustrated in here, because I don't have enough room." She recognized immediately that he might have the thinking talents of making order and precision. As she continued asking him similar questions, he responded with many new ideas as well as suggestions for how to get things done more efficiently. This told her that procedural and innovative cognitive styles were driving his thinking.

Jan told Mike that she had noticed how meticulously he organized things when he worked and asked how he had learned to do that. He lit up immediately, recalling that since childhood he loved to label, organize, and keep everything in perfect order. Jan told him how much he contributed to the excellence of her company and how she appreciated his reliability as well as his new ideas. He tried to shrug it off as nothing. She leaned in closer, explaining that she felt a tremendous pressure to get projects finished on time and would appreciate his ideas on how to accomplish that. He stood up, tilted his head, and winked. "Sure. I'd love to help; just give me some time to think about it." She recognized that thinking alone could very well be another of his talents. He walked away, beaming and whistling. For the first time Jan felt a rapport between them. I explained to her that this connection had been created because she became curious enough to notice and acknowledge his ideas, precision, and value.

When we make an effort to recognize what generates energy for another person, as Jan did, a collaborative contagion begins to spread. But it's not always easy with someone who thinks differently from you.

ENGAGING WITH A PERSON WHO CHALLENGES YOU

In the same way that Jan did, you need to become curious about the thinking talent that may lie beneath an annoying behavior in someone around you. Use the shadow-attributes map below and ask yourself the following questions to recognize and engage that talent:

- What specifically annoys or frustrates you the most?
- Which thinking talent could this represent?
- Is this related to a blind spot you or they have?
- How could you learn from them?
- How could you create a partnership where you support each other's blind spots?

In the story that follows, Nick, the CEO we met earlier, demonstrates how this strategy can be used to increase your perception of the options you have when dealing with a "difficult" person.

Nick closed all the doors of his cavernous office as soon as I walked in. He asked his assistant to hold all calls. He told me to sit on the couch, while he paced back and forth in front of me. There were no opening pleasantries; Nick launched right in. "This thinking-talent stuff has been great, and my inner board of directors is working really well. There is still one person I worry about, though: Martin, my boss and chairman of my outer board. I worry before my meetings with him. I'm clenched so tight when we are together that I can't think straight. Then I worry about what did happen and what could happen for days after the meeting." He

THINKING-TALENTS AND SHADOW-ATTRIBUTES MAP

ANALYTIC
Concerned with data, facts, numbers, being "logical" and rational

INNOVATIVE
Concerned with the future, newness, possibilities, strategy, "big picture"

Making Order
Controlling

Thinking Logically
Skeptical

Talents in All Quadrants

Innovation
"There must be a way!"

Loving Ideas
Pie in the sky

Seeking Excellence
Never satisfied

Collecting
Hoarding

Love of Learning
Learning junkie

Thinking Ahead
Crystal-ball gazing

Wanting to Win
Ruthless

Standing Out
Narcissist

Strategy
Scheming

Fixing It
Critical

Humor
Wise-ass

Adapting
Wishy-washy

Reliability
Plays by the rules

Thinking Back
Stuck in the past

Optimism
Cheerleading

Including
Consults everyone on everything

Connection
Enmeshed in ideas or people

Get to Action
Impatient

Thinking Alone
Loner

Having Confidence
Arrogant

Creating Intimacy
Overly loyal

Peace-making
Conflict-avoidant

Enrolling
Creating new relationships

Focusing
Obsessive about one thing

Equalizing
"It's not fair!"

Goal-Setting
Driven

Storytelling
Exaggerating

Particularize
Nosy

Believing
Righteous

Taking Charge
Bossy

Precision
Nitpicky

Mentoring
Preachy

Feeling for Others
Co-dependent

PROCEDURAL
Concerned with process, operations, logistics, tactics

RELATIONAL
Concerned with feelings, morale, teamwork, development of people

stopped pacing and stood frozen in front of me, his hands clenched into tight fists. "How am I supposed to fix *this,* Dawna?" I could hear the urgency in his request, but before I could offer help, I needed to know more.

Decades as a thinking partner have taught me one thing: *It isn't the difficult person you have to change; rather, it's how you relate to that person.* I reminded Nick of John Wooden's coaching—that each player needs to be at his or her best during adversity, when the best is what's needed. I asked him what was keeping him from relating to Martin with his best thinking.

He looked down and then responded, "He just complains constantly about how we can't go on in the future making the same mistakes as we have in the past. Then he ticks off a laundry list of all the things he knows *could* go wrong in the future and how that will affect the stock price. I worry before, during, and after our meetings."

I pointed to his hands and commented that they looked like the hands of a *warrior,* not a worrier. I asked which one he wanted to feel like when meeting with Martin. He crossed his arms over his chest and said emphatically, "The warrior, of course! But he's like a rock in the middle of a river that I can't get rid of or even move. So I'm just stuck!"

I got up, stood next to him, and explained that by studying what energized Martin's thinking, Nick could change the way he was *relating* to him. I had made a talent map as Nick described what drove his boss's thinking. I wrote Nick's talents on it also, so we could compare them and find where and how they could connect.

Nick hovered over the map as if it were the Rosetta stone. (See Team Map Example 1.) He was stunned. "No wonder!" he mumbled, shifting his eyes back and forth. "No wonder he always begins with what he wants to have happen in the future. Look at his innovative quadrant—exactly where my blind spot is, where I worry!"

I pointed out that, conversely, Martin's blind spots were in procedural and relational thinking, where Nick had an abundance of

TEAM MAP EXAMPLE 1

ANALYTIC
Concerned with data, facts, numbers, being "logical" and rational

INNOVATIVE
Concerned with the future, newness, possibilities, strategy, "big picture"

 Making Order

 Thinking Logically

 **Talents in All Quadrants**

 Innovation *Martin*

 Loving Ideas *Martin*

 Seeking Excellence

 Collecting

 Wanting to Win *Martin*

 Love of Learning

 Thinking Ahead *Martin*

 Fixing It *Nick*

 Humor

 Standing Out

 Strategy *Martin*

 Adapting

PROCEDURAL
Concerned with process, operations, logistics, tactics

RELATIONAL
Concerned with feelings, morale, teamwork, development of people

 Reliability

 Thinking Back

 Thinking Alone *Martin*

 Optimism *Nick*

 Including

 Connection

 Get to Action *Nick*

 Having Confidence

 Creating Intimacy

 Peace-making

 Enrolling

 Focusing

 Equalizing

 Goal-Setting

 Storytelling *Nick*

 Particularize

 Believing

 Taking Charge

Precision

Mentoring *Nick*

Feeling for Others

thinking talents and never worried. Pointing to his boss's map, he exclaimed, "I get it, I get it! That must be why he stresses about how we are going to get things done and doesn't seem to care about the effect he has on people at all. I keep throwing my best ideas about operations and people right at the very places where he has blind spots—what you're calling his procedural and relational quadrants."

Nick's excitement over these realizations was contagious. We both recognized how much each of them was causing the other to worry. Rather than suggesting they were doomed to be adversaries, the maps showed the way to them becoming a pair of powerful thinking partners. Nick needed to learn how to develop rapport with his boss so he could change the flow of the conversation. Knowing that Nick had been a supreme and natural salesman, I asked, "What if this were the map of one of your most difficult and important customers?"

Pacing in front of me, Nick replied, "That's a no-brainer. What I would do is let the customer tell me about his vision for the future. Then I'd offer suggestions for how to fix what isn't working and point out specifically how the people of the organization could make his vision a reality." He turned and punched me gently in the shoulder. "Aha! Now I get what you are saying about how to relate to Martin."

I explained how acknowledging Martin's future visions would calm him down and enable him to be much more open to following Nick's suggestions on how to get to action.

"You make it sound so easy," he said. "Are you really saying that just changing the sequence I use to talk to Martin will make him a kinder, nicer person?"

I emphasized that trying to change his boss was like banging his head against that rock. If, instead, he used his warrior-like mastery of finding and developing rapport with a very difficult customer, the way he related to Martin would change. He could use worry as a signal that rapport was needed. This increased the possibility that they could become collaborative partners and each have the other's back.

Nick threw his head back and laughed out loud. "Now, *that's* a Possibilist's story!"

In the months that followed, he made that story of partnership into a reality. He used his relational talents to become a thinking partner with Martin and as a result was promoted to CEO of the parent company, a position where he could truly foster the greatness in the people he led. (See Team Map Example 1, which maps the talents of Nick and Martin's team.)

HOW TO USE THINKING TALENTS TO BECOME MORE EFFECTIVE AS A TEAM

If you ever feel lost, overwhelmed, or disengaged when working with your group, consider it as a signal that the intellectual capital of your team is not being fully engaged. Rather than just accept the situation, you can transform it. The most powerful way to do this is by first inventorying the total intellectual capital of your group.

- Begin by taking a blank map, like the one you used for yourself in the chapter Uncovering Your Thinking Talents, and write your name below your thinking talents.
- Then ask the people you are working with to complete the assessment for themselves and share their talents with you.
- Compile the results into a single map by writing each person's name below his or her thinking talents.
- When finished, share this map with the team. It will display the specific intellectual capital of this group. It reveals who has which talents, as well as the ones that are missing. This map is a fundamental tool for recognizing whether your team has the resources to create breakthroughs and think collaboratively.

TEAM MAP EXAMPLE 2

ANALYTIC
Concerned with data, facts, numbers, being "logical" and rational

INNOVATIVE
Concerned with the future, newness, possibilities, strategy, "big picture"

Making Order

Thinking Logically

Talents in All Quadrants

Innovation
Leslie, Jamie, Daniel

Loving Ideas
Maggie

Seeking Excellence

Collecting
Daniel

Love of Learning
Jamie, Daniel

Thinking Ahead
Maggie

Wanting to Win
Jamie, Jody

Fixing It

Standing Out
Maggie

Strategy
Jamie, Daniel, Maggie

Humor
Leslie

Adapting

Reliability
Jody

Thinking Back
Daniel

Optimism
Jamie

Including

Connection
Maggie

Thinking Alone
Leslie, Jody

Get to Action
Daniel, Maggie

Having Confidence
Daniel

Creating Intimacy

Peace-making

Enrolling

Focusing
Jody

Equalizing
Leslie

Goal-Setting
Jody

Storytelling

Particularize

Believing
Jody

Taking Charge

Precision
Leslie

Mentoring

Feeling for Others

PROCEDURAL
Concerned with process, operations, logistics, tactics

RELATIONAL
Concerned with feelings, morale, teamwork, development of people

Now comes the fun part. "Read" the overall strengths and gaps of the team. It doesn't matter whether there are two or fifteen members; there is immense value in seeing the total talent profile, because in a very real way it illuminates the intellectual capital of the group. For instance, in Team Map Example 2, this particular team is strong in innovative and procedural thinking, with a few relational talents, but has a large gap in the analytic domain. More on the implications for this team in a bit.

In addition to mapping the team as a whole, you may also want to map any sub-team or small group that consistently interacts. A functional team may have thirteen people who meet once a month, as well as small groups of two or three who interact daily. It would be useful to create maps for both.

WHAT TEAM MAPS CAN TELL YOU

After using this process to assess the intellectual capital of his company's senior leadership, Jeff Dunn, CEO of Bolthouse Farms, said, "Using these maps helped us realize that our results would only change if we changed the way we were thinking. They showed us exactly how to find the way to do that."

Your team map will enable you to quickly gauge what kinds of talents and cognitive styles are present and what is missing in a team. If a talent is needed but absent, you can add new members to your team or ask them to join meetings as advisers. For example, after Angie helped them create their talent map, the senior-leadership team illustrated in Team Map Example 2 was amazed to discover their predominance of innovative and procedural thinking and their lack of analytic talents. This explained why ideas arose and the team immediately turned them into action without evaluating the financial implications or the competition. Once they understood this inherent void, they added a new team member, who was strong in analytic thinking, and had her create a list of questions to use in vetting every new idea.

Another team we worked with was highly compatible because there were so many members with the same thinking talent: "seeking excellence." They all fell predominantly within the analytic quadrant. (See Team Map Example 3.) Without consciously realizing it, the CEO had hired people who were "smart" the way she was. But that did not make them highly effective. It just gave them the same blind spot. As a result, they approached any challenge that arose and overworked it from this one perspective, trying to achieve perfection on the smallest of issues while ignoring other important factors. In addition, people with a different perspective tended to silence themselves rather than go against the collective grain. If they did risk speaking, they were disregarded or disrespected. Too much of any one kind of thinking can result in major mistakes.

Think of a time when someone on your team proposed an action and everyone else jumped quickly on board. Your question or reservation kept you from agreeing, but you didn't want to stop that forward movement. Whether you risked saying something or not, you may now realize that your perspective was very important, because it could have shed light on a collective blind spot. A team map can help everyone recognize a blind spot and create an opening for you to speak.

It also can reveal whose thinking is present and whose is missing in the room in real time. When someone is absent or there is a change in membership, the thinking dynamics and results change. Look at the team of five people in Team Map Example 4.

When Jane is absent, the thinking becomes drastically different. There's no one to create a story for communicating what the rest of the team generates; there is no one to get others on board and enroll them in their vision or give an effective elevator speech at the next leadership meeting. The map reveals the value that she brings, and it enables the team to be explicit in asking her to find a way to contribute even when she is not there.

A team map can also tell you how to re-aim a shadow attribute constructively. A boutique engineering firm we worked with in

TEAM MAP EXAMPLE 3

ANALYTIC
Concerned with data, facts, numbers, being "logical" and rational

Making Order
Tom, Corienne, Chuck, Pete, Maria

Thinking Logically
Corienne, Chuck, Maria

Seeking Excellence
Corienne, Pete, Tom

Collecting
Tom, Maria

Fixing It
Chuck

INNOVATIVE
Concerned with the future, newness, possibilities, strategy, "big picture"

Innovation

Loving Ideas

Love of Learning
Chuck

Thinking Ahead

Standing Out

Strategy
Maria

Adapting

Talents in All Quadrants

Wanting to Win
Chuck, Pete

Humor
Tom

Thinking Alone

Goal-Setting
Pete, Maria

PROCEDURAL
Concerned with process, operations, logistics, tactics

Reliability
Tom

Thinking Back
Corienne

Get to Action
Chuck, Tom

Having Confidence
Pete

Focusing

Equalizing

Taking Charge

Precision

RELATIONAL
Concerned with feelings, morale, teamwork, development of people

Optimism

Including

Connection

Creating Intimacy

Peace-making
Corienne

Enrolling

Storytelling

Particularize

Believing

Mentoring

Feeling for Others

TEAM MAP EXAMPLE 4

ANALYTIC
Concerned with data, facts, numbers, being "logical" and rational

INNOVATIVE
Concerned with the future, newness, possibilities, strategy, "big picture"

Making Order

Thinking Logically

Innovation

Loving Ideas
George

Seeking Excellence

Collecting
Joseph

Love of Learning
Joseph

Thinking Ahead
Jane

Fixing It
George,
Susan

Standing Out
Jane

Strategy
Susan

Talents in All Quadrants

Wanting to Win
Sarah

Adapting
Joseph

Humor
Joseph

Reliability
Susan, Sarah

Thinking Back
Joseph

Optimism
Jane

Including

Connection
Jane

Thinking Alone
George

Get to Action
George

Having Confidence
Jane

Creating Intimacy

Peace-making

Enrolling
Jane

Focusing
Susan

Equalizing

Goal-Setting

Storytelling
Jane

Particularize

Believing
Susan

Taking Charge

Precision

Mentoring

Feeling for Others

PROCEDURAL
Concerned with process, operations, logistics, tactics

RELATIONAL
Concerned with feelings, morale, teamwork, development of people

New York illustrated how this can happen. They gathered every week to discuss how to allocate their resources by looking at their workload and divvying up engineers, junior architects, and other personnel so that each team leader had the necessary resources to get the work done. Trent never seemed to have enough people and battled for every staff member he could get. After we mapped their collective thinking talents, they saw that Trent had "wanting to win." No wonder he always fought to get more people! It was natural for him to compete, even against his own colleagues. We suggested they put Trent in charge of winning clients rather than being in charge of a project area. Months later they reported that, as a result of doing this, they were getting more clients than ever before.

You can integrate this strategy with your own team by creating a collective thinking-talents map and considering the following questions:

- Which thinking talents and cognitive styles (quadrants) dominate?
- What kind of thinking is habitual for your team?
- What are the blind spots? What is hard or avoided altogether?
- When your team stresses or worries, which cognitive style or thinking talent is involved?
- Where is support needed? Where and how can you find it?

Refer to the thinking-talents appendix for detailed information about how to help discover and activate the thinking talents of others.

BREAKTHROUGH PRACTICE: BENDING TO BLEND WITH ANOTHER

Influence is the ability to accept and evoke change. This requires knowing how to shift your mind from rigid certainty to flexible curiosity without losing what is called in the Japanese martial art of aikido your "virtuous intent." This does not come naturally to those of us educated in a market-share economy, where we have been taught that being right means we will be respected. Media, politicians, and corporate leaders, unfortunately, model this rigid righteousness.

The word "respect" means "to relate to," "to show consideration for," "to see again." Developing a mind-share mentality means that all of us need to reconsider what we think is possible for ourselves and those who differ from us.

The following deliberate practice of blending, derived from ki aikido, makes it obvious that the most important and difficult aspect of thinking with others is bending. We must bend our minds to truly recognize where others are coming from and what is important for them. And then the next step is to blend with them, moving in their direction and then being aware and present enough to notice when they're ready to bend and go in our direction.

There are two things you need to be aware of to get the most from this practice:

1. You will not be able to bend your own mind if you are not aware of what is important to you and where you ultimately want to go. You will just become as compliant as a jellyfish following a strong tide. You cannot betray yourself to become loyal to someone else. If, on the other hand, you respect and have confidence in your intention, your mind will gladly bend to blend, knowing you will eventually get where you need to go.

2. We have been taught that rugged individualists win. Thus when we are stuck or in need, we tend to isolate ourselves. We have also been trained that the further away we are from someone who is different, the safer we will be. If you have ever worked with horses, you know how untrue that can be. When you walk around a horse's rear end, you learn quickly that *the closer you are, the safer you will be,*

because the horse cannot reach out to kick you if you are right up against it.

Blending with other people to understand their perspective brings you closer to them and thus makes you safer.

This breakthrough practice will allow you to physically experience blending, helping you to integrate this strategy and make it habitual.

BREAKTHROUGH PRACTICE PART 1: IN YOUR OWN TWO HANDS—BLENDING WITH A DIFFICULT PERSON

Place the palm of one hand flat up against the palm of the other. Imagine the right hand is trying to move toward the left and the left hand is trying to move toward the right. The more they try to move in those opposite directions *while maintaining connection*, the more tension you will experience between them. You, of course, know how to disconnect one from the other. We all do that repeatedly and habitually when we find ourselves up against someone who thinks differently. But what if we stayed connected?

Notice how you can allow the right hand to keep pushing, but the left hand bends and follows until it senses that the other has gone as far as it can. In that moment, the left hand, maintaining connection, bends and moves gracefully in the opposite direction. The right hand, having been fully received, is now willing to bend and be carried to the right.

Aikido sensei Terry Dobson used to call this "the only dance there is." It seems simple at first. Allow yourself to do it repeatedly, until it feels like a smooth and graceful dance.

Then imagine as vividly as possible that your right hand represents someone in your world whom you think of as oppositional, or difficult, or just so different from you that you would habitually disconnect as soon as you could. Keep repeating the blending slowly, as you wonder what would be needed to actually do this in words and actions with this person. Allow your hands to teach your mind.

BREAKTHROUGH PRACTICE PART 2: WHOLE BODY PRACTICE—
RELATING INSTEAD OF CONTROLLING

Find a friendly person willing to learn with you for five minutes. Each of you should bring to mind a distinct time at work when your best efforts to advocate for an idea or to influence someone were met with a backlash, resistance, or opposition.

- Stand across from each other. Each of you extend your right arm so the palms touch, representing the connection between you.
- One person (A) begins to push against the other person's hand. The other person (B) responds first by pushing back against A.
- Now try another response to A's push. This time, B collapses or just gives in and complies.

Both of you now pause and take a moment to notice the effect of this way of relating. Share what popped into your minds. For example, Person B might feel at first, "I had to be forceful against you, the way I am when I'm trying to get my fair share of this quarter's budget." In the second scenario, B might feel, "This person's got the most authority, so there's no point in pushing for what I want."

- Now Person B should think of what is really important while taking a deep breath that goes all the way down to his belly.

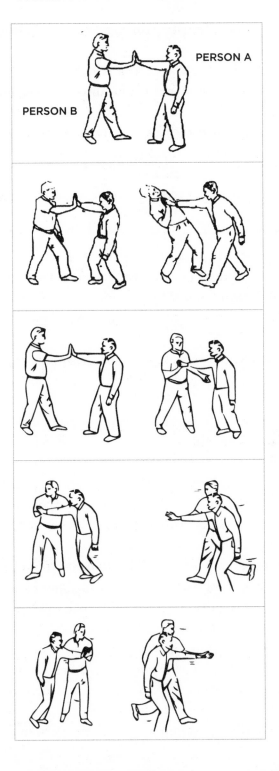

Then both people place palms against each other and push as
they did before.

- Person B imagines that he is a revolving door being pushed
  by A, turning to face in the same direction and allowing himself to be carried by the momentum.
- Rather than pushing back, B keeps moving in A's direction,
  sensing his strength and being curious about the moment
  when he can be influenced.
- In that moment, B redirects A in the original direction he
  wanted to go.

Take a moment to notice the effects of relating in this way and
share what comes up. For example, Person B might say, "Wow, it
turns out the vision I had for this campaign was wrong all along!
The new direction we ended up with together is much more engaging."

After reversing the exercise so A has a chance to practice blending, we suggest that both of you reflect on the following questions:

- How was your relationship (the connection represented by
  your palms touching) affected in the different ways of responding?
- What specific change in your thinking is required for you to
  blend? For example: "When I sense opposition, I need to
  breathe and ask questions until I understand what is important to the other person."
- What mental models or stories come up for you? For example: "There were six kids in my family and I was the youngest, so I have always been afraid I will never get a word in
  edgewise."
- Under what conditions will you allow yourself to be influenced by others? For example: "If I can see their thinking
  talents on a chart, it helps me recognize where they are coming from and what they have to offer."
- What are your most important takeaways from this practice?

A contract is what bridges business partnerships in a market-share economy. A relationship is what bridges business partnerships in a mind-share economy. Market-share skills instill independence, dependence, and co-dependence. Mind-share skills foster interdependence: receptivity and connection, influence and inquiry. Rather than opposing or agreeing with the other person, you accept and acknowledge the other's position until you can understand what is important about it. This requires a willingness to flex, bend, and search in order to understand someone else's needs. Once you know this, you can pivot and create an opening for that person to understand what is important to you. In a relatively short time, your facility in doing this will increase the depth and grace of your ability to connect. Inquiry is the means to accomplishing this, and we'll explore it in depth in the next part of the book.

CHAPTER SUMMARY

KEY CONCEPTS OF THIS CHAPTER	GUIDELINES
Understanding thinking talents can strengthen your rapport and connection with other members of your team.	Use the following questions to identify someone else's thinking talents: • "Tell me about a time in your past when you felt truly engaged. What were the conditions that allowed that to happen?" • "In your current work situation, what are the positive factors that energize you and make you want to be a part of the team?"
When someone challenges you, explore which shadow attributes could be their behavior, and turn this into a thinking talent.	When partnering with those who think differently, ask yourself the following: • What specifically annoys or frustrates me the most? • What shadow attributes and thinking talents could they have that this represents? • Is this related to a blind spot that they or I have? • How could I learn from them? • How could I create a partnership where we support one another's blind spots?

Creating a thinking-talents map makes the intellectual capital of a team visible, showing how each person adds value.	Use the team map to quickly gauge what thinking is present and what is missing. • Which thinking talents and cognitive styles predominate? • What kind of thinking is habitual for your team? • What are the blind spots? What is hard or avoided altogether? • Which of the cognitive styles or thinking talents is represented when your team stresses or worries? • Where is support needed? Where and how can you find it?

Additional Resources

- The Thinking Talents appendix.
- Mapping teams online: To work with teams more effectively, we developed software called "the Smart Navigator." Team members can do an assessment to determine their mind pattern and thinking talents and to create team maps and search for thinking talents within the entire organization. More information is available at CQthebook.com.

THE WISDOM TRAIL

My grandmother never set foot in a school, but she was the wisest person I've ever known. One day in answer to my question about how she had learned so much, she traced a wide loopy spiral in the air with a bony index finger. Then she did my favorite thing: She told me a story. This one was about the Wisdom Trail. In a voice as soft as a whisper, she said, "Each of us travels a path that is shaped like this spiral. It goes round and round a core of questions that live at the very center of who you are. As you go through your life, it may seem as if you are coming to the same place, the same struggle, over and over." Her hand traced the spiral again in the air. "As you walk this trail, life will ask you one of those important questions. It wants you to move forward and gather wisdom. Each question is meant to shift you from the foot of risk, where you will learn something new, to the foot of mastery, so you can practice what you've just learned." She kissed my forehead, as if to seal the understanding into my mind. She continued, "If you only pay attention to the questions that keep you on your foot of risk, you'll live unsteadily, hopping through your days from one thing to another, in a frenzy. If you only explore the questions that shift you onto your foot of mastery, you'll feel stuck, bored, or numb in your life, unable to grow."

She paused and combed her fingers through my hair, then whispered, "Sometimes you may think you're moving backward or that you aren't making any progress at all. But that's not true.

You've just forgotten that the Wisdom Trail is a spiral. Each pass around, if you've really explored those important questions, you will have gathered more wisdom, and you'll find that you travel with more grace. What you need to remember is that, wherever you go on the path, there's no way to escape those questions or what you came here to do."

INQUIRY

Bridging Our Differences

THINK MIND PATTERNS TALENTS **INQUIRY** MIND SHARE CQ

Bridging differences
by understanding
your and others'
inquiry styles

DISCOVERING YOUR
INQUIRY STYLE

The power to question is the basis of all human progress.
—Indira Gandhi

I've had a lifelong fascination with the relationship between great questions and expanding possibility. At a very young age I learned that having the right answers to questions was a fast track to approval. I became so good at accumulating correct answers that I ended up in college at age fifteen and in a doctoral program at eighteen. As a graduate student in clinical psychology, I was taught to develop mastery in answering questions about how people get sick and crazy. But it was there that I also discovered the work of Milton Erickson, M.D., a brilliant psychiatrist famous for his innovative work in clinical hypnotherapy, which led me to explore the question, "How do people get sane and healthy?" While my clinical supervisors were teaching me to focus my attention on the history of pathology, diagnosing and classifying disease, I was learning through Dr. Erickson to open my mind in wonder, to become comfortable with uncertainty, to explore a limitless range of possibilities.

Questions such as "Why do I keep doing this?" "Did I make a

mistake?" "Will I never learn?" can close your mind and restrict access to the full range of your own intelligence. They are questions that divide your mind in half: Good/bad. Smart/not smart. Learning to inquire artfully can open your mind to wider and deeper ways of knowing. It can also transform how you talk to yourself. Questions such as "What is important to me right now?" "Am I being effective?" or "Is this growing my capacity?" will open your mind and connect you to what you are experiencing, the effect you are having on others, and where you want to go. As Daniel Pink points out in his book *To Sell Is Human*, social scientists have proven that this kind of interrogative self-talk is more valuable than declarative self-talk, such as repeating affirmations.

Learning to shift to an inquiry mindset doesn't involve special training. It just requires you to have genuine, simple curiosity. When asked why he became a scientist, Isidor Isaac Rabi, winner of a Nobel Prize for physics, replied, "My mother made me a scientist without ever knowing it. Every other child would come back from school and be asked, 'What did you learn today?' But my mother used to say, 'Izzy, did you ask a good question today?'" Sara Blakely, the billionaire founder of Spanx, attributes her success to the enthusiastic questions her father asked each day about how she had failed. "I never associated failure therefore with something bad. Just that I was taking a risk, which meant I was learning," she stated in an interview with Fareed Zakaria.

While inquiry doesn't require fancy tools or techniques, it does require a profound shift in our thinking. In a market-share economy, the kind of questions that have value are those we can answer quickly with resolve and certainty. We're taught to *provoke* and motivate ourselves by pushing for answers. This approach often results in a closed mind that is forceful and arrogant. Mind share, however, requires that you learn to *evoke* thinking and inspire growth. The focus is on exploring the question itself rather than on being certain about your answer. You strengthen your mental muscle by holding uncertainty. Market share focuses on getting the answer; mind share focuses on exploring the question.

George de Mestral went walking in a field one day and got a burr stuck on his pants. When he returned home, he asked himself, "What could this possibly be good for?" Thus the idea for Velcro was born.

As described in the bestselling book *Moneyball,* Oakland A's general manager Billy Beane questioned the status quo of baseball talent evaluation by asking, "If we weren't already doing it this way, is this how we would do it?" Beane's question, which flew in the face of time-tested baseball management, allowed the early 2000s A's to change how they were working and not only become competitive against teams with vastly deeper pockets but also become a blueprint for other teams to follow, including the 2004 World Series–winning Boston Red Sox.

At the beginning of every new idea, there is a great question. Between every breakdown and every breakthrough, there is a great question. The strategy of inquiry is the art of asking great questions. Asking great questions increases your influence in three significant ways: It connects you to your own wisdom and intention; it bridges and leverages thinking differences; it fosters new possibilities by enabling you to see things from a different perspective.

Asking great questions can be challenging, especially for people in leadership positions. From a young age we're taught that a specific relationship exists between answers and rewards. We orchestrate competitions based on quick responses. In kindergarten, answers are rewarded with gold stars; in middle school, with good grades; in college, with degrees; at work, with promotions and raises. It seems only to end when we retire. Until then, unanswered questions annoy us.

Thus, the strategy of inquiry requires a jump from the raft of "knowing" into the river of "not knowing." Though it feels awkward, it actually makes it more possible for us to learn. Imagine what would happen if, in the midst of a disagreement with someone, you were to ask yourself, "What do I need to be learning right now?" How would that be different from asking yourself, "Who is right and who is wrong?" The first question enables you to approach the situation with the wonder that is necessary for something new to emerge. The second will take you back to the impossible place you've been stuck in many times before.

INQUIRING FROM THE INSIDE OUT

To develop mastery with the strategy of inquiry, it's necessary to embrace what Stanford psychologist Carol Dweck calls a "growth mindset." She has conducted groundbreaking research with subjects around the world, showing that people navigate through life using one of two mindsets: fixed or growth. In a fixed mindset, you believe everyone has been born with a certain unchanging level of intelligence. This results in hiding what you don't know so people won't think you're not "smart." Thus you avoid challenges and negative feedback because it could reveal what you don't know. You consider every setback or obstacle a personal failure rather than a learning opportunity. A fixed mindset limits artful inquiry, because you expect yourself to have all the answers.

When you shift to a growth mindset, on the other hand, you see intelligence as something that can evolve. Obstacles and negative feedback become learning opportunities. You approach challenges by asking yourself three simple questions:

- What can I learn from this?
- How can I grow my capacity?
- How can I do this better?

According to Dweck's research, people who use a growth mindset go on to ever-increasing levels of achievement, because they harvest each and every experience they have for what they can learn. Thomas Edison, arguably the greatest inventor of the late nineteenth century, exhibited a growth mindset in his famous quote when he was criticized for failing seven hundred times to invent the incandescent lightbulb. He said, "I have not failed seven hundred times. I have not failed once. I have succeeded in proving that those seven hundred ways will not work. When I have eliminated all the ways that will not work, I will find the way that will work." It took him one thousand tries. He thought of each one as a learning opportunity.

A growth mindset makes collaboration possible because it enables you to seek out both inspiration and help from others rather than be threatened by what others know. And it allows you to use the strategy of inquiry, because you understand that revealing what you don't know will enable you to grow your capacity.

In working with Dweck's model, we realized two things. First, most people have certain areas of their life where they use a growth mindset and other areas where they use a fixed mindset. For example, someone may strive to grow his sales capacity any way he can while at the same time limiting himself in the physical domain by thinking of himself as uncoordinated or a "klutz."

Our second realization was that you can have a fixed mindset with certain people and a growth mindset with others. When you have a fixed mindset about someone, you feel as if you have to perform up to his expectations or make him perform up to yours. Your opinions about him seem to be set in stone. On the other hand, when you have a growth mindset about him, you are consistently wondering how to grow your own capacity with that person. In the pages that follow, you will discover how you can use inquiry to shift from a fixed to a growth mindset in order to make collaboration possible.

THE THREE KINDS OF INQUIRY

Each of the three categories of questions we will introduce takes your thinking in a different direction to achieve a different result. Together they can be used like a compass to create clarity and collaboration. The first type is success-based inquiry; when you are stuck, this helps you access your own wisdom by focusing on what has worked in the past. The second is intentional inquiry; when you feel lost, overwhelmed, and confused in your thinking, it helps you reconnect with what really matters to you. The third, influential inquiry, helps when you feel disconnected or ineffective in your own thinking or with others.

1. Success-Based Inquiry: Accessing What's Worked in the Past

This form of inquiry is most useful when your mind goes blank, when you feel clueless about what to do next or keep thinking the same thing over and over. Success-based inquiry can help you create a breakthrough by using your past experiences and knowledge to uncover your own unique formula for enabling future successes. When your mind thinks back to a similar challenge that you resolved effectively, you unconsciously access neural pathways that are already wired into your brain. You don't have to create a whole new set of connections. You will feel more confident going forward because you have previous experience to draw on.

Try it for yourself. Bring to mind a challenge you are facing now. Then think of a time in the past when you've experienced a similar challenge that resulted in a positive outcome. Consider all that you did to create that success. What did you learn that could help you now?

This kind of inquiry de-compartmentalizes your knowledge from one experience in your life and transfers it to another. Rather than causing you to reflect on all your past mistakes and failures, it shifts you toward a growth mindset. Because you're using your own life experience as a guide, you will feel much more confident in your ability to create effective ways of engaging with new people or projects. If instead you only remind yourself of what hasn't worked in the past, you block your forward motion and can feel like a perpetual amateur.

The process of answering success-based questions is like recounting a great adventure when someone asks, "How did you do that?" The magic is in examining each detail of the choices you made at tough intersections—the strategies you tried, the tools you used, the emotions you experienced, all the different elements that contributed to how you pulled it off. Planning your next expedition involves distilling this knowledge into elements you can use to your advantage. Here are some success-based questions to access this kind of intelligence:

- When in the past have you been successful in a similar situation? What did you personally do to make that happen?
- How was the breakdown transformed into a breakthrough—when it all started to go wrong, what shifted to make it go right? What was your part in making this happen?
- If you cannot think of a similar situation, think of an area of your life where you have been successful. It could be in health, helping your family, or an outside interest like chess. What did you specifically do that was effective? How could you apply what you did to this situation?

2. Intentional Inquiry: Discovering Your Virtuous Intent

Stephen R. Covey wrote, in *The 7 Habits of Highly Effective People,* that we often become so busy and carried away by what appears to be urgent that we forget what is essentially important to us. Knowing what is essentially important to you is what aikidoists call "virtuous intent." Intentional inquiry uses questions that help you tap in to a place of clarity about what really matters to you. It is most helpful when you feel lost, carried away by another's thinking, or burned out by the pressure of the urgent. Intentional questions are like the magnetic needle of a compass. They help you determine what is important to you in the moment and become clear about where you want to go. They are open questions—meaning that no one but you could possibly know the answers. They require your mind to open so you can search for your unique truth.

When fully explored, intentional-inquiry questions give you the strength to face uncertainty, challenge, and complexity. They should be asked with a respectful and curious inner tone of voice that a dear friend, trusted colleague, or confidant would use. Here are some examples of key intentional questions:

- What is most important to you about this?
- What is surprising to you right now?
- What is inspiring you?
- What is challenging you?
- No matter what, how can you grow your capacity in this situation?
- What do you want to learn from this?
- What feeling do you want to have when you leave this meeting?

3. Influential Inquiry

This kind of inquiry is most helpful when you feel as if you are not making a connection with someone or are being ineffective at resolving a problem. Influential inquiry uses questions that will help you identify where you have natural strength in thinking and competency for influencing people as well as where you may need support.

To make it easier for you to use influential inquiry, we have organized questions into the four cognitive styles you charted in the chapter Uncovering Your Thinking Talents.

THE INQUIRY COMPASS

Asks for logic behind this.

Asks for facts and data to explain things.

Asks questions for clarity.

Questions how to make things efficient and excellent.

Asks what is wrong, and suggests how it can be fixed.

Curious about "Why?" in order to pull idea or problem apart for understanding.

Asks out-of-the-box questions.

Asks questions about the future of "What if . . . ?"

Wonders about alternative scenarios and likes to explore options.

Explores through questions about ideas that help give a new perspective.

Inquires to create the new, rather than repeating the usual.

Inquires to synthesize and create ideas.

ANALYTIC   **INNOVATIVE**

INQUIRY

PROCEDURAL   **RELATIONAL**

Probes to make sure process is done right.

Asks about the past and how it is a blueprint for the present and future.

Asks questions about the outcome, the end result.

Inquires about best practices, structure, routine, timelines, and rollout.

Questions who is responsible, and owns commitments.

Curious about how others are feeling.

Wonders about how things are being communicated.

Inquires into how to connect different people, ideas, places, things.

Asks questions that engage and enroll others, developing rapport.

Asks about how to develop people.

Analytic: "Why?" The person with thinking talents in the analytic quadrant naturally asks questions such as: "What are the facts?" "What does the data indicate?" "What is the most logical way to approach this?" "Why is this true?" This person has an affinity for:

- Logical understanding.
- Interesting facts and data that explain things.
- Helping to make order from chaos.
- Evaluating.
- Making comparisons.

- Seeking to clarify and quantify.
- Pulling an idea or problem apart in order to understand it.
- Maximizing and focusing on making things efficient and excellent.
- Asking what is wrong and easily suggesting how it can be fixed.

Procedural: "How?" The person with thinking talents in the procedural quadrant will ask questions that focus on the detailed sequence of action needed to get things done: "How will we do this?" "How much time will it take?" "What's the deadline?" This person has curiosity about the planning and sequencing of events. He or she likes having history and context and has an affinity for:

- Wanting to know the step-by-step process.
- Executing the plan.
- Looking to the past for reference and context.
- Making things predictable and repeatable.
- An awareness of time and how long things take.
- Clarifying priorities.
- Taking responsibility for commitments made.
- Focusing on the end result and orienting to the destination.

Relational: "Who?" The person with relational thinking talents asks questions like: "How do you feel about that?" "Who could help you?" "What kind of support do you need?" This person values and engages with others and holds the fundamental belief that people are a resource. This person has an affinity for:

- Exploring the feelings and needs of others.
- Wondering how a situation will affect people.
- Understanding the quality of relationships.
- Exploring how to extend networks and create connections.
- Empathy for others.

- Focusing on supporting the well-being of a team.
- Pursuing how to help people grow and develop.

Innovative: "What if?" The person with thinking talents in the innovative quadrant tends to focus on the future and likes to formulate new ideas and strategies. This person asks, "What could we do that no one's ever done before?" "What are all the ways we could approach this?" "What's our vision?" He or she is curious about underlying patterns and likes combining different ideas and concepts into something innovative. This person has an affinity for:

- Finding the cutting edge.
- Pursuing new ideas, new people, new concepts, new contracts, and new work.
- Synthesizing ideas, concepts, or people into something new.
- Exploring the most imaginative and creative possibility.
- Drawing others into the future.
- Finding a vision of the big picture.

Each of us has a natural tendency to be strong in one, two, three, or even all four of these kinds of inquiry. We all tend to have default settings, so to speak—sources of inquiry that direct much of how we influence our own and others' thinking. On the compass on page 181, notice where your questions naturally orient and put a star on which quadrant(s) you most often use. If there is a quadrant you rarely use or that is challenging for you, place a different kind of mark there. When you become aware of your preferred style of inquiry, you'll be mindful of what types of questions come easily and most naturally to you. You might notice that this directly correlates with the cognitive style you discovered in Uncovering Your Thinking Talents. In addition, you will become aware of your blind spots and what kinds of questions you could be asking to expand your perspective.

Many people we work with have one domain they primarily use to inquire at work and a different one at home. Ayla, a director of marketing at a large tech firm, was genuinely curious about people, but because of her tough exterior with those who reported directly to her, you would never know it. She wasn't actually the predator everyone thought she was. Using relational inquiry, she had become a successful client negotiator, but she didn't think this was the proper way to be a "leader."

Like Ayla, many of us limit our influence by compartmentalizing ourselves. We don't do this consciously; these behaviors are deeply entrenched in our family, culture, and social systems. Ayla thought a woman in the corporate world would not be taken seriously if she was too soft and showed that she cared about people. But that is a market-share notion. In a mind-share environment, relational intelligence is required. Additionally, multiple studies show that both happiness and effectiveness are directly related to bringing all of yourself to work. The same is true of your home life. Self-awareness is the first step. The next and more difficult step is self-permission. In Ayla's case, when she actually did allow her relational curiosity to emerge, she was initially self-conscious but then noticed quickly that others were finding her more approachable and thus trustworthy.

BEFRIENDING YOUR BLIND SPOTS

A quadrant where you habitually do not ask questions qualifies as a blind spot. For example, someone may repeatedly ask you how you are feeling (relational) but never ask about your future plans (innovative). As with cognitive styles, knowing your blind spots can be extremely helpful in expanding your ability to inquire. They are suitably named because, if someone asks you influential questions from a quadrant that you habitually avoid, you can be blindsided and misunderstand their questions as a challenge or attack.

Pay attention to your blind spots and get input from someone who is strong in this form of inquiry. Adopting a growth mindset will enable you to ask for support, because you know it does not mean you are incompetent. It actually indicates you are self-aware of your mastery—and of areas where you need backup. This is the essence of collaboration.

Often, breakthrough thinking happens when we explore the quadrant we most often avoid. A director of HR we worked with was a fabulous teacher, funny and engaging, who knew her content thoroughly. However, when asked to lead groups, she got mediocre evaluations. After going through the four quadrants of the inquiry compass (see previous diagram), she realized that she had a procedural blind spot and had not spent any time inquiring about how to deliver her content in a detailed, sequential way. She recognized that this was why she scrambled at the end of workshops and appeared disorganized and rushed. She had thought being procedural would make her rigid and boring, but, in fact, working with someone who could inquire procedurally enabled her to be more effective in how she delivered material.

USING THE INQUIRY COMPASS

Imagine a work challenge that you are currently facing. Thinking alone about it can lead you to overlook important perspectives. To make sure you have a well-rounded way of thinking, scan the compass and consider the issue from all four directions. Here are some typical questions from each quadrant. Some will seem habitual to your way of inquiring, others will not. When you find yourself stuck in your thinking, refer to the questions from the quadrant that is *not* habitual:

Analytic Questions: Thinking about "Why?"
- What is the logic behind this?
- Why am I attending this meeting?
- What is the purpose of this call?
- What are the facts that I know so far?

- What are the measurements and data used?
- What is clear and known?
- Why should I do this?
- What's the bottom line?
- What will this cost?

Procedural Questions: Thinking about "How?"
- When can I expect this to happen?
- What's the plan?
- How long will this take?
- What resources are needed?
- How does this relate to what I am already doing?
- How can I minimize the risks?
- What methodology do I have in place?
- What have I done in the past that ties to this?

Relational Questions: Thinking about "Who?"
- How can this help others?
- What do people need?
- Whom else do I need to talk to?
- How do they feel?
- What does the customer need?
- Is the team connected?
- What effect will this have on the people involved?

Innovative Questions: Thinking about "What If?"
- What's the big picture?
- What new ideas can I enact?
- Is there another way to think about this?
- What are all the possibilities?
- What is unique and interesting about this?
- What's going to be on the cutting edge?
- What are all the ways this could be done?
- What could be created that has never existed before?

WHY DOES INQUIRY MATTER?

George had just been appointed the senior VP of business development for one of the world's largest technology firms and was now on the executive team. He had always struck me as laid back and relaxed, but he sounded desperate when he called. "This leadership team really needs help, Dawna, especially the new CEO, Peter—he's impossible! Can you fly to London to meet with him?"

I asked if Peter himself was requesting the help or if George simply wanted him to *have* help. As I feared, it was the latter. Normally I would not consider such an "arranged" partnership, but as George went on, I became intrigued by his dilemma. He explained how the stock price had dropped twenty points the day after Peter's first meeting with the Wall Street analysts. The ensuing executive-team meeting was a "fault fest"—where everyone was trying to lay blame on someone else.

I asked to see a video of Peter's meeting with the financial analysts so I could learn more about him. It was even worse than I'd imagined. He was tight as a fist responding to the analysts, punching back in response to their questions. I've always been a sucker for the person everyone else deems "un-teachable." I discovered that Peter's father had also worked for this company, and Peter himself had worked there his entire adult life. At fifty, he was the youngest CEO ever appointed. I called George back and agreed to meet with Peter for one session, *if* the request came from Peter.

The glass-walled offices overlooked the Thames. I waited for thirty minutes in the anteroom, counting the revolutions of the London Eye Ferris wheel, before his assistant told me Peter was ready to see me. He began to talk before I sat down. He reminded me of a man who lived permanently on the loud edge of chaos. He complained that George was wishy-washy and weak, always asking questions instead of saying what he really thought. He went on to describe the flaws of every other person on the executive team and how their poor presentation caused the analysts to eviscerate the company's results. Then he leaned back in his burgundy leather chair, folded his arms across his chest, and stared straight at me, proudly declaring that no coach had ever been able to work with him.

I stood up without saying a word, slung my computer bag over my shoulder, and walked out of the office. As I waited for the elevator, he charged up to me and demanded, "Where do you think you're going?" If it had been a real question, I might have paused to answer, but in this case I didn't say a word. I turned my back on him and walked over to the watercooler. I put a paper cup under the faucet and, as he was watching, let the water fill the cup and continue to run over the sides onto the floor until there was a puddle at my feet. Then I tossed the cup into the garbage, went back to the elevator, and rode down to the lobby.

Peter caught up with me as I stepped into the revolving door to exit the building. He followed me out onto the street and told me he wanted to know what was going on. There was the slightest tinge of genuine curiosity in his voice, indicating his mind might possibly be beginning to crack open. I walked down the street with him following at my side. I told him that, like the water cup, his mind was so full of itself that there was no room for anyone or anything else in it. I did not, therefore, want to waste my most precious resource—my time—with him. I explained that thinking together, which was what I loved to do, would be impossible. He continued walking next to me without a word for the rest of a very long block. Finally, as we turned the corner, he said, "People are always telling me I have to listen more and ask more questions, but I was trained as an engineer. I'm supposed to solve problems, fix things, give people the right answers." He shrugged and told me that he really didn't understand what people wanted from him. I looked at him and, strange as it seemed, really believed what he was saying.

I know a great deal about the need to be right. Most of the CEOs I partner with are deeply entrenched in this habitual way of thinking. Unfortunately, being rewarded for being right all the time often stands in the way of senior leaders being able to inquire so they can think collaboratively. Obviously, this was true for Peter. I knew I wasn't going to get through on words alone, so I stopped, turned toward him, and stretched out my hand in a fist. I said, "Peter, a human mind, like a hand, is capable of being open or closed. When you are so sure you're right, your mind is closed like this." I punched him on the shoulder. "It might make you seem strong, but if this is how you are all the time, you end up in arguments with people. And clearly you're not able to receive or learn anything from them either. I don't think I'm telling you anything you don't already know, am I?"

He didn't say a word. He just looked down at his feet.

Then I issued him a challenge. I suggested that each time he noticed his mind was closed like a fist, when he was certain he was right, that he ask himself if he would rather be right or effective. And if he decided that he'd rather be effective, then he would have to inquire of himself what was most important to him in that moment. This intentional inquiry would allow his clenched mind to open a bit. Then he needed to observe, like any good engineer, what effect he was having on those around him.

I knew this very simple suggestion would take him to the edge of his comfort zone, but I had to find out if the desire to be a leader was stronger than his habit of being a boss. His response surprised me. "I will do this experiment of asking this question and observing the effect," he replied. Then he actually winked, saying, "Just as an experiment. I'm not guaranteeing anything."

A month later, he invited me to attend the executive-team meeting. He told me that the experiment was very useful in finding what I had called his virtuous intent: He wanted to think with others in an open and collaborative way, but he had observed that the consistent effect he had on others—especially the analysts— was to shut them down. He couldn't understand why and wanted me to work with him in "real time" as he related to his leadership team. I surprised myself by agreeing to go. If he had learned to open his mind that far in a month, the least I could do was to open mine to him.

As the team began to work through the agenda, I calculated how much money it was costing the company for one hour of the twelve of them "working" together. My guess was more than six figures for the constant bickering, complaining, and backstabbing. Challenges were not addressed, everyone blamed someone else, and the air sizzled with tension. Peter directed the agenda in his booming voice. Each person reported on his or her own business unit without any signs of engagement. In four hours, nobody asked a single question, except what time lunch would be served. They were operating on the old market-share model of command and control, trying to exert power over one another through force-fully arguing their point of view. Each time someone spoke, he or she looked immediately to Peter for approval. The company had just spent an obscene amount of money for them to report *to* one another but not to think *with* one another.

That evening I joined Peter for a family dinner. I witnessed an entirely different man. As his daughter, Sophia, entered the room, he gave her a bear hug and asked what had surprised her that day at school. My ears immediately perked up as he continued to draw her out with evocative questions and devote his full attention to her answers. As she talked about challenges, he did not jump in to "fix" her but asked instead how she was going to deal with them.

Later, when we were alone, I asked how he had come to form such a close connection with his daughter. He explained that when she had become a teenager, he realized that for the few remaining years she was still living at home, he wanted to be a positive influ-ence on her. He wanted them to enjoy each other's company, so he started to take her sailing. He intuitively realized that a boat was the place where his mind was the most open and curious, so he could draw her out through interesting questions and really listen to her. I asked him what his relationship with his daughter and mastery of sailing could teach him about effective collaboration with those he was leading at work. I could almost see Peter's mind open one of its drawers and transfer the contents to another.

"Well, the obvious thing is that I ask her questions to draw her out. While I am sailing, I have to harness the wind by consistently making micro-adjustments and tacking. . . ."

I could almost feel the breeze on my cheeks as he went on, "I need to hold sight of where I want to go and keep asking myself about the wind direction and waves, so I can tack accordingly and maintain speed and forward direction."

I observed that, at work, Peter was more like an archer than a sailor, using his authority over people as a bow and his opinions as arrows. I explained there are situations where this strategy is highly effective; however, collaborating with teammates is not one of them, because people end up feeling as if they are targets. I asked him to consider how he would communicate if he sailed through meetings instead. He tilted his head inquisitively, stared out the window, and considered what I was suggesting.

"Rather than using statements like arrows that you shoot at the analysts or the executive team, what if you used questions like a tiller to achieve influence? What if you thought of George as a changing wind, being curious about where he was coming from and how he might be steered on course toward the desired destination?" Step by step, I was explaining the concept of success-based inquiry.

Peter sat silently for what seemed a very long time, as if becalmed. Then he suddenly leaned forward, smacked his palm flat on the mahogany desk, and said, "This is good. I already know everything I need to. All I have to do with the analysts and George and my team is use the same strategy I do to connect with my daughter and the wind!"

I ended our session with his favorite three words: "You are right!"

Not willing to be bested, he replied, "Yes, but can I be effective? *That* is the question!"

The following month, I heard, saw, and felt the answer. Peter set up a meeting for us with George and asked him a dozen questions, which were all in service of understanding what quadrant George was coming from. At first it took every ounce of self-restraint for Peter not to jump in with comments, but he couldn't help but see the positive effect he was having—he was finally getting a complete picture of the company's current problems. The two of them began to play off each other's perspectives and explore possibilities.

The words "What if we . . ." came much more frequently out of Peter and George's mouths in the next day's executive-team meeting. Their collaborative energy slowly spread to the rest of the team like a positive contagion. Their increased use of inquiry resulted in people feeling that their input was valuable. This made it possible for the team to tackle together the pressing and complex issues the company was facing. At the end of four hours, I thought it truly had been a million-dollar meeting.

The following month we turned our minds toward improving Peter's communication in meetings with the analysts. By using the inquiry compass, he recognized that he was extremely strong in procedural inquiry but avoidant in innovative. Thus, when the Wall Street analysts prodded him about the future of the company, he froze; he couldn't think effectively beyond the present moment. Whenever he was asked questions about the future, he became defensive, because he didn't want anyone to probe his blind spot. His blind spot had become a company pitfall. When I pointed out this dynamic, he began to turn to the innovative intelligence of his teammates. George, the person he initially had been so frustrated with, now prepared him for these types of future-oriented questions.

At the next analysts' meeting, Peter made sure George and his CFO were by his side. Each time an analytic question was asked, the CFO responded; each time a question about the future was asked, George stepped forward to answer; and each time a question was asked about how something was going to be accomplished, Peter himself responded. The analysts were quite satisfied they were getting honest and complete answers to their questions, instead of Peter's previous defensive replies. They therefore wrote much more positive reports, which caused the stock price to rise. The real value, however, came as a result of Peter's willingness to open his mind to reach for collaborative intelligence.

BREAKTHROUGH PRACTICE: EMBODIED INQUIRY, INSPIRED BY SENSEI RICHARD KUBOYAMA

You have just learned three forms of inquiry: success-based, intentional, and influential. We now invite you to experience one last form: embodied inquiry. It is often the passageway into our intuition and integration. Thinking through your body is an integral part of your unique intelligence; it will help improve the way you respond to challenges. The first part of the following inquiry practice is for you to do anytime you want to notice how something or someone is affecting you. The second will help you master inquiry with another person.

BREAKTHROUGH PRACTICE PART 1: USING INQUIRY TO BECOME CENTERED IN YOUR BODY

This can be done in an airplane, boardroom, restaurant, or office.

- Take three deep breaths that reach the center of your belly.
- Bring to the forefront of your mind a challenging person or situation you are dealing with.
- Ask yourself: "What sensations do I feel in my body as I think of this?"
- As you breathe and notice these sensations, ask yourself, "What metaphor best describes them?"
- Place one hand on your belly and ask what the sensation needs. For example: "If I am feeling tightness in my chest, like ropes, they might tell me that I need to give myself room to breathe."

BREAKTHROUGH PRACTICE PART 2: USING INQUIRY WITH ANOTHER PERSON

Find another person who is willing to explore this practice with you. It should take less than five minutes. Designate one of you X and the other Y. Switch roles so you both take a turn in each position.

Step 1: Convincing—Trying to Change Someone's Mind

Person Y extends one arm with a closed fist. Person X grasps Y's wrist firmly. X attempts to move or steer Y's arm in any direction, while Y does everything possible to keep from being moved. After a minute of effort, both people pause and note the effects of relating to each other in this fashion.

What is a phrase or metaphor that comes to mind when you do it this way? Examples: "closed-minded," "pushy," "insensitive," "firm," "heavy-handed," "controlling," "manipulative," "like a bulldozer pushing a boulder."

Step 2: Inquiring—Butterfly on Wrist

Person Y begins as before, with an arm extended, and again makes a great effort not to be swayed from this position. This time X

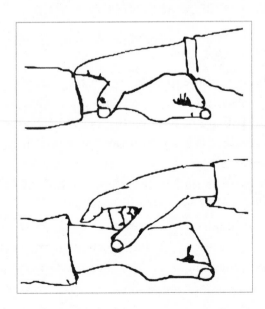

takes a breath, relaxes, and very lightly—like a butterfly landing on a branch—makes contact with Y's wrist. After making contact, X feels the movement that already exists in Y's arm. Because only the dead are truly motionless, there will always be movement, even if it is very slight. Sensing Y's motion, X follows it, joins it, and influences it by gently amplifying the motion until the two hands move together, without clashing or forcing.

Moving together in such a fashion, X can notice where opportunities exist to lead Y's arm in the direction X originally intended. Person X can notice a multitude of paths to get to that direction rather than the one originally attempted, some of which lead to struggle, some to harmony and a better relationship with person Y by extending, leading, following.

Questions to Consider
- Which took more energy and hard work: holding rigidly to your position, or the butterfly hold?
- What if the butterfly equated to questions you asked and the wrist was the most rigid person you know? How would you be asking those questions?

This breakthrough practice is pivotal in helping you recognize how you relate to current challenges and discover where you need support. In the following story, Angie illustrates this with a senior leader of a nonprofit who was at her breaking point.

Claudia had been the director of a prominent community arts center for nearly three months. Soon after she started working there, she was faced with countless staff challenges and a weathered landmark building that needed a lot of structural TLC. There was no honeymoon: The stress, challenges, and employee problems were beating her down quickly. Claudia is an eternal optimist who typically has a smile for everyone, but bit by bit her positive nature was being eroded. This is when she hired me as a thinking partner.

When we first met in Claudia's office, the windows were so drafty that she sat wrapped in an overcoat. Her attention kept going to the water dripping from a leak in the ceiling. In contrast, around her desk, icons of possibility stood out: stunning artworks ready for display; framed magazine profiles that had been written about her; books signed by distinguished authors. Her office mirrored the contradiction that she faced: dreams, aspirations, and creativity struggling to find their place amidst a crumbling infrastructure and financial uncertainty.

After Claudia painted the picture of her struggles, I asked her to pause and take three breaths, bringing to the forefront of her mind her most immediate challenge: her staff. "What sensations do you feel in your body as you think of them?" I asked. Her shoulders caved, and her head sank lower. She reached around to massage her lower back.

"I feel tons of tension, and I feel like a piece of Silly Putty that has been stretched too far. People keep pulling me in different directions," she said with a sigh.

I had her put her hand on her belly. "What does this sensation of tension need right now?" I asked.

She grimaced and said, "I need support and for people to do their jobs and stop nagging me." It was obvious her staff problems were taking up most of her attention and sucking the life out of her.

I put my arm out and asked her to imagine that it represented her employees and to demonstrate physically what her interactions with her staff felt like. She grabbed my wrist and barked out requests, attempting to push my arm back and forth. I responded immediately by locking my elbow and becoming rigid. "I can't budge you," she said with frustration. I then asked her to relate to my arm as if she were inquiring like a butterfly on my wrist. It had a totally different effect this time: I didn't feel forced, and she wasn't pushing. Soon our two arms moved together in circles.

As we talked about the experience, her shoulders sagged again and she said, "This is what I wanted it to be like when I first started here. I've always thought of myself as a people person, but I am so frustrated with all of their problems. I just need to push to get things done around here." She went on to describe how she used to have patience and cared about her staff. I discovered that now she had the entire staff of sixteen people reporting to her directly and was embroiled in the minutiae of every problem. No wonder she had lost interest in connecting with them. I then reached out for her wrist, landing on it like a butterfly, and asked what ideas she had for a different structure that would free her. Her face lit up as she described a small group that would surround her and be the interface with the rest of the staff.

When I returned the next month, Claudia proudly reported that she had established a management team of four as her critical support network; they were using inquiry to help one another think through issues and tackle the challenges of the organization together. This freed her to excel where she was brilliant—using her relational influence. In the months that followed, she created a vibrant, supportive community, gained national media exposure, and increased membership by 25 percent, and the number of people the center served annually went from forty thousand to ninety thousand. At the end of the year, she led a successful campaign that raised funds for a new building.

As it did with Peter and Claudia, the strategy of inquiry will help you access your own wisdom and connect to those who think differently from you. It will allow you to see things from a broader perspective and enable new possibilities to emerge. In the next chapter, we will explore how to use this strategy with teams.

CHAPTER SUMMARY

KEY CONCEPTS OF THIS CHAPTER	GUIDELINES
Inquiry helps us get beyond either/or.	Ask questions that lead you away from differences into a common future.
We approach challenges and people with either a growth mindset or a fixed mindset.	To move to a growth mindset with both people and challenges, use questions such as: "What can I learn from this?" and "How can I grow my capacity?"
Being awkward means your mind is shifting from focusing on what you already know to what you don't know. This is a positive state; this is growth.	Stand up a little straighter every time you feel awkward. It means you're getting smarter. Do the same for others.
We tend to see things just from our cardinal viewpoint; this limits us.	Welcome a diversity of viewpoints. Inquiry will help you to adopt a wider perspective and to increase your influence.

There are three kinds of inquiry:
  1. Success-based inquiry
  2. Intentional inquiry
  3. Influential inquiry
	Use these kinds of questions when you are stuck in your thinking and need to broaden your perspective.

Success-based inquiry helps you gain confidence by accessing past successes.	When thinking isn't moving forward, use success-based inquiry to discover what conditions have worked in the past.
Intentional inquiry reminds you of what is important to you.	Use intentional inquiry to gain clarity about what really matters to you.

Influential inquiry uses questions to help you identify where you have natural strength and competency for influencing people and where you need support.	Inquire from all four of the compass directions:
	  Analytic questions: thinking about "Why?"
	  Procedural questions: thinking about "How?"
	  Relational questions: thinking about "Who?"
	  Innovative questions: thinking about "What if?"

DISCOVERING THE INQUIRY
STYLES OF OTHERS

The fact that we are different doesn't mean that one of us is wrong.
It just means that there's a different kind of right.

—Faith Jegede

When Henry Ford launched the Model T, he created a major breakthrough in the automotive business that exhibited all four directions of inquiry. Initially he had a procedural issue to solve: To meet growing demand for the Model T, he had to double his workforce and minimize the bloated overhead that was limiting profits. His solution was to introduce the assembly line to his Highland Park plant in 1913, which made production so efficient that he nearly doubled output with the same workforce the following year. This produced an analytic win but raised an unforeseen new nightmare: Employees began to quit en masse because of the arduous, repetitive work.

Ford approached this innovatively and relationally, by improving working conditions and doubling the employees' wage rate to five dollars per day, a previously unheard of increase of ten million dollars annually. Within a year, his gamble paid big dividends: Annual labor turnover fell from 370 percent to 16 percent; productivity was up from 40 to 70 percent. Ford soon became the world's greatest automaker and a billionaire and changed the landscape of society by making cars affordable even for his factory workers—which was an analytic win after all.

To master the strategy of inquiry, we must begin with the fundamental belief that the thinking of others *does* matter. It requires releasing market-share habits and beliefs that minimize your influence. It requires you to partner with others who think in a different way to help you maximize your influence. The realization that you cannot be good at everything makes this possible; you will come to realize how much you truly need others to extend your reach.

HOW TO GET PAST CLASHES IN STYLES OF INQUIRY AND MOVE TOWARD COLLABORATION

When we try to collaborate with others, there are a number of ways we can get stuck. Analytic and procedural thinking are considered "left hemispheric." To understand a problem this way, your mind rationally breaks it into small pieces, converges on one answer, and then creates a process to enact that one solution. Mind-share thinking occurs primarily in your "right hemisphere," where innovative and relational inquiry happen. Here your mind is interested in exploring the whole of something, rather than the parts, as well as the pattern of connections between one idea and another. In this way, many new possibilities are generated.

When left- and right-brain thinking meet in a conversation, they often collide rather than create collaboration: Instead of "It's a cool new innovation," Jesse might respond to an analytic question from her boss, Jonathan, with "It's too risky, we've never done it before," and then illustrate that comment with a story about the effects of a decision on people (relational). This would cause Jonathan to check out or even grow annoyed, and Jesse would be left wondering why she failed to connect with him.

The following graphic illustrates the above dynamics.

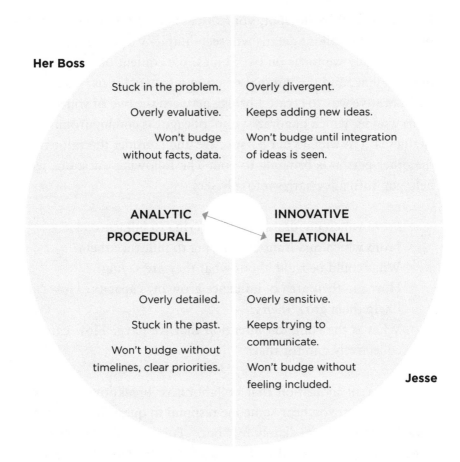

Her Boss

Stuck in the problem.

Overly evaluative.

Won't budge
without facts, data.

Overly divergent.

Keeps adding new ideas.

Won't budge until integration
of ideas is seen.

ANALYTIC

PROCEDURAL

INNOVATIVE

RELATIONAL

Overly detailed.

Stuck in the past.

Won't budge without
timelines, clear priorities.

Overly sensitive.

Keeps trying to
communicate.

Won't budge without
feeling included.

Jesse

In this example, tension arose between relational and analytic types of inquiry, but breakdowns can occur when any of the four perspectives clash. A vital part of collaborative intelligence is understanding how to bridge these diverse perspectives in order to move beyond "either/or" to what can be possible. When someone quickly jumps in and asks questions from a different quadrant, your tendency may be to feel that you're under attack. If relational inquiry is a blind spot for your colleague, when the conversation turns to people, team building, or feelings, he could get bored and think the meeting is off-track. If innovative inquiry is your boss's blind spot, big ideas, divergent comments, and risk-taking will make him uneasy, as if you are wasting time. If procedural inquiry is a co-worker's blind spot, your discussion of timing, sequence, planning, and rollout details will seem nitpicky and boring.

Habitually we focus on two things: the content of what someone is saying, and the internal reaction it causes for us. Instead, a collaborative way to create a bridge between the two of you would be to wonder which quadrant your colleague is coming from. This enables you to widen your perspective and consider the value that the other person is bringing to you. The following questions will help you turn adversaries into advisers.

- From which quadrant are they trying to influence me?
- From which quadrant am I trying to influence them?
- What could be *right* about what they are saying?
- How can their area of influence grow my capacity? How can I help them grow theirs?
- What is the common intention that we have? How can we collectively aim for that?

A different indication that collaborative breakdowns are occurring is when you hear someone respond to questions by saying "yes," followed immediately by "but." For example, Mitch says, "Yes, we have a powerful vision and a strategic plan that everyone is excited about, *but* there are still too many financial obstacles to enact it." This sentence is factually true; however, it can cause confusion and drive others crazy.

People like Mitch who frequently use "yes, but . . ." are having an inner tennis match between their mental sweet spot and their blind spot, unable to resolve the difference. They are expressing their sweet spot as a "yes" and their blind spot as a "but." In my experience, when people say "yes, but . . ." they intuitively know where they are strong, as well as where they need support. What Mitch was really saying is, "Yes, I have a vision that inspires people. I have asked the right innovative questions, *and* I lack analytic support to figure out how to finance the vision of the program." The impasse is resolved by replacing "but" with "and."

If you notice yourself or someone you work with getting stuck between "yes" and "but," think about what quadrant their "yes" is coming from and what quadrant the "but" resides in. Then you can help tease apart the two, enabling both issues to get addressed.

PUTTING THE THREE KINDS OF INQUIRY TO WORK

Charlotte is the elegant and composed director of a large nonprofit that resides within a larger global for-profit company. She was used to juggling complexities, but sometimes the terrain of money and operations became overwhelming even for her. Her team of nine lived all over the globe, operating in sixty countries, in multiple time zones, and in seven languages, to support teachers, volunteers, and children.

Charlotte was constantly pulled between the needs of the company, the nonprofit, and the schools she was trying to support, as well as the ever-changing governments, CEOs, and directors; I was amazed that she could function at all.

When we began to work together, her outer calm belied the inner chaos she was feeling. We met in a small French restaurant so no one could find her and pull her in yet another direction. After ordering a simple green salad and a glass of chardonnay, she whispered that she was ready to resign. She ran her carefully manicured fingers through her coal-black hair and explained, "Angie, I've been working for this company for thirty years, longer than any woman in a leadership position." She took a sip of wine and tears formed in the corners of her eyes. She continued, "In the beginning, everyone ignored me and left me alone, but I've had nine different bosses in the past ten years. The latest one just told me to present a written proposal for funding, even though my team and I spent three months in the last quarter doing exactly that for my previous boss. I'm not sure I can deal with all the disruptions and challenges this man will bring—at least not alone." She placed her glass carefully on the linen tablecloth and asked me if, as her thinking partner, I could help her find a way through. "There are two hundred thousand kids who benefit from the work we do. I can't let them all down."

I couldn't either. I believed that we could find a way for her to collaborate with her boss.

The next morning at her downtown New York office, it was time to make that belief into a reality. I asked her to tell me how she had led the last meeting with her new boss. She reported that she had asked him a string of questions—how he was feeling about the previous quarter, what was exciting to him about the next, and how the individual members of his team were doing. She thought she had been establishing rapport and connection by asking these kinds of relational questions. It had worked in the past when a boss had a relational cognitive style, as she did. Problems arose, however, if a boss had a different style. Then she had to figure out what he wanted and re-orient her entire strategy in order to get the funding they needed. I pointed out that valuable time and resources were wasted on pleasing each boss instead of executing the company mission. In addition, this strategy left her completely out of the picture, scrambling to satisfy the boss but ignoring the very real needs of her team.

Based on this new boss's behavior, we began with the assumption that he thought differently than she did. I suggested she prepare for the next meeting using the three kinds of inquiry to find out what approach would be most effective for both of them.

Step 1: Success-Based Inquiry

I asked Charlotte to call on colleagues who knew the new boss well and inquire about past successful presentations to him: what had engaged him, what kinds of questions did he typically ask, who was successful with him and why. Then I suggested she study his presentations to others, because we generally present to others in the way that is most natural for us.

She distilled the information she had gathered into guidelines that would increase her and the team's chances of success. Her detective work led her to conclude that he preferred analytic inquiry to relational. Then we shifted the focus of inquiry back to her past successes. A key element was for her to think about how she had helped each team member develop and grow toward accomplishing a common goal. Thinking in this relational way reignited her self-confidence in the meeting.

Step 2: Intentional Inquiry

Intentional inquiry was an important step, because Charlotte had previously become so focused on trying to meet others' needs that she forgot her own intention and that of the organization she was leading.

The intentional questions I asked helped her become clear about what really mattered to her: helping to support all those children her program served. I suggested she bring their brochure to every meeting with her boss. It was filled with photographs of the lives they had touched and could serve as a reminder of both past successes and their deepest sense of purpose.

My intentional questions helped her set her internal compass and become clear about her *own* goal: to help her boss understand the strategic value the organization brought to the company, while still being open enough to hear his wishes, and ultimately to get the necessary funding approved. As obvious as it may sound now to you and me, realizing she could align with him without losing her own direction was a radical and exciting possibility to her.

Step 3: Influential Inquiry

In the past, Charlotte had used anecdotes from the field to build the case for her budget: She had sought endorsements from managers in various countries to show the web of relationships that supported her cause.

Given what she discovered in her detective work, I advised that it would be more effective to start with his cognitive style, analytic inquiry, and then bend him around into her own approach. Instead of starting with stories, she could begin with charts and numbers, answer his questions about facts and data—how many children were served, how many communities impacted, et cetera—without betraying how important relationships were to her success. She could even sneak in some heart-wrenching examples of the direct impact of her organization—but only after she felt he was fully engaged.

The CQ homework she did before the meeting prepared her to explain why the program needed to exist. Rather than interpreting his scrutiny as an attempt to ruin her and the initiative, she was ready to hear his questions with a sense of partnership. The result? After Charlotte implemented this approach, her boss not only immediately approved the budget for the following year, he even agreed to an increase in funds. More important, Charlotte felt as if she had a positive influence on him and he on her.

Now it's your turn to learn how to modify your style in order to get your way, as Charlotte did. Bring to mind someone you have had difficulty collaborating with recently. Take yourself through the three kinds of inquiry:

1. Use success-based inquiry to gather as much data as possible about the other person's inquiry preferences. Talk to people who have been effective with him or her, in order to get a sense of how they were successful in the past. What worked? What didn't? Then use success-based inquiry to discover your *own* winning formula.
2. Use intentional inquiry to clarify your objective for meeting with this person. What's really most important to you?
3. Use influential inquiry by consulting the compass of inquiry to prepare for the meeting, translating as much of your presentation as possible into the other person's habitual style. How will you know when the time is right to translate from her style into your own? How can you give in to get your way?

Her Boss

Asks for logic behind this.

Asks for facts and data to explain things.

Asks questions for clarity.

Questions how to make things efficient and excellent.

Asks what is wrong and how it can be fixed.

Curious about "Why?" in order to pull idea or problem apart for understanding.

Asks out-of-the-box questions.

Asks questions about the future: "What if . . . ?"

Wonders about alternative scenarios and likes to explore options.

Explores through questions about ideas that help get a new perspective.

Inquires to create the new, rather than repeating the usual.

Inquires to synthesize and create ideas.

ANALYTIC ◄

PROCEDURAL

INNOVATIVE

RELATIONAL ►

Probes to make sure process is done right.

Asks about the past and how it is a blueprint for the present and future.

Asks questions about the outcome, the end result.

Inquires about best practices, structure, routine, timelines, and rollout.

Questions who is responsible and owns commitments.

Curious about how others are feeling.

Wonders about how things are being communicated.

Inquires into how to connect different people, ideas, places, things.

Asks questions that engage and enroll others, developing rapport.

Asks about how to develop people.

Charlotte

HOW DO I USE INQUIRY IN TEAMS?

The challenge of every team is to build a feeling of oneness, of dependence on one another. Because the question is usually not how well each person performs, but how well they work together.

—Vince Lombardi

We are all frustrated by how much time most of us waste in meetings, thinking in the same old ways and getting the same tired results. Angie and I want to encourage you to ask, "If we weren't already doing it this way, is this how we would do it?" Consider meetings a precious opportunity to make use of mental resources and to challenge yourself and your team to try new processes, until you find the ones that really work to maximize your collaborative intelligence. We encourage you to experiment with the practices that follow, which we developed over our years of working with multiple global teams.

THREE-STEP INQUIRY

You can use the same three-step process with a group that you did with one other person. It's especially effective when launching a project or facing a new work challenge, as well as when you find yourselves going around and around on the same issue repeatedly. This process will help the team interact more authentically while opening to one another's influence. It will increase your chances of creating something extraordinary, because people will be *utilizing* their differences instead of blocking, ignoring, or being frustrated by them.

Step 1: Success-Based Inquiry

Discuss with your team what has been effective when you faced a similar challenge in the past. Be as specific as possible. Examine the conditions used to make the success happen. Create a visual track so you can collectively see the elements that can be applied to *this* challenge or project. Discuss what each of you has learned from successes on other teams. Each team is distinctive, and moving forward needs to be built on each person's past wisdom.

Another success-based-inquiry practice is to end every meeting by asking, "What worked? How can we do more of what worked next time?" as well as "What didn't work? How can we do less of that next time?" Use each project, each client, each meeting, as an opportunity to refine your team's own handbook of effective processes that bring out the best in each of you. Be picky, be honest, be diligent, and don't sit back and be too busy for this. Invest energy and have collective ownership of the time spent thinking together. The return will be worth it.

Step 2: Intentional Inquiry

Take time to be clear on what specific result you want and to agree on your desired outcome. Have each person answer the question, "What is my intention here?" and then ask the group, "What matters to us all?"

Create a chart or visual reminder for the group to regularly check their decisions and actions against. We work with many virtual teams who do not share a physical office space; we suggest they use Post-it notes on their computers or create a repeated reminder of their intentions in their calendars. You can also be metaphorical. Charlotte's executive team posted a picture in their conference room of a Malaysian child holding a science award. It was a constant reminder that their intention was to support children falling in love with learning through the sciences. When new challenges arose, the team faced them with more confidence, because they literally held the image of this child in their minds.

Step 3: Influential Inquiry

Using the four directions of inquiry, map each team member's natural cognitive style by writing names in the domains where each person is strongest. Then discuss what the team profile indicates. Where are you strong as a group? Are there quadrants that are unpopulated? As a team, do your discussions tend to veer to one quadrant? Do you need help thinking in a particular vacant quadrant? Where can you find this help? Post the compass where you can see it so when thinking gets stuck, you can determine which kinds of questions are needed to get you unstuck.

See Team Compass Map Example 1 on page 211. Here is a compass of a team we worked with at a prominent health spa in California. After seeing their profile, they realized they had no procedural inquiry. This explained why they had been able to generate countless ideas to improve their services but few actually got implemented. This time they decided to use CQ to help them overcome this gap. They chose one idea they all wanted to implement: turning a garden into a natural, outdoor speaker venue. They enrolled a colleague from another department—operations—to help them come up with a plan and budget. Both departments proudly held the scissors in the ribbon-cutting ceremony six weeks later.

FOUR-DIRECTIONS ROUND TABLE

The following process will help you eliminate many of the blockages that occur when a group thinks together about a sticky issue. It uses both the right brain and left brain, convergent and divergent thinking, working the same issue from all four perspectives simultaneously.

- Create sub-teams representing the four different quadrants of inquiry: innovative, relational, analytic, and procedural.
- Have team members split up, joining the sub-team where they are the strongest. Each sub-team works the challenge from this perspective only.
- Ask each sub-team to come up with solutions to the problem at hand, capturing the essence of their discussion on a flip chart or using Post-it notes and placing them on a wall where everyone can see them.
- At the end of the allotted time, have each group present their work to the whole team.

TEAM COMPASS MAP EXAMPLE 1

Asks for logic behind this.

Asks for facts and data to explain things.

Asks questions for clarity.

Questions how to make things efficient and excellent.

Asks what is wrong and how it can be fixed.

Curious about "Why?" in order to pull idea or problem apart for understanding.

Asks out-of-the-box questions.

Asks questions about the future: "What if . . . ?"

Wonders about alternative scenarios and likes to explore options.

Explores through questions about ideas that help get a new perspective.

Inquires to create the new, rather than repeating the usual.

Inquires to synthesize and create ideas.

Peter
Henry
Maria

ANALYTIC | **INQUIRY** | **INNOVATIVE**

PROCEDURAL | | **RELATIONAL**

Probes to make sure process is done right.

Asks about the past and how it is a blueprint for the present and future.

Asks questions about the outcome, the end result.

Inquires about best practices, structure, routine, timelines, and rollout.

Questions who is responsible and owns commitments.

Curious about how others are feeling.

Wonders about how things are being communicated.

Inquires into how to connect different people, ideas, places, things.

Asks questions that engage and enroll others, developing rapport.

Asks about how to develop people.

George
Philippe
Ryan

BREAKTHROUGH PRACTICE: THE PIVOTAL MINDSET

When breakdowns in thinking together occur, most of us don't know what to do to turn the situation around.

When fragmentation happens, it can mean people have shifted back to a habitual market-share way of thinking or to a fixed mindset. Typical triggers for this are:

- Something happens (or doesn't happen) that you don't like, want, expect, agree with, or intend.
- You make an assumption and create a rigid opinion or belief.

Asks for logic behind this.

Asks for facts and data to explain things.

Asks questions for clarity.

Questions how to make things efficient and excellent.

Asks what is wrong and how it can be fixed.

Curious about "Why?" in order to pull idea or problem apart for understanding.

Asks out-of-the-box questions.

Asks questions about the future: "What if . . . ?"

Wonders about alternative scenarios and likes to explore options.

Explores through questions about ideas that help get a new perspective.

Inquires to create the new, rather than repeating the usual.

Inquires to synthesize and create ideas.

ANALYTIC ←→ **Pivotal** ←→ **INNOVATIVE**

PROCEDURAL ←→ **Mindset** ←→ **RELATIONAL**

Probes to make sure process is done right.

Asks about the past and how it is a blueprint for the present and future.

Asks questions about the outcome, the end result.

Inquires about best practices, structure, routine, timelines, and rollout.

Questions who is responsible and owns commitments.

Curious about how others are feeling.

Wonders about how things are being communicated.

Inquires into how to connect different people, ideas, places, things.

Asks questions that engage and enroll others, developing rapport.

Asks about how to develop people.

- You become invested in defending your position and in proving the other position wrong.
- Your ability to inquire into the other's perspective diminishes because all you can hear are the voices in your own head convincing you about who and what is right and wrong, so tension increases.

The pivotal mindset helps you to shift gears, so you can think from a neutral, open space in order to give the other person the quality of attention needed. It often takes no more than thirty seconds. When you listen through a filter instead of your own habitual perspective, all you really will hear is your own thinking. The conversation will then become a tennis match, with each of you on different sides of the net. This practice that follows helps you jump the net and pivot from where the thinking is stuck to where it needs to go. It synthesizes everything you've learned in this chapter to transform a breakdown into a breakthrough.

1. Shift your attention from its habitual quadrant(s) into neutral, the center of the compass. Quiet your mind as you notice the inhale and exhale of several breaths. This will settle your mind and allow it to open.
2. Now listen to another person, being curious about which quadrant she is thinking from.
3. Respond with some indication that shows you have an understanding of her thinking. It does not necessarily mean you agree, only that you have heard her. A statement such as "I get what you just said" or "I now know what matters to you" is sufficient.
4. Share thoughts from your perspective in a way that adds on to the other person's view rather than opposes it. You could say, "I've heard what's important to you; now can I share where I come from?" or "Are you open to hearing my thoughts?" When there is a breakdown, we secretly wish the other people would just "listen to us." However, an influential mind is also a mind that can be influenced.

A pivot is an essential move in almost every human sport and art form. We do it naturally while holding a ball, club, sail, paintbrush, flute, and loom. It has enabled our species to hunt, swim, and celebrate. You could say pivoting is in our DNA. What our bodies and hands remember, though, our habitual market-share mentalities seem to have forgotten. Each time you use all the styles of inquiry, each time you use the compass and wonder about how to pivot to connect with someone who thinks differently, you will be helping all of us reclaim an essential aspect of our collaborative intelligence.

CHAPTER SUMMARY

KEY CONCEPTS OF THIS CHAPTER	GUIDELINES
Inquiry helps us get beyond either/or.	Ask questions that lead you away from differences into a common future.
We tend to see things just from our cardinal viewpoint; this limits us.	Welcome a diversity of viewpoints. Inquiry will help you to adopt a wider perspective and to increase your influence.
Use the three steps of the inquiry process to increase your chances of creating something extraordinary. This will allow you and those around you to utilize your differences instead of blocking, ignoring, or being frustrated by them.	Use success-based inquiry to integrate and build on the wisdom each team member already has. Use intentional inquiry to clarify the specific result each team member desires. Use influential inquiry to make sure all perspectives are explored. Using the inquiry compass, map each team member's natural cognitive style by writing names in the domains where each person is strongest.

MURMURATION

In the vineyards where I used to live, just after harvest and just before sunset, the sky darkens and the air fills with the sound of thousands of glossy black starlings. I call it a startle of starlings, but I think it's really called a murmuration. Above our heads, huge clouds of them would gather, wheel, turn, and swoop in unison, a perfectly coordinated Möbius strip held together by an invisible force. If any one bird turned and changed speed, so did all the others.

I wondered for years what makes this uncanny coordination possible. How is it that they never leave a single bird isolated when under attack by a falcon or eagle? Here's what I have learned so far: They gather at harvest time to keep warm at night, exchange information, and protect one another from raptor challenges. A simple rule explains how they remain so incredibly cohesive: Each one keeps a fixed number of its neighbors—seven other starlings, irrespective of their distance—in its awareness. When a neighbor moves, so does that bird. Each starling's movement is influenced by every other starling. It doesn't matter how large the group is or if two birds are on opposite sides of the vineyard. It's as if every individual is connected to the same network. It is a system poised on the brink, capable of near-instantaneous transformation, like an avalanche or a ballet.

MIND SHARE

Creating a Collaborative Future

THINK   MIND PATTERNS   TALENTS   INQUIRY   **MIND SHARE**   CQ

Creating a
collaborative future
by shifting your
mindset

SHIFTING YOUR
MINDSET

It's no failure to fall short of realizing all that we might dream:
The failure is to fall short of dreaming all that we might realize.
—Dee Hock

I've seen the possibilities of mind share many times in my life and career, but perhaps the greatest large-scale realization of these principles that I've witnessed was inspired during the Los Angeles riots of 1992, after the beating of Rodney King. I kept encountering the phrase "random acts of violence" on the news and in the papers. I felt as if I were being pelted by the belief that the world was a chaotic and hostile place, and it drove me to my knees. Deep in my bones, I yearned to find a different way of thinking so I could foresee a future for my son and myself.

Around this time, I heard Maya Angelou give a speech in which she quoted what a woman named Anne Herbert said: "Practice random kindness and senseless acts of beauty." *There it was*—the opposite profound truth that could bring balance back to the wounded world. I began to ask people in the groups I was teaching to create thank-you cards to strangers who had performed a random act of kindness, some senseless gift of beauty that helped them believe that anything could be possible again. Those in my group told tales of a man who had stopped to help change a flat tire in the middle of the night, or of feeling one's grief salved by listening to Mozart. I asked them to tell one another stories of the random acts of kindness that *they* had done. The energy in the room was electric.

A few weeks later, I was driving on a back road in Kauai with M. J. Ryan, publisher of Conari Press. We began to have a philosophical conversation about whether, as Einstein had posited, the universe could really be a friendly place. I mentioned the practice I had been doing in the groups I was teaching and its enlivening effect on people. By the time we reached our destination, we had decided to compile these inspiring stories from all over the country into a book called *Random Acts of Kindness*.

We sponsored parties across the country, asking people to share their stories, as I had done in the training groups. In the book, we asked readers to send in their stories. Within a few short months, the publisher was inundated. We felt as if a movement had begun. We decided to extend it to children, and *Kids' Random Acts of Kindness* was published. Schools around the country, then around the world, began to host Random Acts of Kindness days. As I write this, there are participating groups in eighteen countries, extending from Canada to Singapore, New Zealand to Japan. The revenues from the original book went to support one of the first AIDS foundations, while the publicity surrounding it fostered a flood of further stories. Three more *Kindness* books followed, selling a total of nine million copies.

The Kindness movement began with one inspiring idea that pulled me toward what could be possible by redirecting my attention, intention, and imagination. It grew into a simple, replicable model that required neither central leadership nor a cumbersome infrastructure to move others from thinking apart to thinking together.

In the beginning of this book, we discussed how we are in the middle of a shift from a market-share to a mind-share mindset.

Random Acts of Kindness is one inspiring example. Thus far we've described three strategies for learning how to think with people who think differently. The fourth strategy—mindset—will teach you how to embrace mind share in three distinct ways, by using your "attention," "intention," and "imagination." We will also focus on how to shift your mindset toward the realization of what you want. This is a dynamic state we call "future pull," an aligned course of forward action and influence. In the next chapter we will focus on how you can do this with others.

TEN THINGS YOU CAN DO TO SHIFT FROM A MARKET-SHARE TO A MIND-SHARE MINDSET

MARKET SHARE	MIND SHARE
1. Uses power over others to win.	1. Uses influence with others to connect.
2. Leads as a hero.	2. Leads as a host.
3. Perceives differences as a deficit.	3. Dignifies differences as a resource.
4. "I have it and you don't."	4. "The more we share, the more we have!"
5. "How smart am I?"	5. "How *are* we smart?"
6. Analytic and procedural thinking are the most valued.	6. Analytic, procedural, innovative, and relational thinking are all valued equally.
7. Asks who is right and who is wrong.	7. Asks what can be possible.
8. Considers value to be created by and carried by things.	8. Considers value to be created by and carried by exchange of ideas and connections.
9. "What will others think of me?"	9. "How can this grow my capacity?"
10. Values independence.	10. Values interdependence.

THREE KEY ASPECTS OF MIND SHARE:
ATTENTION, INTENTION, AND IMAGINATION

Attention, intention, and imagination form the connective tissue of the human mind. Attention connects you to the present moment, where you have the power to act. Intention identifies what really matters to you. Imagination explores how you can realize future possibilities. When these three aspects work together, they create an unstoppable force. Without attention, you lack vitality and focus. Without intention, you lack passion. Without imagination, your vision lacks direction and influence. Together, these three create a mind-share mindset.

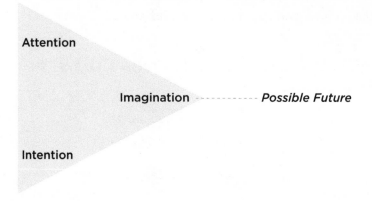

AIMING YOUR ATTENTION

Researchers in the field of neuroscience are just beginning to understand the significant way that attention itself changes the brain. When you aim your attention by consistently directing it toward one thing, you can in fact rewire your brain. Habitually your brain is chaotic, noisy, like an orchestra warming up. When you give something your full attention, however, it's like bringing an orchestra together to play a piece of music. Professor Robert Desimone from MIT calls this "neural synchrony." This is no small feat in the digital age. How often have you attempted to share an idea or experience with someone who is texting while you are talking? What effect does it have when all the participants in a meeting are trying to hide the fact they are actually checking their emails? Linda Stone, former Microsoft executive, calls this "continuous partial attention."

To aim your attention, you don't have to learn anything new;

in reality, it's more like unlearning—stepping out of the engine of your thoughts and checking in with what is real and where you want to go. What you have to do is simply redirect your attention to what you are experiencing in the moment and aim it toward a goal. It's important to recognize when your attention is fading and to develop strategies to help you re-aim it. Doing this is much like sailing: a constant recalibration of sail and tiller to stay on course.

You know what the absence of attention feels like, both for yourself and when working with others. As this happens you may feel stressed, agitated, distracted, or indifferent. In the strategy of mind patterns, you discovered the specific way your mind focuses; now you can apply that to becoming fully present.

There are many mindfulness and meditation practices to help you redirect your attention to regain awareness of the present moment. I have noticed that one differs from the next, depending on the mind pattern of the person who developed the particular methodology. One teacher, whose mind used the KVA pattern, taught me to bring my attention to the present by walking in silence, with my breath and step aligned. Another, who used the AVK pattern, taught me to chant a mantra while sitting still. Another, whose mind used the VAK pattern, taught me to stare at the horizon and listen to the sound of my own breath while sitting motionless.

Knowing your mind pattern can help you make the small continual adjustments needed to align your attention in different situations. Revisit the following chart for a reminder on how to do this.

Visual, Auditory, and Kinesthetic **VAK PATTERN**		
V1	**FOCUSED THINKING**	To Trigger Concentration: VISUAL
A2	**SORTING THINKING**	To Trigger Sorting: AUDITORY
K3	**OPEN THINKING**	To Trigger Imagination: KINESTHETIC

Visual, Kinesthetic, and Auditory **VKA PATTERN**		
V1	**FOCUSED THINKING**	To Trigger Concentration: VISUAL
K2	**SORTING THINKING**	To Trigger Sorting: KINESTHETIC
A3	**OPEN THINKING**	To Trigger Imagination: AUDITORY

Kinesthetic, Auditory, and Visual **KAV PATTERN**		
K1	**FOCUSED THINKING**	To Trigger Concentration: KINESTHETIC
A2	**SORTING THINKING**	To Trigger Sorting: AUDITORY
V3	**OPEN THINKING**	To Trigger Imagination: VISUAL

Kinesthetic, Visual, and Auditory **KVA PATTERN**		
K1	**FOCUSED THINKING**	To Trigger Concentration: KINESTHETIC
V2	**SORTING THINKING**	To Trigger Sorting: VISUAL
A3	**OPEN THINKING**	To Trigger Imagination: AUDITORY

Auditory, Visual, and Kinesthetic **AVK PATTERN**		
A1	**FOCUSED THINKING**	To Trigger Concentration: AUDITORY
V2	**SORTING THINKING**	To Trigger Sorting: VISUAL
K3	**OPEN THINKING**	To Trigger Imagination: KINESTHETIC

Auditory, Kinesthetic, and Visual **AKV PATTERN**		
A1	**FOCUSED THINKING**	To Trigger Concentration: AUDITORY
K2	**SORTING THINKING**	To Trigger Sorting: KINESTHETIC
V3	**OPEN THINKING**	To Trigger Imagination: VISUAL

Aline is a senior executive of a global ad agency. She is also the mother of three and an avid runner. She was caught in the cycle of too much to do and not enough attention to go around. Layering tasks became her norm: leading conference calls while watching Little League, sending emails while preparing lunches. Her seven-year-old son drew a picture of Aline holding her BlackBerry and looking away, instead of holding his hand and looking at him. Her husband and best friend both asked her why she seemed so stressed.

She knew things had to change. She sat next to Angie in her office and discovered that her mind used the VKA pattern. She realized that her habit had been to disconnect from the present by looking at emails (V-1) while talking (A-3). Thus, she was never fully present for either.

Angie helped Aline to experiment until she discovered that she was most present when she looked directly at her son (V-1) while touching him (K-2) and asking questions or listening to him (A-3). In meetings, she could be much more present when she projected her talking points on the wall, using pictures (V-1) and standing (K-2) while speaking (A-3). Having a common visual enabled her to move around and not be flooded with all that she heard.

Angie suggested that Aline look at her calendar each day and circle the meetings or family commitments where it was most important for her attention to be fully present. They then strategized about how she could create the conditions to enable this. Aline knew that managing time would continue to be a challenge, but she now had a way to distribute her attention so she wouldn't miss the precious moments she had with her son or be less than all she could be with her team.

Bring your mind back to that situation when you felt stressed and discouraged. Consider what interferes most with your attention being fully present. Is it people talking? Visual clutter? Or being physically uncomfortable? What is your internal signal that you're not present and need to align your attention through your senses? For example, if you have been listening for a long time, you may need to move or to look at something visual. If you have been talking nonstop, you may need to pause and take a couple of breaths. If you have been staring at a spreadsheet, you may need to let your eyes wander. Just as when trimming a sail to adjust for the wind, becoming present means exploring which adjustments are needed.

AIMING YOUR INTENTION

Your intention is what drives your actions. Your thinking can take you away from or direct you toward what you want to make happen. In the first case, you imagine what could go wrong, such as: "If I don't work harder, my colleague will get promoted before me." Your energy is wasted in pushing against obstacles or interferences. On the other hand, if you aim your intention toward what's important to you, your undivided energy and knowledge will be directed forward.

The most effective way to aim an intention is to be as specific as possible. Compare the following three intentions: "I don't want to gain weight, because I might have a heart attack." "I am going to lose weight to stay healthy." "I am going to lose fifteen pounds in the next six months, so I can cross the finish line with my colleagues during the company's 5K run." Which would create "future pull" for you? What is it about the way the intention is framed that makes it more effective?

When you direct your attention toward your purposeful intent, you find yourself serving what you love, and what you love serves you. A client of Angie's didn't know what her intention was five years ago, but what has always magnetized her is reading and writing stories about inspirational thought leaders. By first recognizing her thinking talents of belief, storytelling, and thinking ahead, she uncovered that her intention was to help people tell their story as a way to inspire others. She then followed that pull forward and has now interviewed hundreds of leaders around the world who are making a difference. She subsequently crafted their stories into inspirational narratives that reach thousands of global professionals through a newsletter and videos.

Living your dream doesn't necessarily mean it is the source of your income or that you do it every minute of every day. It means you identify what makes you feel most alive and purposeful. Inquiry is an effective strategy to support you doing this.

Bring to your mind a situation where you feel stressed and discouraged. Use the following inquiry compass so you have a greater chance of recognizing and directing your intention.

Inquiry Compass for Intention

Analytic Questions
- What is the predominant motivation for you right now in your current situation? Is it moving you away from what you are afraid of or moving you toward what you want?
- If you analyze your intentions in different areas of your life (work, family, other interests), what is one common denominator?

Procedural Questions
- When in the past have you aimed your intention?
- What were the conditions that made this possible?

Relational Questions
- Who are the people who inspire you?
- Who are the people in your world who are most supportive of you realizing your intentions?

Innovative Questions
- What would you be doing in the future if your intentions were aligned?
- If all your intentions were voices in a choir singing one song, what would it be?

AIMING YOUR IMAGINATION

Your imagination is where possibilities are created and explored. Aiming your imagination involves envisioning what you want to achieve and then directing it toward your intention. Doing so is more likely to result in your feeling inspired and fulfilled.

One of the greatest challenges of life is how to enact our intentions within everyday constraints. Every time Elton John sits down to play the piano, he has to work within the constraints of the size of his hands. Artists don't notice borders of the canvas; they create inside them. A hang glider isn't deterred by changes in the wind; she adapts to them. The challenge is not to "survive" within the constraints or interferences but to design a passionate and creative output within them.

The following chart highlights typical constraints or interferences that can arise when you are trying to aim your imagination. Constraints may be such things as: minimizing the intention's importance, ignoring it, or convincing yourself that you won't be able to enact it by thinking about past failures. This chart offers suggestions for how you might approach these challenges differently, using the strategy of mind share.

AIMING YOUR IMAGINATION	WHAT IS THE INTERFERENCE?	HOW DO YOU ACCOMPLISH THIS?
Knowing how to use your mind pattern to evoke imagery.	You don't recognize the value of your dream. You don't know the conditions your mind needs to create imagery.	Use each of your thinking talents to realize the value of what you are imagining. Use your mind pattern to open your attention, which facilitates imagination and creative thought.

ACTIVATING YOUR IMAGINATION	WHAT IS THE INTERFERENCE?	HOW DO YOU ACCOMPLISH THIS?
Identifying all the tasks and which talents are needed to make this happen.	You burn out because tasks are misaligned with your innate talents. One of the following is unclear: process, timeline, resources, best practices, or skills needed.	Match your thinking talents to tasks, and seek thinking partnerships for your blind spots. Ask for support from someone who is strong in procedural thinking to help create a unified plan of action.
	Thinking is focused only on problems, challenges, or interferences.	Remind yourself regularly of your intention with a meaningful picture, an object, or a quote placed where you will see it often. Each time you notice it, imagine you're realizing it.

USING ATTENTION, INTENTION, AND IMAGINATION TO CREATE FORWARD MOMENTUM

Raymond, the marketing director of a major automobile company, paced around me on the patio of his suburban home. We had just mapped his thinking talents, and I challenged him with a question that was not easy for him to answer: "Given what you now know about your capacity, what is it that only *you* can do?"

Because his mind used the VAK pattern—visual (focused attention-1), auditory (sorting attention-2), kinesthetic (open attention-3)—I suggested that he move while thinking about this question so he could access his "right brain" imagination and intuition. Walking in circles, hands clasped behind his back, he intermittently stopped and tilted his head as if listening to someone I couldn't see. Then he glanced at the chart lying on the glass-topped patio table and repeated the question as if it was a mantra.

The map showed that Ray's thinking talents fell into three quadrants: storytelling, optimism, and mentoring in the relational quadrant; get to action in procedural; and fixing it in analytic. Instead of working together on his behalf, however, his talents were habitually in conflict with one another. His inner dialogue often sounded like a scrimmage on the fifty-yard line: "Do this." "But that won't help anyone!" "We've never done it that way before." "Exactly. Times are hard. We need something that will lift everyone's spirits." We agreed that he needed to learn how to make his talents work collaboratively.

On the horizon for Ray was designing a big marketing campaign for a halftime event at a major college bowl game, which his company was sponsoring. It had to be both inspirational and relevant. I asked Ray to imagine that his thinking talents were an internal board of directors who would advise him on the project. After several minutes, Ray said that his relational talents wanted this event to tell a story that would inspire and align everyone—players, fans, and the television audience. "Fixing It" in the analytic quadrant and "Get to Action" in the procedural domain wanted the event itself to model how the nation could heal its overall morale problem during the war in Iraq.

Suddenly Ray's face lit up. He sat down, and the pen in his hand raced across the page as if taking dictation. I didn't say a word. It was clear he knew exactly what he wanted to create and how he was going to do it.

Two months later, during the halftime show, in front of tens of thousands of fans and millions of television viewers, Ray was standing on the football field, surrounded by a group of fifty or so children and adults. He grasped the microphone, and his face shone brighter than the spotlights as he boomed out the following announcement: "We proudly present . . . all the way from Iraq . . . twelve of our troops who have been fighting for you!" Breaking through a huge paper banner imprinted with the company logo, twelve soldiers ran into the arms of their surprised family members, who stood standing around Ray. Separated by a year or more of war, husbands, wives, and children now clung tightly to one another, causing a tidal wave of emotion through every person

Making Order

Thinking Logically

Innovation

Loving Ideas

Seeking Excellence

Collecting

Love of Learning

Thinking Ahead

Fixing It
Raymond

Standing Out

Strategy

Talents in All Quadrants

Wanting to Win

Adapting

Humor

Reliability

Thinking Back

Optimism

Including

Connection

Thinking Alone

Raymond

Get to Action
Raymond

Having Confidence

Creating Intimacy

Peace-making

Enrolling

Focusing

Equalizing

Goal-Setting

Storytelling

Particularize

Believing

Raymond

Taking Charge

Precision

Mentoring
Raymond

Feeling for Others

who watched. Raymond announced that when these soldiers completed their tours of duty, each of them was guaranteed a job with his company.

The value of this "marketing promotion" was much more than its effect on the bottom line. This was a grand collaboration that resulted from the alignment of all the people in the company on behalf of something that mattered. It caused a literal breakthrough, made possible by one man contributing the full range of his capacity.

BREAKTHROUGH PRACTICE:
CREATING FUTURE PULL

Consider two simple words: "What if . . . ?" You might say to yourself, "What if I run out of money?" Or you might say to yourself, "What if I really go for what I want?" The first will trigger fear and isolation; the latter will trigger future pull.

The following practice, drawn from ki aikido, creates an embodied understanding of how we habitually react in response to the pressure of stress or collapse. You will explore an alternative option that can aim you toward the future. The most effective way to do this is with another person; if that's not practical in this moment, you can also imagine it as vividly as possible.

- Sitting in a chair, bring to mind the person "above you"—a boss, the chairman of the board—to whom you report directly.
- Ask your partner to stand behind you with the weight of his forearms pressing heavily down on your shoulders. Or imagine this scenario.

- You, of course, want to get out from under all that pressure. One option you can try is to stand up by pushing against it. Where in your body do you feel that?
- An alternative response would be to collapse in the chair, trying to appease the power above you or not caring, so you can slide out from under and move away. When and with whom in your life do you habitually use this option? How does it affect you?

You have just been practicing getting rigid or collapsing as responses to pressure. Both are habitual market-share strategies that do not carry you forward.

Let's explore another option of response:

- Shift your *attention,* away from the pressure that holds you down, to an awareness of your breath, your body sensations, the sounds you hear, and the things you see around you.
- Place one hand on your belly and think about your *intention,* something in the future that you *really* want to make possible.
- Imagine it so completely that you can feel a yearning for it in your belly, the center of gravity of your body.
- Look to the other side of the room, imagining as vividly as possible that over there lies the accomplished breakthrough you want to create. Feel it pulling you forward like a magnet.
- Imagine all the people in your life who want you to accomplish this standing by your side, supporting you.
- Now use the pressure you feel from above to propel you forward all the way to your aspiration—as if you took the top off a tube of toothpaste and the pressure caused the contents to surge forward. You are now pulled forward from your center out of the chair *toward* your desired future.

By aiming your attention, intention, and imagination away from an up–down power struggle and toward what you want to create, you have made the cognitive shift toward a possible future.

WHY IS COLLABORATION EASIER FOR WOMEN THAN FOR MEN?

According to recent advances in brain imaging reported by Barbara Annis, Shelley E. Taylor, and Leonard Schlain, our knowledge of the differences in men's and women's brains, and the role that hormones play, has revolutionized our understanding of human behavior. Advances in brain imaging now allow us to literally see the dramatically different ways that men and women communicate, listen, solve problems, make decisions, handle emotions, deal with conflict, and manage stress. The following discoveries indicate that women, in general, have a collaborative edge.

- *A woman's corpus callosum is larger on average. It is also shaped differently and contains more nerve fibers that enable women to travel back and forth between the left and right sides of the brain more easily. This means that women tend to engage logical and creative thinking at the same time. Their logic flow doesn't necessarily stop their creativity.*
- *The size and shape of a woman's corpus callosum also enable her to decode unspoken components of a meeting or exchange, such as body language, tone of voice, and facial expression, while at the same time staying engaged in the content of the discussion. Women often take a more inclusive perspective of situations and typically view the various elements of a problem or task as interconnected.*
- *Women typically have a larger anterior cortex than men do. Many scientists attribute women's superior ability to integrate memories and emotions into more-complex patterns of thought to this finding. They tend to weigh more variables, consider more options, and visualize a wider array of solutions.*
- *The prefrontal cortex, the part of the brain that controls*

judgment, decision-making, and "executive function," is larger in women and develops earlier. It biologically steers women toward win–win solutions to conflict. As a result, they tend to look for ways to compromise and serve the needs of others.

- *Oxytocin, known as the social-attachment hormone, is produced in greater quantities in women. It affects social recognition and bonding as well as the formation of trust between people.*

While it may be true that collaboration is more natural to most women, the four strategies of this book foster and nurture it in all of us.

Angie takes us to Colombia to experience this mind-share strategy in real time.

At 9:00 P.M. I checked in to a well-guarded hotel in downtown Bogotá. I'd been traveling for a week, delivering a series of workshops to teachers, volunteers, and students. My goal was to help them recognize mind patterns and thinking talents in every child by using a game we had developed. Utterly exhausted, I took five minutes before bed to catch up on emails and to review the next day's schedule, which had just been sent to me: pickup at 7:00 A.M. for an hour-long bus ride to a school for the deaf, with an estimated fifty to sixty kids. I reread this line over and over, trying to get my head around the implications. I hadn't been told I'd be presenting to deaf students. I called the local coordinator to ask about this, and she confirmed it was a school for orphaned deaf children. She reassured me that everything would be fine. I didn't believe her for a second.

I looked at my well-crafted, rehearsed workshop agenda. I was confident about its timing, visuals, sequence, and content—all the cornerstones I needed to facilitate a successful workshop. I calculated in my head the extra time needed for translation and for working with such a large group. I tried to imagine how the content could be translated into signing; would there even be a sign for each of the thinking talents? How would I know if the students understood? How would I understand their questions? I was a wreck—my mind raced, my attention jumped from one thing to another. All I could imagine was falling flat on my face in failure. I just wanted to run away. I was so anxious I couldn't sleep.

The trip took an hour and a half longer than expected, due to flooding and bad roads. The bus was noisy, but I tried to focus on my notes. One teacher's laughter was so contagious that it drew me out of my own stressful thoughts. Why was I imagining that the workshop was going to fail? Another teacher leaned over and told me in a thick Spanish accent, "I was so nervous my first time working with deaf children. I wondered how I could possibly teach when I couldn't communicate with them. I decided I would just do my best. Teach with your heart, and it will all work out." She reminded me of my true intention—to help people of all ages recognize their thinking differences and use these differences to enable one another to do more than they ever believed possible.

With that intention pulling me forward, I realized that instead of using my imagination to make up scary stories of everything that could go wrong, I needed to focus my imagination on things going well—that what I had to offer would be useful, even if we didn't cover everything on the program. I stared at the passing scenery, but in my mind's eye I saw a movie of those children uncovering their unique gifts and talents. I imagined that, as a result of today, all of these kids might be able to do better tomorrow and then five years from now. I wondered what I would be able to do better tomorrow as a result of learning with them today. I began to feel more alive and focused.

When we arrived at the campus, it looked more like a quaint farm than a school. Lush green fields and a series of low whitewashed buildings formed a perfect square. Kids in blue uniforms were running around. Everywhere there was the inescapable silence. I took a slow walk, which helped my KVA mind focus my attention. I connected with myself in the present moment by looking at the children around me and asking myself questions that helped me wonder how I could realize my intention.

The day unfolded like an awkward and beautiful dance. Translating every word was a two-step two-interpreter process: from English to Spanish, and then from Spanish to Spanish sign. Comments or questions went from Spanish sign to Spanish, then from Spanish to English, and back again. It was dizzying, but somehow we made it work.

On a break, I kicked around a soccer ball with the kids. One gangly student walked over to me, grinning through crooked teeth. Eyes shining, he made a fist and used it to pound his heart. He then wrapped his other hand tightly around the fist and pushed the fist up as the constraining fingers slowly opened, until each was fully extended in a reach. The gesture captured me totally, and his smile said everything. Two translators came over and told me he was expressing his thanks for helping him grow today. His hands showed a seed breaking open to express his feelings. I signed the same gesture back to him. Shifting my mindset had made this moment possible.

CHAPTER SUMMARY

KEY CONCEPTS OF THIS CHAPTER	GUIDELINES
There are three aspects you can shift to help create a mind-share mindset: attention, intention, and imagination. To create future pull—a unified course of forward action—you need to aim the three aspects of a mind-share mindset.	**Aim your attention** by redirecting it to what you are actually experiencing in the moment. You can use your mind pattern to help you explore which sensory adjustments will bring you to the present. **Aim your intention** forward, toward what you want to create, by using existing pressure to pull forward. **Aim your imagination** by using your mind pattern to open your attention, vivify your intention through multi-sensory imagery, and activate it with your thinking talents.

SHIFTING THE MINDSETS
OF OTHERS

When we think about leaders and the variety of gifts people bring to corporations and institutions, we see that the art of leadership lies in polishing and liberating and enabling those gifts.
—Max De Pree

On July 7, 1990, the night before the FIFA World Cup final in Rome, a performance at the ancient Baths of Caracalla by the Three Tenors—Plácido Domingo, José Carreras, and Luciano Pavarotti—gave birth to one of the most successful musical collaborations of all time. An estimated eight hundred million viewers witnessed the distinct moment that their three voices went from competing to joining, elevating, and resonating off one another. Listen to a recording of the concert and you'll hear for yourself how they pulled one another forward to excellence in a way each could never have achieved alone.

The story I heard about what made this possible is that the conductor, Zubin Mehta, understood the challenge of having three immense egos singing together. The night before the concert, Mehta asked them to prepare a meal together, because he knew they all loved to cook. He also did this to give the singers an experience of alignment that they could draw on as a reference point during the concert. He clearly knew what he was doing, because the world vibrated with the synergy that resulted from that historic musical collaboration.

Five years later, another such moment occurred on a different continent. In post-apartheid South Africa, Nelson Mandela asked the mostly white Springbok national rugby team to travel from one black township to another, playing with the local children and raising goodwill and support, so they could bridge racial gaps and truly become South Africa's team. By embracing the national team and hosting the 1995 rugby World Cup, South Africans aligned. They aimed their focus toward what united rather than divided them: their team's success. On June 24, the world witnessed South Africa defeat New Zealand, 15–12, in the final game in Johannesburg. Moments later, Nelson Mandela emerged onto the field, wearing his number-16 green Springboks jersey, to shake the hand of team captain François Pienaar. As he prepared to hand over the cup, he said, "François, thank you for what you have done for our country." Pienaar, with extraordinary presence of mind, replied, "No, Mr. President. Thank you for what you have done." It was a mind-share victory against all odds: for the team, for Mandela, and for South Africa.

Nelson Mandela is an outstanding example of how a leader can align attention, intention, and action to pull an entire country toward a possible future. While the challenges for South Africa still exist, Archbishop Desmond Tutu summed up its significance: "The lesson is simple and wonderfully encouraging: If it happened once, it can happen again."

What Mehta and Mandela did took place on a public stage in front of millions, but you too can influence moments where people shift from thinking apart to thinking together. Great leaders can do this by mastering the cognitive shifts you read about in the last chapter.

SECRETS OF TWO COLLABORATIVE LEADERS:
AL CAREY, JACKI ZEHNER

We asked Al Carey, CEO of PepsiCo Americas Beverages, and Jacki Zehner, CEO of Women Moving Millions, to answer three questions:

- *What is one thing you've done to shift the limiting mindset of others?*
- *What do you know that you want others to know about collaboration?*
- *To increase your collaborative intelligence, where could you grow?*

JACKI ZEHNER

What is one thing you've done to shift the limiting mindset of others?

I have acknowledged the limiting mindset of myself.

What do you know that you want others to know about collaboration?

Collaboration requires a different mindset than what we are used to. We have to move away from trying to one-up each other with our intelligence, our ideas, our credentials, in order for it to work. It is about creating a new kind of space that is truly respectful, inviting, and inclusive.

Collaboration requires skills that few of us are taught; in fact, we are more likely to be taught how not to collaborate. To work together effectively, we will have to challenge what we think we know and be open to doing things differently.

To increase your collaborative intelligence, where could you grow?

I need to know more about how to balance getting everyone's best thinking on what to do with actually getting it done.

AL CAREY

What is one thing you've done to shift the limiting mindset of others?

I don't believe negativity comes naturally. It's mostly a protective habit.

I believe inspiring other people to their own greatness is one of the most essential parts of my job. I ask a lot of questions, to make sure I know where a person is coming from. I have to find out as much as I can about what he or she needs to achieve outcomes at the maximum level of their capacity. I've done a great deal of work on my own thinking so I can create a positive mindset about each person I lead. They are naturally attracted to that. It's contagious if it's genuine. Mine is. I believe in the people I lead and the possibilities they can create. By changing the way I think about people, the people I think about change.

What do you know that you want others to know about collaboration?

I came up through the ranks in sales, and I learned that the best sales I made were when I listened more than I spoke. I listen underneath people's words for what they really need and what's important to them. As a leader, I am in service to them. Collaboration makes it possible for you both to serve each other's success.

To increase your collaborative intelligence, where could you grow?

I believe in what's called the "adversity advantage"—using challenges to learn with others and grow forward together. This is very challenging in a time when companies are thought of as financial instruments only. I don't know yet how to collaborate with the mindset that tears companies apart, leaving ten thousand people out of work and nothing of value remaining. Since I believe that almost all collaborations can work in time, I still have to learn when the effort is unproductive.

AIMING COLLECTIVE ATTENTION

Attention can be thought of as the currency of mind share. What if, for instance, you thought of attention as something you give, something you earn, something you invest and spend, instead of something you "pay"? William James, psychologist and philosopher, described attention as the brain's conductor, leading the orchestra of the mind.

The linear definition of attention is the self-regulated flow of energy and information within and between us. Aikido sensei Wendy Palmer put it this way: "Energy follows attention." These days we are tossed and turned by data floods and pummeled by clashing streams of rapid-fire imagery. We participate in fleeting virtual meetings that are rescheduled a half dozen times and punctuated by pings and beeps and multitasking. Dee Hock, former CEO and founder of Visa, has described a spectrum of attention: Data at one end is distilled to information, then to knowledge, then to understanding, and finally to wisdom. However, Hock states, "We are now at a point in time when the ability to receive, utilize, store, transform, and transmit data . . . has expanded literally beyond comprehension. Understanding and wisdom are largely forgotten as we struggle under an avalanche of data and information."

As shareholders, co-workers, advertisers, and social-media platforms all grab for it, attention is in dwindling supply. No matter how much power or money you have, you cannot buy attention. As any parent or teacher can tell you, you can force someone to look but not to see; you can pressure them to listen but not to hear. Over and over we tell our children and ourselves to "pay attention."

In the midst of a time when distraction has become a disorder, our research and work with influential global leaders has proven it *is* possible to influence the direction of the attention of a group, whether of two or twenty-two, by focusing it on the assets of the people present. For instance, remember how Nick, the CEO we wrote about earlier in the book, begins his senior-leadership team meetings by asking everyone to leave their phones and devices in a basket at the door as they enter. He starts the agenda by going around the room and telling each person something specific he or she has done in the previous month that contributed to the success of the company. People light up as Nick calls forth the best of who they are. In this way he focuses the attention on the intellectual assets in the room and then directs them to the task at hand.

How could you do the same with a team you lead?

Guidelines for Aiming Collective Attention

- Focus on the assets and successes that are present in the room, on what is working and what has worked. Do it in as multi-sensory and experiential a way as possible.
- Remember that different people give their attention in different ways. Recall what you've learned about mind patterns. Observe the factors that switch people on—i.e., is it standing, talking in dialogue, asking lots of questions? For some it happens when they look right at you, for others when they are looking away. Some find their focus when they're walking beside you, and for still others it's when they are engaged in heated debate. This will help you enter the model of the world of those with whom you will be thinking and find the conditions and circumstances where they are naturally fully attentive. Then you can replicate them as much as possible.
- Recognize that people have a natural rhythm of "here now, then gone, here now, then gone." They shift between open and focused attention. This rhythm is different for each person. Sometimes "gone" simply means that a person may be incubating a new idea or digesting what has just happened.
- Tell people what *you* need to be present: "I need to walk while I listen to you," or "I need you to show me what you mean so I can follow you." Knowing and naming what you need to be fully present increase your effectiveness.

- Be aware that people may feel awkward in a non-habitual thinking environment. You might need to "host"—help them find comfort as you would a guest at a dinner party in your home.

AIMING COLLECTIVE INTENTION: QUESTIONS FOR LEADERS

Aiming collective intention describes the state of a group aligned in the same direction toward a collective goal. It magnetizes everyone involved. Nelson Mandela's intention to unite all of South Africa was accomplished by aiming everyone's intention toward winning the 1995 World Cup. Collective intention inspires collective excellence. Without it, people may comply but they won't truly commit.

Inquiry is one of the most effective ways to bring about the alignment of collective intention. For example, compare the following three collective intentions: "We don't want to develop any new products, because our resources will be too taxed." "We need to streamline existing products, so we can make sure we have enough resources." "We are going to focus on streamlining existing product lines for the next six months, so we can gain needed resources to develop and grow new cutting-edge products by the end of the year." Which do you think would create the strongest future pull for a group?

The following questions will help you recognize whether a group is aligned or not, and they can also help connect your intention so you can pull one another forward.

Analytic Questions
- What is the predominant motivation for you right now in your current situation? Is this moving you away from what you are afraid of or moving you toward what you want?
- If you analyze your intentions in areas of your life where you are in a group/team (work, family, other interests), what is one common denominator?

Procedural Questions
- When in the past has the team's intention been aligned?
- What were the processes and conditions that made this possible?

Relational Questions
- Who are the people who inspire your team?
- What is the story that inspires your team's intention?

Innovative Questions
- What would your team be doing in the future if its intention was aligned?
- What might be a new way to evoke and align the individual intentions?

Travel with us to a meeting in Nigeria to experience how we helped create the conditions where attention and intention could be aimed forward in a situation of extreme fragmentation.

Several years ago, Angie and I were asked by the then-CEO of Royal Dutch Shell to design and facilitate a workshop on collaborative intelligence between its senior leaders and the Ministry of Energy and Mineral Resources. Shell had the reputation of ravaging the country for decades. I was informed that in a previous meeting with company leaders, the minister had walked out after five minutes. When I asked where the meetings usually took place, the head of HR looked at me quizzically and replied that they used the main conference room of the company headquarters, which was equipped with the latest technological support.

Six months of research into Nigerian history, tribal customs, and culture told me that the corporate conference room was not the place and PowerPoint was not what was needed to align the attention and intention of these two groups. I had learned that Nigeria is a very musical culture and that storytelling is a natural and habitual way of thinking among the Igbo, Hausa, and Yoruba tribes, who would all be represented in our meeting. Therefore, we designed a meeting in the ballroom of the main hotel in Lagos, which we hoped would captivate everyone's attention and make it possible for a common intention to emerge.

We covered the walls with huge evocative photographs of local people, places, and things. Below each one was a sheet of newsprint. At the top was the question: "What if, ten years from now, you could tell your children a story about how you helped Nigeria thrive?" We removed all the chairs, because I had learned that many Nigerians tended toward the KAV pattern, so they were accustomed to thinking on their feet. As the minister entered the room, music by the famous Nigerian singer Fela Kuti was playing over the speakers.

We asked people to choose the photograph that grabbed their attention and gather around it, with an equal number of people from Shell and Nigeria in each group. They were instructed to align their individual ideas into a story that would reveal how they could create a future together.

The Nigerians began to laugh and talk immediately. Telling stories was innate to their way of thinking. The corporate Europeans and Americans, however, trained in market-share analysis and procedure, were awkward and adrift. Finally, though, they were carried forward by the energy and excitement of the Nigerians and began to participate actively. The minister stayed for the whole day, including that evening, when we invited family members of the group to join in with music and dancing. As each small group shared their stories about what could be possible ten years from now, the room filled with energy, laughter, and even some tears.

To the amazement of many, the minister returned the next day. We began by asking the group what they had learned thus far about thinking together that could inform how they would work that morning. They were unanimous about wanting to meet on their feet in the same groups, with big paper on the walls. They wanted to think about one action they could take that would move Nigeria closer to the stories they had crafted. By the end of the morning, the whole group had agreed to co-create a technical university to train young people in Nigeria to use the latest technology. As I write this, several years later, they've broken ground on the building.

Multi-sensory thinking aimed the intention of everyone in this meeting, including the minister, and made forward movement possible: visually with the photographs, auditorily with the music and stories, and kinesthetically through dance and the shared experience of thinking on their feet.

Guidelines for Aiming Collective Intention

- At the beginning of each meeting, state your intended outcome and check to make sure each person is aligned with it. If the thinking diverges from this intention, bring people's attention back to it.
- "Walk-and-talks" and wall murals make it possible to include everyone's thinking in the overall intention.
- Use small groups and non-habitual pairs to create new connections and shift away from numbing thinking habits.
- Find a "What if . . . ?" question that will be meaningful and evocative to draw out the intentions of each person in the room.
- Create a multi-dimensional representation that unifies all the diverse intentions. For example: a collage of images or photographs cut out of magazines, or a model or sculpture using the available materials in the room.

AIMING COLLECTIVE IMAGINATION

One of the most unused collective resources is imagination. How many meetings have you attended in which someone called for a pause, during which all were to imagine what could be possible in this situation? I have never heard this question asked in a corporate meeting, yet everyone would agree that imagination is what makes progress possible. Until we come to value it as a legitimate way of thinking and learn how to create the conditions that foster it, we will not be able to fully access our intellectual capital. Those who know how to evoke collective imagination will lead the mind-share economy.

Aiming collective imagination means knowing the value your shared intention brings, evoking it through multi-sensory imagery, and aligning and enacting it with the available thinking talents in your group.

The following chart will help you aim and enact the imagination of a group:

	WHAT INTERFERES?	HOW DO YOU ACCOMPLISH THIS?
Aiming Collective Imagination	The value each person brings to the collective intention is not being recognized.	Use thinking-talents map to display the value each person brings to the group.
	We are not in touch with the conditions our different mind patterns need to think creatively.	Create the conditions needed for multi-sensory thinking.
	Fear that we lack capacity and energy to accomplish certain tasks.	Create thinking partnerships that will complement different cognitive styles so you can balance talents and blind spots.
	The misunderstanding that imagination takes too much time and is not a valid way of thinking together.	Ask each person to share a story of a time when something they imagined was realized. Then ask if the time they just spent was beneficial, and how.

Enacting Collective Imagination	One of the following is unclear: timeline, resources, process, best practices, accountability, or responsibilities.	Create a unified plan of action, which includes a clear timeline, resources, best practices, defined accountabilities, and responsibilities. Identify all the tasks and talents that are needed to make this happen.
	Thinking is directed toward problems rather than possibilities.	Use analytic inquiry to help discern which possibilities would be the most effective, and which problems need to be solved.
	Imagination and action are not acknowledged as enablers of each other.	Create a multidimensiional representation of the collective intention as a "magnetic north" to remind people of what to aim toward (e.g. collage, sculpture, mural).

For those who like acronyms, we use CARE as a pragmatic reminder of the process that integrates imagination and action. Using this sequence will help you aim attention, intention, and imagination.

C—Create ideas.
A—Analyze ideas for effectiveness.
R—Refine your best ideas into an action plan.
E—Execute your plan by aligning task and talent.

BREAKTHROUGH PRACTICE: ENACTING MIND SHARE

The most important things we need to know about how to think well together are often hidden because of our assumption that we all think in the same way. We have developed a simple process to make accessing the collaborative intelligence of any group possible.

Create a Collaboration Handbook
- Each person fills out one page on how to best work with him or her. This might include thinking talents, mind patterns, cognitive styles, and whatever helps to think together with others. Be as specific as possible. (See the example below.)
- Combine them all to create a team handbook.
- In the group, ask each person to explain the information on his or her page.

COLLABORATION HANDBOOK

Name _____

- My best guess of my mind pattern (VAK, etc.):

- My thinking talents are:

- My inquiry style is:

- My blind spots are:

- If you want to treat me with respect:

- How I prefer to receive information (e.g., email for short messages; phone calls for longer issues; never voice mail; etc.):

- How I prefer to receive difficult feedback:

- One thing I'd like you to know about me is:

Angie offers a story of how a new CEO took the first steps of enacting mind share.

Karen had been in her new position as CEO of a Fortune 500 beverage company for just two weeks when she hired me to bring cohesion to her leadership team. She warmly greeted me, and as we rode the elevator she shared how unprepared she felt for the meeting I was going to attend with her. Her predecessor had planned the off-site, so she hadn't even seen the agenda. "I have heard they are competent individuals but not a competent team and are very fragmented. I have no idea what to do," she said nervously. As the elevator doors opened, I put a hand on her shoulder and said, "We have a lot of wisdom and experience between the two of us. Let's assume we can pull this off, okay?"

I went on to suggest that we let the meeting begin as it normally would, so we could observe how the team thought together. The CFO started by showing a PowerPoint of the agenda and then talked it through. The rest of the team sat passively, glancing at their Black-Berries under the table. As he moved through the agenda from one slide to another, the CFO talked about how challenging the numbers were, how the economy was in a downward spiral, and how poorly the product launches had gone. People made defensive statements, which all began: "What if we can't . . ." "The board won't . . ." "Customers aren't . . ." "The competition is . . ." By the time the break came, each person had presented, reported, and shared information with one another, but none of them were thinking together. We had no idea what intention was pulling them forward.

Even the espresso that was served didn't help. The two of us noticed how the team seemed swallowed by problems that were too big for any one of them to solve alone. We strategized how to rescue the meeting. It was time to shake up their thinking habits.

After the break, Karen stood up and asked the room, "Is this meeting moving you all forward?" Noticeable groans, sighs, and shuffling made the answer obvious. She said, "All right, I suggest we begin by aligning our intention, attention, and imagination. Let's do this by going on a 'walk-and-talk.' Choose a person with whom you typically do not interact, go outside, and explore the following open question: 'What would we do differently to unleash the potential of all fifty thousand employees of this company?' Remember, there's no right answer. What you need to do is consider what you'd really like to make possible."

When they returned a half hour later, I had covered the entire length of the conference room wall with a blank mural. As the team stood around it, I wrote that single question at the top. At first there was absolute silence, and then one by one people came up and spoke passionately about their intentions; I summarized what they said on the mural in words and images. A few of the ideas were:

"We would become the strongest employment brand in the world."

"We would ask each employee what he or she needed to feel energized about coming to work every day."

"Our true competitive advantage would be the happiness of our employees."

After fifteen minutes, the wall was covered with ideas. We all stood back and absorbed the finished product, stunned and excited at what it represented: an aligned collective intention created by each of them that inspired them all. Karen suggested they use it to pull themselves forward as they worked through the remaining agenda items. They broke up into small groups and divided the tasks according to areas of interest and expertise. Occasionally they looked up at the mural as a reminder of where they were going together. They decided to hang it in the main entry hall of the building, as a collective compass.

At the end of the meeting, I asked them to think about their experience that day and what had shifted their thinking from where they had started to where they were now. Karen stood up and said, "As your new leader, I really want us all to think better together than we do on our own. To learn how to do this, Angie has suggested we create a collaboration handbook."

Chairs were pushed aside, and people hastened to share with one another the conditions that brought out their best thinking. Most wanted multi-sensory meetings in a larger room, where they could break into pairs and small groups, move around, and use images and

several flip charts. Others asked for periods of silence within meetings for reflection. Still others needed to make input by putting Post-
its on a whiteboard instead of having to speak. Karen was so excited
by what had happened that she promised to give each person a T-
shirt, in the color of his or her choice, that said, "I think better when I
think with you!" as a reminder of the collaborative intelligence that
existed between them.

CHAPTER SUMMARY

KEY CONCEPTS OF THIS CHAPTER	GUIDELINES
To generate future pull, aim the collective attention, intention, and imagination of your group.	Aim your team's attention by: • Shining the light on the assets of the people present. • Focusing on possibilities rather than constraints. • Thinking in multi-sensory ways so all diverse minds can contribute. Aim your team's collective intention forward by using analytic, procedural, relational, and innovative Inquiry. Aim your team's collective imagination by understanding what each person needs according to their mind pattern in order to think creatively, and enact it by using the CARE process (create, advance, refine, and execute).
Enact mind share in your team by creating a collaboration handbook.	Have everyone prepare a one-page summary of what supports his best thinking, then share with team, deciding what to stop, start, and continue in meetings. Create an operating agreement to enact this going forward.

THE RANDORI

My husband and I walked in to an immense Quonset hut in Kauai, Hawaii. The fluorescently lit hall, or dojo, was filled with white-suited class members kneeling on bright blue mats that covered the floor. As if by some secret signal, they bowed to the teacher, or sensei, who then bowed to them. He was Japanese, perhaps fifty, perhaps seventy; there was no way to tell. He wore a white tunic and long black skirtlike pants, the garb of a martial-arts master.

Half a dozen burly men circled him menacingly. As they began to close in, he was absolutely still, calm, poised. Suddenly, with shouts that reverberated off the metal walls, they attacked him in unison from all angles. The master seemed to flow like water into their mass, swirling *between* them, his black skirt surrounding them. Each time they reached to strike his body, he was not there. As a gyroscope spins faster and faster, its motion appears still. So it was with the sensei as he met and diverted the energy of his attackers, redirecting them one by one out of the melee. He seemed to lay each down on the ground tenderly, protectively, respectfully.

His actions were so effortless that I knew there was a force at work that could not be readily seen, something implicit. After class was over, I approached him, keeping a respectful distance. When he turned to face me, I felt every molecule of his attention surround me. I was only going to thank him for allowing me to observe the class, but curiosity got the best of me. I had to ask one question. "Excuse me, Sensei, but how long did it take you to learn to do that—what you did with those men?"

"You mean the Randori?" he asked.

"Sure, if that's what you call it. You made it look so simple!"

His students were lining up, waiting to perform the closing class ritual, but his attention was totally present with my question and me. "I have been practicing Randori for forty years, but I am sorry, I have not learned it yet. Still, I practice. That's all there is. Simple. Practice. Like life, yes?" He bowed, turned, and was simply and completely gone.

The multiple challenges of a Randori, with its chaotic forces closing in from many directions, are familiar to any person in a leadership position today. What was there beneath the surface that enabled the sensei to respond in such a way? How did he manage to remain balanced and calm, simultaneously relating to both himself and others with respect?

CONCLUSION

RANDORI: LEADING WITH A NEW QUALITY OF MIND

From the standpoint of daily life, however, there is one thing we do know: that we are here for the sake of each other—above all for those upon whose smile and well-being our own happiness depends, and also for the countless unknown souls with whose fate we are connected by a bond of sympathy. Many times a day I realize how much my own outer and inner life is built upon the labors of my fellow men, both living and dead, and how earnestly I must exert myself in order to give in return as much as I have received.

—Albert Einstein

While the sensei was fully aware of his "virtuous intent"—the internal force guiding his sense of purpose in the world—he was also attending to external forces without being distracted by them. He did not see others as opponents but as people on their own journey. This freed his mind to choose how he was going to relate to them. He moved between them, with them, around them, but gracefully used the energy of their movement to aim himself toward his goal. He was like a revolving glass door that uses the push of people who move through it to turn.

"Randori" is a term used in the Japanese martial art of ki aikido to describe freestyle practice. It literally means "grasping freedom." We are always free to choose how we respond. The more complex challenges we face, the more diverse thinking styles and mind patterns we have to collaborate with, the more critical it becomes to notice how we can cultivate the quality of mind that will free our thinking.

Collaborative intelligence will help lead you from what was to what can be. Making the transition from market-share to mind-share thinking requires activating all the intellectual capital available to us. We have been trained, however, to foster self-sufficiency, individual competence, and independence. Hence we now find ourselves walled off from one another, fragmented, and isolated, at a time when collaboration is what is most needed. Perhaps our only true refuge lies in learning to respect and serve the value in one another.

Thus far in this book, we've offered four strategies for thinking with people who think differently. What's truly needed to master them, however, can't be taught, because it is a quality of mind that can only be nurtured. As you've turned one page after another, we have asked you to explore intellectual diversity so you can bridge the differences that tear us apart. We have pointed to the talents you bring that can transform burnout into passion, inquiry into inspiration. We have encouraged shifting your mindset to aim your attention, intention, and imagination.

What will differentiate you as a leader is not something you are born with or taught in business school. It is cultivating respect for the value of our differences, even in the midst of stress and speed. How do *you* know when you are respected? Each person I have asked responds differently. For instance, one person might say, "I know I'm respected when someone listens to me." Another person may say, "I know I'm respected when someone looks me in the eye." How, then, do you demonstrate respect when we are using one word to express myriad behaviors?

The root of the word "respect" means to look again, to see or consider oneself, other people, situations, and challenges as if for the first time. In my experience, it is this single most important quality of mind that enables us to think well with people who think differently.

Each of the people around you has a dormant seed of greatness inside, often devalued and repressed, waiting for nothing more than recognition and respect to emerge. Therefore, no matter with whom you are working, you are always collaborating with a hidden possibility.

How do you remember this when faced with work's multiple challenges and the chaos of today's world? My grandmother, who was a midwife, said that the moment a newborn infant opened his or her eyes and looked at her—the first human the baby had ever seen—that seed of possibility was obvious. She lived in the slums of New York City, but those moments of wonder were her true wealth, and she wore them like a jeweled necklace. Maybe they were why I never heard her swear or curse at anyone. Not even on the day her youngest son, my uncle Allie, was run over by a motorcycle. She held her apron over her face and wept for days, but she never cursed the man who killed her son. All she said was that she prayed for him by imagining that, someday in the future, his hidden seed of possibility would grow.

When I lead a group of people, I do what I can to follow in my grandmother's footsteps. Rather than thinking about whether they like me or if I am smarter than they are, rather than analyzing what is wrong with them and figuring out how I can fix it, I take one long, slow moment to incubate both respect for myself and for them with the following breakthrough practice:

> Bring to mind those who stand behind you, those who dreamed of you and prayed that one day there would be one such as you who could move beyond the limitations of their previous history.
>
> Now bring to mind those who stand next to you, those who, in small and large ways, make it possible for you to do the

work you do, make the difference you make, and have the influence you have.

Last, bring to mind those who will come after you, those whose lives will be enriched and improved by what you are doing now, those who will think back with gratitude to your efforts and accomplishments.

Shift your awareness to one person you are working with (perhaps he is particularly difficult or challenging).

Enjoy a long, slow breath and then bring to mind those who stand behind that person, those who have prayed for and dreamed of him.

Consider those who stand next to this person and make it possible for him to do the work he does.

Last, think of the future that is pulling this person forward, and imagine that he is realizing the specific gifts and talents that are the contribution only he can bring to the rest of us.

Conclude by asking one open question that inspires your respect, such as, "What can we make possible together?"

This practice and the quality of mind it engenders will determine what you are serving as you lead, whether you reach out, listen, and guide with respect or control, whether you see yourself and the people you work with as broken and damaged or as unfinished works of art. It can sustain you and every person with whom you think.

The future may depend less on your expertise than on your capacity to connect with others who think differently. It may require the wonder of your imagination to bridge those differences and realize those possibilities.

May you know, through the journey we have shared, that there is a collaborative intelligence larger than any one of us, which cannot be measured but can be trusted: May you use it well.

UTILIZING MIND PATTERNS IN WORK SITUATIONS

VAK PATTERN

Visual, Auditory, and Kinesthetic VAK PATTERN			
V1		FOCUSED THINKING	To Trigger Concentration: VISUAL
A2		SORTING THINKING	To Trigger Sorting: AUDITORY
K3		OPEN THINKING	To Trigger Imagination: KINESTHETIC

Best Ways to Focus Your Attention
- To get logical, focused, and organized, it is best for you to write or draw.
- You are a natural list-maker and generally like to take notes. The act of note-taking alone may be enough to get you fo-

cused on an idea—you may not even need to go back and re-read them.

Best Ways to Explore Options and Think Through Confusion

- Think out loud with a partner, ideally someone who is a good listener and who will allow you to go back and forth and weigh different options without providing the answer for you.

Best Ways to Innovate or Create

- Try moving. Get up from your desk and walk around. Take time to do some physical activity that allows you to go at your own pace, like yoga, swimming, or walking. While doing this activity, allow yourself to "space out," not thinking about anything in particular.
- Driving can also be very effective for unlocking creativity. Allow your mind to wander from one idea to the next as you drive, and try talking out loud to yourself.

Your Most Effective Decision-Making Strategies

- You tend to make decisions best by first writing about an issue, and then talking with a good listener about what you discovered through your writing. Pay attention to the physical effect that what you are saying has on your body—your gut reaction when you consider one decision versus another. Is there one option that you're more drawn to? Or one that you instinctively want to move away from?
- In a meeting when joint decisions are to be made, it is best if you are visually prepared with a written memo or minutes from the last meeting.

Your Best Working Environment

You may be very particular about your physical environment. It is important to you that it looks just the way you want and that you can see what you are working on, rather than having it stored away in drawers or files.

Your Best Learning Process

- Manuals, directions, and textbooks are important tools for you, since you naturally learn best by reading about something first, and then discussing it with someone else before you have to do something new with it.
- When you are learning something technical, you naturally prefer to read text and look at diagrams, and then ask questions as needed, rather than trying a hands-on approach first.
- If you do get stuck, you prefer to show someone else what you know, while narrating your process, and then have the other person show you where you've gone wrong as they explain.

Communicating with Others

- Since you characteristically communicate by storytelling, listeners who need logical details may feel impatient and want you to "get to the point."
- Stay aware of this and ask yourself frequently: "What is the main point I want to convey?" Then try to summarize your message in a headline.
- Try presenting a visual message when you want to get to the point or communicate more efficiently.

Receiving Feedback

- You generally prefer to receive difficult, critical feedback in writing first—in notes, in emails, in written reports—with an opportunity to discuss face-to-face later, once you're ready.
- More intimate and positive feedback will be more deeply received if you hear it while seeing the person's face.

Dealing with Conflict

- You most likely prefer direct, truthful communication about difficult issues and are usually willing to verbally discuss the source of conflict. You may dislike feeling that you are being talked about behind your back.

- It can be helpful for you to prepare for a discussion of a particularly loaded issue by writing or reading about it first.

Receiving Support or Guidance

- You may naturally need a lot of time to talk through your experiences: what you've done, how you feel, what you like, or what's hard for you. You may not fully know how you feel about something until you talk about all sides of it.
- You may dislike being told what to do or what you are feeling. Usually, when you are working through something, you just want space to figure out what is going on in your head.
- If someone is teaching or mentoring you, ask that person to explain things using metaphor and analogy as much as possible.

The Most Effective Way to Relax

- You tend to relax by reading, watching TV or movies, or listening to music of your choice.
- To really relax and get a sense of what you are feeling in your body, it helps you to close your eyes and be still, perhaps while listening to music. A long shower or bath, a massage with music, or driving while listening to music or an audio book may also help you to relax.

To Enhance Your Physical Well-Being

- You may have a difficult time with a regular, structured exercise regimen. You do best with physical activity that is not too repetitive or competitive and can be done at your own rhythm—walking, swimming, yoga, biking.
- One way to encourage movement is to find a partner to share such activities and converse with, as long as that partner does not try to push you too fast or too far. You might also enjoy listening to music or a fascinating interview or audio book while moving.

Famous People Who Use the VAK Pattern

Martin Luther King, Jr.: He told stories to inspire others; he
spoke in colorful metaphors and painted a vivid picture of
his vision. He stood very still while speaking. He was a voracious reader.

Oprah Winfrey: She makes extended, direct eye contact with
her guests, and she sits very still through interviews. Her
face expresses whatever she's feeling, and her physical appearance is very important to her.

Working and Communicating with Other Patterns

KVA

- People who use the KVA pattern tend to be very independent
workers who can grasp physical and technical tasks quickly.
Refrain from showing and telling them what to do; they generally prefer to figure things out on their own.

- Allow for a great deal of silence when working with those
who use the KVA pattern and try to not answer their questions unless they specifically ask you to.

- Don't assume you know what KVAs are feeling by reading
their faces. People who use this pattern often do not show
their feelings this way. Their facial expressions are not necessarily indications that they are angry or don't like you.

- Use email rather than verbal communication with them as
much as possible.

- If you supervise KVAs, give them as much independence as
you can and communicate as much as possible in writing,
particularly if it is about something important.

KAV

- People whose minds use this pattern are natural partners for you, particularly in metaphoric thinking.
- KAVs are good at moving your ideas into concrete action.
- Be careful not to overwhelm them with visual information—communicate as much as possible verbally, although if you want to praise them, a short email will have a huge impact.
- As much as possible, don't force eye contact—sit next to (not across from) them, so their eyes can move where they want to.
- If you find yourself in conflict with someone who uses this pattern, suggest that you go for a walk to talk it out, and allow the person to speak without looking at you.
- If you supervise people who use the KAV pattern, allow them to move around in meetings; they will be able to pay attention better and contribute more.

AKV

- People who use the AKV pattern are visually sensitive, so avoid too much visual information—emails, faxes, written memos, visual directions.
- Don't draw or show too many diagrams when speaking to them.
- Allow them to not make eye contact with you.
- If you supervise those who use this pattern, suggest that they get up and move around as they feel inclined, even in meetings; it will enable them to get in touch with what really

matters to them and it will help them have patience with those who speak more slowly.

AVK

- Usually, people who use the AVK pattern are comfortable work partners for you, particularly in a brainstorming situation, when ideas are flying.
- They are very good at seeing the big picture and the details. However, they may be slow to move into action, or struggle to discover what, concretely, they need to do.

VKA

- People who use this pattern are natural collaborators who make very good team players.
- They meet you easily in the visual world—how things look is very important to them as well.
- Communicate with them as much as possible in writing— email, written memos, and letters.
- If you supervise VKA people, be aware that they are very sensitive to your tone of voice.

VKA PATTERN

Visual, Kinesthetic, and Auditory VKA PATTERN		
V1	FOCUSED THINKING	To Trigger Concentration: VISUAL
K2	SORTING THINKING	To Trigger Sorting: KINESTHETIC
A3	OPEN THINKING	To Trigger Imagination: AUDITORY

Best Ways to Focus Your Attention

- You depend on detailed written reminders, lists, instructions, and directions to keep yourself organized, and it is through writing that you express yourself in the most detailed, organized manner as well.

Best Ways to Explore Options and Think Through Confusion

- Experience is your best teacher in sorting things out. Actually trying out the various options, or thinking back on what has worked for you in the past, is the ideal way to determine what is best for you.

Best Ways to Innovate or Create

- A great way for you to get in touch with your innovative capacity is through speaking, allowing yourself the freedom to brainstorm verbally and "talk in webs." Ideally you would have someone write down what you say and then read your words back to you. But if you don't have someone to do this for you, try getting alone in a room, walking around, talking into a tape recorder, and then transcribing your ideas.

Your Most Effective Decision-Making Strategies

* Write down all your options. Then try them out one at a time, and talk about the results with someone who will record or verbally repeat what you've discovered. Give yourself the freedom to change your mind when you have experimented with options.
* Talk to yourself while looking in the mirror to discover what you really want. It is easier for you to get in touch with your true intentions when you are looking at only yourself, as opposed to when you are around other people.

Your Best Working Environment

* Most likely, you are very particular about the way your physical environment looks; you can't think well with visual clutter.
* You also tend to be very sensitive to auditory distractions and need quiet in order to do your work. It may help you to touch base frequently with your team and feel the energy of all the people who are working with and around you.
* A lack of visual precision on the part of those you work with can be extremely frustrating. It helps to remember that while this is a strength of yours, others have different abilities.

Your Best Learning Process

* You learn best by watching a demonstration or reading the directions for a task and then experimenting, without being told first how to do it.
* If you get stuck, you might want to ask questions and receive some explanation from others. You do not do well in general, however, with lectures or long verbal explanations.

Communicating with Others

* Most likely you communicate well one-on-one and in small groups. Try to get very clear about where you stand and what you want to say by jotting down some notes before you

talk with others; you may find yourself being swayed by others' opinions and agreeing to something you really don't believe in.

- If you must speak in front of a large group, prepare visually in advance, move around to find your words, and draw on a whiteboard or use bullet points to keep you on track.
- Suggest to others that they communicate with you in writing as much as possible.
- In meetings, take notes for yourself or volunteer to be the official note-taker standing at a flip chart or whiteboard in order to best remember what was said.

Receiving Feedback

- Since you are sensitive to auditory feedback, it is best to receive negative feedback in writing. Positive feedback can be delivered in writing or verbally, ideally with good eye contact.
- You may want to tell people of other patterns who use sarcasm that you are highly sensitive to a biting tone of voice and as a result may misunderstand the other person's intention.

Dealing with Conflict

- It is best for you to deal with any conflict in writing or while walking. Otherwise you can easily be swayed by what the other person is saying and come away from the interaction conceding or agreeing with something that is not really true for you.

Receiving Support or Guidance

- Those who wish to give you help or guidance should encourage you to write, to allow your thoughts to come into focus and help you communicate more succinctly.
- Writing is also an effective way for you to express the many feelings you have inside.

- Remind others to allow you time to speak and not to finish your sentences, interrupt you, or put words in your mouth.
- Ask others to mirror back to you in words or in writing what you have said.
- You may need to ask a lot of questions when receiving guidance from another person. Don't be afraid to take notes during phone conversations or in other important verbal communications, and write down the questions you are wondering about. This will help you to think for yourself.

The Most Effective Way to Relax
- You may need to engage in some kind of strenuous physical exercise every day in order to relax.
- In addition, you may relax most naturally by reading, journaling, or exercising to music.
- Listening to music with headphones can help you come back to yourself or stop the voices in your mind.

To Enhance Your Physical Well-Being
- A physical outlet can help you when you are very keyed up and tense. Generally you do best with activities with a great deal of intensity—running, skiing, tennis, volleyball—and need to be encouraged to also do some receptive physical practices such as yoga.

Famous People Who Use the VKA Pattern

Princess Diana: She always seemed to take in the world through her eyes. Her appearance, rather than her words, seemed of utmost importance. She took action based on what she saw and experienced. She was generally quiet, but what she said seemed to have deep meaning to her.

Dustin Hoffman: He makes very direct eye contact both in acting roles and in interviews. When he speaks, the emphasis is more on his tone than on what he's saying. He often speaks in questions rather than statements. He seems to have pent-up energy always bursting to get out; he seems most comfortable speaking when he is moving.

Working and Communicating with Other Patterns

KVA

- People who use the KVA pattern are good work partners for you since you are both auditorily sensitive; you communicate naturally with one another via email and memo and move smoothly together into action.
- Sometimes, people who use the KVA pattern can be frustrating for you because they work so independently. Be aware that they may not want to interact as much as you do or come to as many meetings as you think are appropriate.

KAV

- You can also partner well with people who use the KAV pattern, particularly when creating something concrete.
- Be careful not to overwhelm them with visual information—communicate as much as possible verbally, although if you want to praise them, short emails will have a huge impact.
- As much as possible, don't force eye contact—sit next to (not across from) them, so their eyes can move where they want to.
- If you find yourself in conflict with a person who uses the KAV pattern, suggest that you go for a walk to talk it out, and allow him or her to speak without looking at you.

- If you supervise people who use the KAV pattern, allow them to move around in meetings; they will be able to pay attention better and contribute more.

AKV

- People who use the AKV pattern may inadvertently hurt you with their verbal sarcasm; try not to take it personally.
- People who use the AKV pattern are visually sensitive, so avoid giving them too much visual information such as long emails and reports, visual directions, and a great deal of metaphors.
- Don't draw diagrams when speaking to them, unless you want to challenge them to be very innovative in their thinking.
- Allow them to avoid making eye contact with you.
- If you supervise people who use the AKV pattern, suggest that they get up and move around as they feel inclined, even in meetings; it will enable them to get in touch with what really matters to them and have patience with those who speak more slowly.

AVK

- People who use this pattern may overwhelm you with their verbal stamina.
- Remind these talkers, perhaps by a prearranged hand gesture, to leave space so that you can speak; it will not hurt their feelings.

- Encourage them to communicate as much as possible with you via email, or email them and allow them to answer via voice mail.
- Be sensitive to how difficult it is for people who use the AVK pattern to do any physical task; it is as hard as you getting up in front of five hundred people and speaking spontaneously.

VAK

- People who use this pattern match you naturally in the visual world—sharing images, conversations about movies and books, brainstorming any visual product.
- You both communicate best via the written word and through pictures.
- Be aware that people who use the VAK pattern cannot usually do work that is as visually detailed as you do and can't estimate well how long a task will take. If you take on those aspects of a project, you both will be happier.

KAV PATTERN

Kinesthetic, Auditory, and Visual KAV PATTERN			
K1		**FOCUSED THINKING**	To Trigger Concentration: KINESTHETIC
A2		**SORTING THINKING**	To Trigger Sorting: AUDITORY
V3	👁	**OPEN THINKING**	To Trigger Imagination: VISUAL

Best Ways to Focus Your Attention

- You are the most organized when you are engaged in activities that include your body.
- You like to make piles of things to get organized.

Best Ways to Explore Options and Think Through Confusion

- You need to sort things out by handling objects and talking out loud. You may begin by speaking with someone about the different choices you have, and by the end of your conversation you will most likely know which option will work best as a result of having talked it through.

Best Ways to Innovate or Create

- You come up with new ideas most effectively when you are allowed to go at your own pace without anyone else around. It may help you to observe nature, doodle and draw, write creatively or journal, create big-picture diagrams, or stare out the window at moving scenery. Listening to or playing music is also very helpful.

Your Most Effective Decision-Making Strategies

- The best way to make a decision is to try out different options and notice how each one feels, and then talk the effects over with someone you trust, who will ask open questions.
- You also can weigh each option by taking note of how it feels in your body.

Your Best Working Environment

- You work best when you feel physically comfortable in your environment. You may go to great lengths to find the office equipment that feels just right.
- You need to do things at your own rhythm.
- You need both contact with others and a lot of personal space.

- You may find it challenging to sit at a desk for long periods of time. A good job for you is one that allows a lot of physical movement.
- Silence may help you do a visual task.
- You organize best by placing things in piles.
- In a meeting room, find or create space to walk around and stretch to help you keep focused.

Your Best Learning Process

- Doing something hands-on.
- You may also learn well through discussion in which you get to express your ideas, experiences, and feelings and hear those of others.
- If you need instruction of some kind, it should allow you to experiment in the moment and then provide someone to talk you through while you perform the new task.

Communicating with Others

- You are generally good at immediately knowing what you are feeling and what is comfortable/uncomfortable for you. And you are at ease communicating this to others.
- You need to realize not everyone is as aware of what is going on for them as you are and that it may be difficult for others to communicate their feelings verbally. Ask those who prefer writing to email you. Read their email while standing or moving, and then respond via phone or in person.
- You may have a tendency to act first and speak later. If others seem frightened by your abrupt movements or actions, or if you tend to express yourself physically instead of speaking about it, for example, ask people to walk with you or do something physical—hitting golf balls, throwing rocks in a river—and then wait and listen for the words that will come.

Receiving Feedback

- Since you are visually sensitive, written feedback can leave a lasting impression. In general, it's best to receive negative feedback auditorily, preferably while in motion.
- The person giving the feedback should be sensitive to the looks he or she gives while delivering the message.
- Positive feedback for you may include a pat on the back, a neck massage, a look of gratitude, a smile, or short written notes or cards.

Dealing with Conflict

- In general, you are very moved by your own feelings, and when you are upset about something, it's usually easy for others to tell.
- You typically don't sit on your feelings for long periods but tend to want to clear the air. You do it best verbally while in motion—taking a walk, going on a run.
- When dealing with people of other patterns around a highly charged issue, you should remember that writing is a more comfortable mode for some people, particularly when there is conflict. Read their messages to you while moving.

Receiving Support or Guidance

- You may feel supported when people do activities with you.
- Those who are giving support or guidance should not insist that you sit still, but rather should keep in mind that moving and fidgeting help you to stay alert.
- Suggest that you talk while doing something: for example, walking, fixing the Xerox machine, working out in a gym.
- Having something to hold and play with in your hands may also help you pay attention, as will physical proximity and standing or sitting side by side instead of face-to-face.
- If you need guidance, ask your helper to speak to you in action or feeling words; explain things in terms of how to do something, how it works, or how it might feel.

The Most Effective Way to Relax

- You generally relax by doing something intensely physical, then sitting still or rocking and listening to music.
- If you really want to relax, watching the right TV show or movie can be good, although it must be exactly right, because you are very sensitive to what you see.

To Enhance Your Physical Well-Being

- You are naturally in touch with your physical well-being and love to do sports of all kinds.
- However, you can, if you get injured or as you age, have difficulty knowing how to be less active and may sink into inertia or even depression. You should be encouraged to cultivate receptive kinesthetic forms, such as yoga, receiving a massage, free dancing, and you should find other ways to be in your body besides as Mr. or Ms. Macho.

Famous People Who Use the KAV Pattern

Michael Jordan: He is very steady and assertive with his physical energy and gestures. He is obviously very competitive physically. His facial expression is usually fairly flat, and he rarely makes steady eye contact.

Mother Teresa: She was constantly "doing"—helping people, hands-on. Her eyes were often downcast while she spoke. She was very energetic physically. The phrase "Do small things with great love" was often attributed to her.

Working and Communicating with Other Patterns

KVA

- People whose minds use this pattern are great partners in activity with you. You can work well together on concrete projects of all sorts.
- Because people who use the KVA pattern have such sensitive ears, communicate visually as much as possible or while walking in nature. Do not expect them to be able to tell you what is going on for them.
- If you supervise a KVA, suggest he or she take notes or construct a model while listening in order to pay more focused attention.

AKV

- People who use this pattern may have trouble doing concrete things in the same systematic way that you do and they may have trouble estimating how much time something will take.
- Since you are both visually sensitive, you meet most comfortably in the auditory and kinesthetic worlds.
- Shared activity with conversation can work very well between you.

AVK

- People who use this pattern can have difficulty doing anything physical, while you love the concrete world of action.
- You can become an ally of those who use the AVK pattern by helping them move their ideas into specific action, particularly if you are sensitive to their kinesthetic awkwardness.

VAK

- People whose minds use this pattern are natural partners for you, particularly in metaphoric thinking.
- They are good at creating a picture that you can then activate or manifest.
- The best way for you to communicate is verbally, so you don't overwhelm them with touch or action and they don't overload you with visual detail.

VKA

- People who use the VKA pattern can be stimulating partners for you because their strength is in visual detail, while yours is in kinesthetic detail.
- Be aware that VKAs have sensitive ears, however, and communicate visually, particularly for important information, or while walking, whenever possible.

KVA PATTERN

Kinesthetic, Visual, and Auditory KVA PATTERN			
K1		**FOCUSED THINKING**	To Trigger Concentration: KINESTHETIC
V2		**SORTING THINKING**	To Trigger Sorting: VISUAL
A3		**OPEN THINKING**	To Trigger Imagination: AUDITORY

Best Ways to Focus Your Attention

- You are most logical, detailed, and organized when doing something or in movement. You like doing many tasks at once.

Best Ways to Explore Options and Think Through Confusion

- Writing helps you to assess what is most important to you and what you really want to do.
- If you find yourself vacillating in an "either/or" situation, try dividing the issue between two columns and writing out the options. Then get up and move around and notice how each option feels in your body.

Best Ways to Innovate or Create

- Listening to evocative music or being in silence helps you think creatively, as does walking in nature.
- It can be very helpful to speak to a trusted friend who will let you "swirl" without trying to impose meaning or order on your words and then write them down for you.

Your Most Effective Decision-Making Strategies

- You make your best decisions when you are allowed to physically experiment with the various options, noticing how each makes you feel in your body rather than thinking of them abstractly. Once informed by your physical response, journal about the decision. If you have less time and need to make a snap decision, look away, or close your eyes while pondering the issue and wait to see what image emerges.

Your Best Working Environment

- You generally work best alone or with a small group of people you know well, with little supervision from or interaction with others.
- When your team does come together, having hands-on models to work with or something in your hands to play with (a rubber band, etc.) while talking helps you engage fully.
- Your physical comfort is quite important and so you may go to great lengths to find the right chair or the right position to sit in.
- It is also important that you be surrounded by silence or by music of your choice when you need to concentrate. Loud noises of any sort—even happy cheers—can be very challenging. If it is impossible to have an office by yourself with a door that closes, it may be effective to wear earphones so that you can choose what you listen to.
- Headset phones are great tools for you because they allow you to walk around while on long calls. This also frees up your hands to write on a tablet or whiteboard while you're on the phone, which helps you listen more effectively.
- In meetings, if possible, take notes on a flip chart or mind map, move around, or play with something in your hands.

Your Best Learning Process

- You learn most easily by doing and watching, while only occasionally asking questions. What this usually means is that it's best for you to be left alone to experiment with something until you figure it out.

- If you can't figure it out on your own, read just enough or look at a diagram or watch another person doing it in order to get what you need to move forward. Listening to lectures or long verbal instructions can be very difficult for you.

Communicating with Others

- You need to feel safe and listened to in order to enter into meaningful conversation.
- Ask others, in writing, to give you as much room to speak as possible.
- Be aware that other people aren't as verbally sensitive as you are and try not to take their tones of voice or phrasing personally.
- Whenever possible, communicate with others in writing—email, notes, and memos—especially if you want to express your feelings.
- Suggest that in meetings with a lot of verbal dialogue, there is a time for silence to write things down.

Receiving Feedback

- You are naturally affected deeply by tone of voice. Harsh or critical phrases can echo in your mind for years. Therefore, whenever possible, feedback (particularly negative feedback) should be written rather than spoken, and you should be allowed to respond in writing as well.

Dealing with Conflict

- If someone comes at you with a problem or conflict, suggest that he or she write to you; add that you will respond in writing by a certain predetermined date.
- If you find yourself stewing internally over an issue with someone, send an email or write a note that goes something like this: "I am imagining 'X.' Is that true?"

Receiving Support or Guidance

- You need to be joined in activity and adventure and feel appreciated for what you know how to do. Let people know that the most effective support for you begins with doing something together, out in nature if possible. This is where your natural leadership style emerges.
- Let others know you need some space when you withdraw and that they shouldn't prod verbally. Suggest they try a silent pat on the back, a hand on the shoulder, or a note in your pocket.
- When giving you guidance, a mentor needs to ask you about past experiences that may bear on the issue at hand.
- Remind others that when they ask you a question, you need silent time to think and respond.
- Other people should be reminded to listen to your explanation all the way through, even if they think they know what you are going to say.
- You tend to navigate through life by asking endless questions, looking for possibilities, and living out the answers. No matter how much people offering help are tempted, they should not attempt to answer your questions. Rather, they should just be silently supportive or answer with an honest "I don't know."

The Most Effective Way to Relax

- You generally relax by taking long, slow walks alone; wondering; listening to mellow music; and staring out the window; or having a massage with background music.

To Enhance Your Physical Well-Being

- You may have a tendency to overdo active physical exercise. Try to balance it with more receptive physical activity (like yoga, stretching, and massage).
- Most likely you know how you feel in your body and just

need to find ways to alleviate tension and be aware of the areas you are overstressing.

Famous People Who Use the KVA Pattern

Mia Hamm: On the soccer field, she led by example rather than verbally. Her physical presence is solid and steady. In interviews, she ponders the questions before answering; her replies are usually slow, thoughtful, and very deep and sincere.

Tiger Woods: He has been known throughout his career for practicing and working out longer and harder than most other golfers on tour, with a very regimented schedule. His game is all about feel and mechanics. In interviews he looks aside to ponder questions then looks back directly to answer. He prefers to work and play in silence.

Working and Communicating with Other Patterns

KAV

- People who use the KAV pattern are great partners in activities. You work well together on concrete projects of all sorts.
- Because KAVs are visually sensitive, try to communicate with them verbally as much as possible.
- If you supervise those who use this pattern, allow them to move around in meetings; they will be able to pay attention better and contribute more.

AKV

- With their quick-tongued sarcasm, people who use the AKV pattern can unintentionally be hurtful to you, but their verbal mastery can also be compelling and mesmerizing.
- People who use this pattern are visually sensitive, so communicate verbally as much as possible—by phone or face-to-face.
- Stand or sit next to (rather than in front of) them, so they can move their eyes where they want to.
- If you supervise those who use this pattern, suggest that they get up and move around as they feel inclined, even in meetings; it will enable them to know what really matters to them and have patience with those who speak more slowly.

AVK

- People who use the AVK pattern can be verbally intense for you. Ask them to communicate with you in writing, or send them emails and allow them to answer via voice mail.
- Remind them to give you space to speak (perhaps by a prearranged signal, such as a raised hand).
- If a person with the AVK pattern gives you the space and feeling of safety to speak, the two of you can be a dynamic work duo, with you taking action and he or she articulating to others what is being done.

VAK

- People who use the VAK pattern can be challenging to you if you see these natural storytellers and salespeople as exaggerating or fabricating the truth.
- Remember that people who use this pattern can be inspiring, which is as vital to any team as your ability to make something happen.
- Ask them to communicate visually with you as much as possible to respect your sensitive ears.

VKA

- People who use the VKA pattern are natural collaborators who make very good partners for you.
- Because you are both auditorily sensitive, you tend not to offend or upset each other with your words, and you both are comfortable communicating in writing as well as through speaking.
- You do well creating things with people who use this pattern, helping one another to concretely visualize your ideas.

AVK PATTERN

Auditory, Visual, and Kinesthetic AVK PATTERN			
A1		**FOCUSED** **THINKING**	To Trigger Concentration: AUDITORY
V2		**SORTING** **THINKING**	To Trigger Sorting: VISUAL
K3		**OPEN** **THINKING**	To Trigger Imagination: KINESTHETIC

Best Ways to Focus Your Attention

- You are most alert and detailed in your thinking when you are talking. Therefore, when you wish to be sequential and logical, talk through your line of thinking, even if it is to yourself.

Best Ways to Explore Options and Think Through Confusion

- Reading, writing, and drawing are your best methods for weighing different options. Since writing is very useful to you in making decisions, if you find that your thinking is stuck, write out both sides of an argument on two separate pages to help you sort out where you stand.

Best Ways to Innovate or Create

- Get moving. Get up from the desk, walk around, or go for a drive. Take time to do yoga or go for a swim to open your mind and stop yourself from thinking about any one thing in particular. That kind of thinking can block creativity.

Your Most Effective Decision-Making Strategies
- Talk about a decision with others first, gathering as much information as possible. Then read about the issue and, finally, write out all the pros and cons.
- It's also often effective to think metaphorically about the problem at hand. For example: Is it like a boulder that won't budge? Often, the answer will come out of nowhere when you are doing something physical—taking a shower, for instance, or driving the car.
- If you must make a snap decision, try this: Get completely quiet, look into the distance or close your eyes, and wait to see what pops into your mind.

Your Best Working Environment
- You tend not to be particularly sensitive to your physical work environment, although you may want to join in others' conversations if you can hear them.
- You may like to do work over the phone and can sit still for long periods of time. You can work alone but like to have the chance for verbal interactions throughout the day. If you spend too much time reading or at the computer, you may become verbally "pent up."

Your Best Learning Process
- You learn best through talking, then reading, then doing or experiencing. When stuck, you do best to get someone to explain verbally and, particularly if it's a technical or physical skill, to show you how to do it while explaining simultaneously as you take notes. Then try it out immediately.

Communicating with Others
- Recognize that others are not as facile with language as you are. Refrain from finishing people's sentences. Allow for silent pauses as often as possible so that others feel they have a chance to talk.

- To receive what others have to say, ask a question that will lead to a kind of topic headline, such as, "Are you saying you need the deadline for this project?"
- To express your feelings, consider doing it in writing, which may be easier for you than talking.

Receiving Feedback

- Verbal communication—whether face-to-face or on the phone—is the most effective way for you to receive any kind of negative feedback.
- Most likely you prefer "direct" communication—you don't like to feel that the other person is holding back criticism. If the feedback is negative, it is best that it be verbal and very straightforward.
- If the feedback is positive, it tends to be more effective for you to receive it in writing, since written communication is felt more deeply than verbal for you.

Dealing with Conflict

- While you are more comfortable with verbal conflict than most others, remember that people of other patterns may have difficulty expressing themselves verbally in highly charged situations. Suggest that people of other patterns email or write their thoughts to you, and then ask them how they would like to proceed after you've read their communication.

Receiving Support or Guidance

- Doing something physical, even something as seemingly simple as changing the paper in the copy machine, can be challenging for you, and you may need to be shown how to do the same physical action several times.
- You may not do well with others watching while you learn to do something. Let others know that you need privacy and to move at your own pace, which may be slow when learning something that's hands-on.

- Explain that you learn best if they demonstrate while talking, then leave you alone to try it for yourself and be on call to help if necessary.
- Ask others to remind you to take care of yourself physically.

The Most Effective Way to Relax
- Typically you unwind by reading, listening to music or lectures, or watching movies or TV.

To Enhance Your Physical Well-Being
- You may have a difficult time with a regular exercise regimen. If so, try a physical activity that is not too repetitious or competitive and can be done at your own rhythm—walking, swimming, yoga, biking. One way to encourage movement is to find a partner whom you can talk to during such activities, as long as he or she will not try to push you too fast or too far.

Famous People Who Use the AVK Pattern

Bill Clinton: He is very pointed and direct in his speech, almost asking questions as statements. His language is very precise and ornate. He is relatively still in his body and looks somewhat awkward when he moves.

Barbra Streisand: Her voice carries a certain surety and power; she speaks very directly and doesn't mince words. She stays very still as she speaks. She tends to glance away whenever she needs to think something over, then looks directly back when speaking.

Working and Communicating with Other Patterns

KVA

- People who use the KVA pattern tend to be very independent workers who can grasp physical and technical tasks quickly.
- Refrain from telling them what to do; they generally prefer to figure things out on their own.
- Allow for a great deal of silence when working with those who use the KVA pattern, and try to not answer their questions but encourage them to answer for themselves.
- Avoid the temptation to finish their sentences. Be aware that they are very sensitive to tone of voice and the words you choose and can be easily hurt by something you say.
- Use email rather than verbal communication as much as possible.
- If you are their supervisor, give them as much independence as you can and communicate as much as possible in writing, particularly if it is something important.

KAV

- People whose minds use this pattern may be challenging for you because they like to do and to discuss their feelings about what they are doing, while you tend to live in the world of abstract ideas.
- Communicate as much as possible verbally, although if you want to praise them, a short email will have a huge impact.

- Sit next to (not across from) them, so their eyes can move where they want to.
- If you find yourself in conflict with a person who uses the KAV pattern, suggest that you go for a walk to talk it out, and allow him or her to speak without looking at you.
- If you supervise those who use the KAV pattern, allow them to move around in meetings; they will be able to pay attention better and contribute more.

AKV

- People who use the AKV pattern are visually sensitive, so communicate verbally as much as possible—by phone or face-to-face.
- Stand or sit next to (rather than in front of) them, so they can move their eyes where they want to.
- If you supervise those who use the AKV pattern, suggest that they get up and move around as they feel inclined, even in meetings; it will enable them to know what really matters to them and to have patience with those who speak more slowly.

VAK

- Usually, people who use the VAK pattern are comfortable work partners for you, particularly in a brainstorming situation when ideas are flying. If there are no other patterns on the team, however, there may be slowness in moving into action or a struggle to discover what, concretely, to do.

- The two of you meet naturally in verbal repartee, but be aware that when you get going, you could take up all the air in a meeting.

VKA

- People who use the VKA pattern are natural collaborators who make very good team players. They can be challenging for you because they speak in loops and circles rather than in a straight line.
- Don't finish their sentences for them!
- If you find yourself becoming impatient, take a deep breath and ask them to draw you a picture of what they mean.
- Communicate as much as possible in writing—email, written memos, and letters.
- If you supervise those who use the VKA pattern, be aware that they are very auditorily sensitive, so choose your words carefully.

AKV PATTERN

Auditory, Kinesthetic, and Visual AKV PATTERN		
A1	FOCUSED THINKING	To Trigger Concentration: AUDITORY
K2	SORTING THINKING	To Trigger Sorting: KINESTHETIC
V3	OPEN THINKING	To Trigger Imagination: VISUAL

Best Ways to Focus Your Attention

- You are most alert and detailed in your thinking when you are talking. Therefore, when you wish to be sequential and logical, talk things out, even if it is to yourself.

Best Ways to Explore Options and Think Through Confusion

- Movement is the best way for you to explore and sort through options. Get up and pace around the room, while taking stock of your physical response to each option.

Best Ways to Innovate or Create

- You can stimulate new thinking by doodling, sketching, or staring out a window at moving scenery.
- Try putting a pen or pencil in your hand and allowing yourself the freedom to draw or write without worrying about details.
- To generate new ideas, it may also help to use the images of your daydreams as starting points.

Your Most Effective Decision-Making Strategies

- You may not know you've made the right decision until you try it in action. Take the first step in a specific direction and notice how it's working and/or how you feel.
- You tend to love pilot programs and aren't afraid to regroup and fine-tune in the middle of a project.
- If you're struggling to take action on a decision, it can help to imagine yourself having made the choice and how you would feel.
- You may also find it helpful to talk with others who have made the choice you are thinking about, to gather information, and try it on for size in your mind.

Your Best Working Environment

- You like to be in charge of what you do and how you do it. You may get uncomfortable quickly if confined to a desk or small space for any length of time, especially if you are asked to deal with a lot of written material. Your best work environment is one that allows for a great deal of freedom of motion and a varied schedule.

Your Best Learning Process

- You learn easily through discussion and lectures or by talking about what to do.

Communicating with Others

- You need to recognize that other people may not be as facile at speaking as you are. Even if you feel impatient when other people speak more slowly or are less to the point than you want them to be, resist the urge to finish their sentences.
- Try to allow for silence so that others feel they too have an opportunity to talk.
- To listen more comfortably, consider getting up and moving around or going for a walk with the other person.
- Be aware that people of other thinking patterns who may take you literally can misunderstand sarcasm.
- Be aware that others may be frightened or alienated by the energy with which you speak.

Receiving Feedback

- You prefer verbal, direct, to-the-point feedback.
- You may appreciate feedback that is as humorous as possible.
- When receiving feedback on something you've written, you may prefer to have the other person's comments written on a separate page.

Dealing with Conflict

- It's important to remember that people of other patterns may have difficulty expressing themselves verbally in highly charged situations.

- Suggest that you do something kinesthetic together while talking, such as walking. Walk side by side, so you can look wherever you are comfortable.
- Request that others email or write up their thoughts in a clear and simple way and then allow you to respond verbally.

Receiving Support or Guidance

- You are a natural coach and prefer to offer guidance and support to others. When you need support, ask for explicit verbal advice and examples of experiences others have had. In a team situation, most likely you want to be met by peers who share your intensity of commitment and energy.

The Most Effective Way to Relax

- You may like to listen to music or go to concerts when you have leisure time.
- You may enjoy exploring on the Internet or playing computer/video games where you can get lost in the speed and number of visual choices.
- Although you're particular about what you watch, you can be captured by a good TV program, movie, or book and use this as a way to wind down.
- Travel of any kind, even day trips, can be very relaxing.

To Enhance Your Physical Well-Being

- You may intuitively know that you need daily exercise to manage stress.
- Individual sports, such as swimming, biking, Rollerblading, weight-training, jogging, long-distance running, or one-on-one sports, like racquetball or tennis, may be particularly enjoyable.

Famous People Who Use the AKV Pattern

> Robin Williams: He was very energetic, first with his words, then with his body language. He could speak to an audience for hours without visual cues (just watch his stand-up routines) but never stayed still for one minute. He seemed to dress for comfort rather than appearance. He seldom made eye contact, either in interviews or in the roles he played.
> Madonna: She speaks and sings with a great deal of energy. Her concerts are fraught with action and frenzied energy and dancing. She always makes a splash when she talks and is often sarcastic. She seems to look through or over people when talking to them and doesn't hold eye contact for long.

Working and Communicating with Other Patterns

KVA

- People who use the KVA pattern tend to be very independent workers, who can grasp physical and technical tasks quickly.
- Refrain from telling them what to do; they generally prefer to figure things out on their own.
- Allow for a great deal of silence, and try not to answer their questions but encourage them to answer for themselves.
- Avoid the temptation to finish their sentences.
- Be aware that they are very sensitive to tone of voice and can be easily hurt by something you say.
- Whenever possible, walk together when you have something important or sensitive to say.

- If you are their supervisor, give them as much independence as you can and communicate as much as possible in writing, particularly if it is something important.

KAV

- KAVs are your natural collaborators. Talk with them about your joint vision.
- Get specific to avoid frustration. You both tend to have images of the way things are supposed to look when complete. Make sure you are envisioning the same thing.
- If you agree to move ahead on a task, give KAVs time to do things their own way first and then respond to questions and offer feedback. Allow them the opportunity to explore different options out loud before drawing conclusions.
- If you supervise those who use the KAV pattern, allow them to move around in meetings; they will be able to pay attention better and contribute more.

AVK

- You meet naturally in verbal repartee, but be aware that when the two of you get going, you could take up all the air in a meeting.
- People who use the AVK pattern are kinesthetically sensitive, so avoid casual contact—punches on the arm, pats on the shoulder, etc.—and be aware that doing anything physical can be extremely challenging for them.

VAK

- The two of you share the ability and desire to speak passion-ately about what matters to you.
- Join forces with a person who uses the VAK pattern and you may have an ally who can communicate succinctly and spe-cifically in writing in ways that could be difficult for you.
- People who use the VAK pattern find taking notes and mak-ing lists the easiest way to keep track of what is said in meet-ings and what needs to be done for follow-up.
- They may need written instructions or time to talk through a task to make sure expectations are clear before beginning it.

VKA

- People who use the VKA pattern are natural collaborators who make very good team players.
- They may talk in circles and ask a great deal of questions that you should refrain from answering. Rather, respond with something like, "What a good question; what do you think?"
- Try not to interrupt or finish their sentences for them.
- When an issue is really important, communicate as much as possible in writing—email, written memos, and letters.
- If you supervise people who use the VKA pattern, be aware that they are very auditorily sensitive, so choose your words and tone of voice carefully.

UTILIZING THINKING TALENTS IN WORK SITUATIONS

COLLECTING

ANALYTIC THINKING

Activating Your Own Talent
- Volunteer when there are re-search opportunities.
- Offer to be in charge of collect-ing data, facts, information . . . whatever needs to be collected.
- Get help in organizing what you've collected.

THINKING TALENTS

Collecting

"What am I interested in here?"

Collects information, things, quota-tions, artifacts, or facts, anything that is deemed interesting. The world is exciting because of its variety; acquiring, compiling, and filing stuff away keeps things fresh.

Developing Your Resources
- Partner with people with strong
  Focusing or Precision talents. They can help you stay on track when you want to follow bunny trails that are interest-ing but not relevant.

Activating This Talent in Others

- Call on people with this talent when research is required.
- Ask them to provide information during meetings.
- Recognize that they love to receive information from you.

FIXING IT

ANALYTIC THINKING

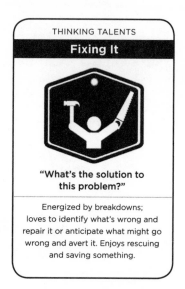

THINKING TALENTS

Fixing It

"What's the solution to this problem?"

Energized by breakdowns; loves to identify what's wrong and repair it or anticipate what might go wrong and avert it. Enjoys rescuing and saving something.

Activating Your Own Talent

- Let people know that you love it when someone comes to you and says, "I have a problem." That's not true for everyone.
- You may come across as negative when pointing out what could go wrong. Learn to communicate your insights in a positive way.
- It can be frustrating to end up in situations where you can see what's wrong but can't fix it. Focus instead on circumstances where you can help.

Developing Your Resources

- Learn to balance your desire to fix with others' needs to learn. Be patient, especially if you're a manager, coach, or teacher; allow other people to solve their own problems.

Activating This Talent in Others

- Turn to them for help with a current problem or for advice on what might go wrong with an idea or a plan. They love to be asked.
- They may come across as negative when pointing out what could go wrong. Help them learn to communicate their insights in a positive way.

- They may struggle when a problem goes unfixed for too long, as they might take it personally. Celebrate when the problem is solved.
- They can become impatient with others' "learning curves." Help them to teach and not "do for" others.

MAKING ORDER

ANALYTIC THINKING

Activating Your Own Talent

THINKING TALENTS

Making Order

"How can I align all these different variables?"

Enjoys managing and aligning many variables into the best configuration. Jumps into confusion and devises new options; organizes what's messy.

- Volunteer to jump into messy situations and put things in order.
- You thrive in situations where many things are going on at the same time and there is a need to create a logical sequence.
- When you're stuck, ask yourself: "What's the best order for this? How else could this be arranged?"

Developing Your Resources

- Learn to document the systems you come up with as you make order of processes; this can leave a legacy of your talent for others.

Activating This Talent in Others

- People with this talent love the chance to jump into messy situations and put things in order.
- They thrive in situations where they have many things going on at the same time and there is a need to create a logical sequence.
- When they're stuck, ask: "What's the best order for this? How else could this be arranged?"

SEEKING EXCELLENCE

ANALYTIC THINKING

Activating Your Own Talent

- You dislike inefficient designs and processes. Place yourself in situations where you can make a process or product more efficient.
- Recognize that you may come across as a perfectionist. Strive for excellence, not perfection.
- At the outset of a project where you are working with others, show them a sample of something you consider excellent as a benchmark. Otherwise, you may be frustrated by the results you get and others may not be able to meet your unarticulated standards.

Developing Your Resources

- Study success. Be inspired by others' stories and experiences of being successful and seeking excellence.
- Don't avoid tasks or situations where you feel unsure (which might be your tendency); instead, find allies and mentors to assist you in defining what excellence and success would be like in these areas.

Activating This Talent in Others

- People with this talent are naturally focused on creating excellence. Activate their talent by asking them how they can personally strive for excellence or how to create an excellent process or product.
- Discuss how they know when they've done an excellent job.
- These people dislike inefficient designs and processes. Ask

them for advice on how to make a process or product more efficient.

- They may come across as perfectionists. Help them understand that success comes from a drive for excellence, not perfection.
- They may be reluctant to do something where the "excellent outcome" is not clear.
- Ask them for a sample of something excellent at the outset of a project, as a benchmark. Otherwise, a person with this talent may frustrate others with unarticulated standards.

THINKING LOGICALLY

ANALYTIC THINKING

Activating Your Own Talent

THINKING TALENTS

Thinking Logically

"Why is this true?"
"Prove it to me."

Dispassionate;
theories must be sound,
logical, based on solid data.
Exposes clumsy thinking;
sees patterns in data.

- For you, getting a task done correctly may be more important than meeting a deadline. This may be frustrating to others.
- Explain that you need logic and facts when being communicated to.
- Volunteer to be the one to gather and present the facts in a situation.
- You tend to recognize patterns in data. Find opportunities to share these patterns with others, but understand that not everyone can naturally recognize these patterns without help.

Developing Your Resources

- Partner with someone who is strong in Get to Action. He or she can push you a bit more quickly through the analytical phase to the action phase.
- Draw on the resources of people with Strategy, Believing, or

Feeling-for-Others talents. Their read on people or situations—sometimes intuitive and intangible, but often accurate—can help you anticipate in advance and understand people's potential reactions to your analysis.

Activating This Talent in Others

- They tend to explain things in a logical, factual way when communicating. Be sure to accurately present data and supporting facts to them.
- When a decision that affects them is being made, take time to present the logic behind it.
- They can see patterns in data and may have trouble understanding that others don't. Put them in situations where they can help by presenting and explaining the patterns to others.

INNOVATIVE

ADAPTING

INNOVATIVE THINKING

Activating Your Own Talent

- Look for short-term assignments that require flexibility.
- Volunteer to help when balls are dropped or plans go awry.
- You may need help when it comes to long-term planning.
- Use your other talents to know where you stand before consulting this one. Otherwise you may end up agreeing to things you regret later.

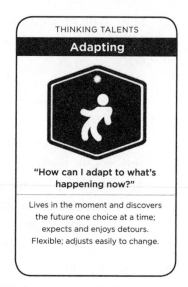

THINKING TALENTS

Adapting

"How can I adapt to what's happening now?"

Lives in the moment and discovers the future one choice at a time; expects and enjoys detours. Flexible; adjusts easily to change.

Developing Your Resources

- Partner with people who are strong in Focusing and/or Strategy; they can help you with keeping sight of the big picture while you innovate and adapt.

Activating This Talent in Others

- Individuals with this talent will likely do well on short projects that require flexibility; structures/processes that seem binding or rigid may be frustrating.
- They are energized by newness and the need for spontaneity. When plans must change, invite them to make suggestions about how to cope.
- They may need help when it comes to long-term planning or sticking to routine.

INNOVATION

INNOVATIVE THINKING

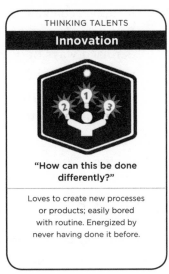

THINKING TALENTS

Innovation

"How can this be done differently?"

Loves to create new processes or products; easily bored with routine. Energized by never having done it before.

Activating Your Own Talent

- You tend to be very forward-thinking. When you want to do your best thinking, ask yourself: "Imagine it is a year from now and we've gotten exactly what we wanted. What will have happened? How will we have gotten from A to B?"
- When you're stuck, ask yourself: "What are all the possible ways I could make this work?"
- It may be challenging to follow standardized ways of doing things, because you tend to quickly lose interest if something's not new. Try to partner with others who take on the procedural aspects of a project.

- Challenge yourself to continue to find new ways of doing things to keep things interesting.

Developing Your Resources

- Partner with someone with a strong Get-to-Action talent; he or she can help you take action today to create the future you envision.

Activating This Talent in Others

- People with this talent tend not to look back. When you want their best thinking, ask them: "Imagine it is a year from now and we've gotten exactly what we wanted. What will have happened? How will we have gotten from A to B?"
- When they are stuck, ask: "What are all the ways you can imagine achieving this?"
- Be aware that it may be challenging for them to follow standardized ways of doing things, because they quickly lose interest if it's not new. Challenge them to continue to find ways to keep things interesting.
- Use their vision to create motivation in a team.

LOVE OF LEARNING

INNOVATIVE THINKING

Activating Your Own Talent

- Explore new things. The process of continual learning energizes you.
- Share what you've been learning with others. Volunteer to lead discussion groups or presentations.
- Focus on the task at hand when

THINKING TALENTS

Love of Learning

"What can I learn next?"

Drawn always to the process more than the content of learning; energized by the journey from ignorance to competence. The outcome is less important than what is learned.

learning. Otherwise, you may find yourself leapfrogging from one thing to the next.

Developing Your Resources

- You may have a nagging feeling that however much you know, it's still "not enough," so find ways to benchmark your learning.
- If there are levels of mastery within the discipline or skill you want to achieve, take time to recognize and acknowledge your success at each stage. If there aren't external markers, create them for yourself.

Activating This Talent in Others

- People with this talent must be constantly learning or they will seek opportunities elsewhere. Help them find new things to keep learning in order to remain motivated.
- Ask them: "What have you been learning about X?"
- Invite them to lead discussion groups or presentations or to become the expert in some aspect of the work you are doing.
- Help them stay focused on the task at hand when learning.

LOVING IDEAS

INNOVATIVE THINKING

Activating Your Own Talent

- You have lots of ideas. Look for situations where you can contribute them.
- Find ways to be present at the start of something. Otherwise, your new ideas may come too late in the process.
- When decisions are being made,

THINKING TALENTS

Loving Ideas

"What's a thrilling idea or theory to explain this?"

Searches for concepts to explain things; loves theories; derives jolt of energy from a new idea.

ask for help in understanding how each one is rooted in a particular theory or concept.

Developing Your Resources

- Partner with someone with a strong Get-to-Action talent; he or she can help you move from idea to reality.

Activating This Talent in Others

- Those with this talent have lots of ideas and need an outlet for them.
- They are great at the outset of a project, when you're considering possibilities.
- They like to understand how ideas come together. When decisions are made, take time to show them how a decision relates to broader big-picture thinking. If it doesn't, let them know it's an exception.

STANDING OUT

INNOVATIVE THINKING

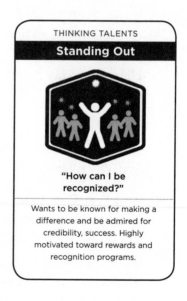

THINKING TALENTS

Standing Out

"How can I be recognized?"

Wants to be known for making a difference and be admired for credibility, success. Highly motivated toward rewards and recognition programs.

Activating Your Own Talent

- You thrive on meaningful recognition for your contributions. Be sure to let others know this. Not everyone is like you.
- Look for occasions to stand out.
- Try not to let your self-worth suffer when others do not give you the recognition you deserve. Ask people to inform you about your performance.
- Behind the desire to stand out is the wish to make a difference in the world. Look for ways to make concrete contributions to your organization.

Developing Your Resources

- Understand that your truest recognition must come from within. If you expect recognition only from external sources, you may grow resentful. Find ways to acknowledge yourself for your contributions, your effort, and your energy.

Activating This Talent in Others

- People with this talent love being the center of attention.
- They need public recognition for their contributions and they love awards, honors, ribbons—as long as they are meaningful rather than rote.
- Their self-confidence and self-worth can suffer and they may become de-motivated when recognition is not forthcoming. Find ways to praise them publicly.
- Behind the desire to stand out is the wish to make a difference in the world. Help them find ways to make a concrete contribution to the organization. Then be sure to recognize them for it.

STRATEGY

INNOVATIVE THINKING

Activating Your Own Talent

- You have the ability to antici-pate problems and their solu-tions in a way that may not be "logical."
- You understand the difference between strategy and planning. Others do not. Help them rec-ognize the difference.
- Find ways to be at the headwa-ters of ideas and projects where this talent can add the most value.

THINKING TALENTS

Strategy

"What are alternative scenarios, and what is the best route?"

Sorts through clutter; recognizes all the possible options; engages in "if this, then that" thinking.

Developing Your Resources

- Partner with someone with a strong Get-to-Action talent; he or she can help you take action today to implement the strategy you envision.
- After your strategy has been implemented and the results are known, partner with people who can help you honestly evaluate your strategy's success, so that your next round of thinking will be even better.

Activating This Talent in Others

- Those with this talent have the ability to anticipate problems and their solutions. Place them in meetings about plans for the future.
- They're great at sorting through all the possibilities and finding the best way forward.
- Offer them even more training in strategic thinking.

THINKING AHEAD

INNOVATIVE THINKING

Activating Your Own Talent

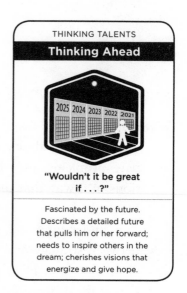

THINKING TALENTS

Thinking Ahead

2025 2024 2023 2022 2021

"Wouldn't it be great if . . . ?"

Fascinated by the future. Describes a detailed future that pulls him or her forward; needs to inspire others in the dream; cherishes visions that energize and give hope.

- You live for the future and as a result must always have something to look forward to.
- Look for opportunities to use your talent to think into the future. Try to place yourself at the headwaters of projects.
- When a group needs to embrace change, step in. You can help others overcome their fears of the future.

Developing Your Resources

- Partner with someone with a strong Get-to-Action talent; he or she can help you take action today to create the future you envision.
- Use people with the Thinking-Back talent to help provide you with context, so that you don't repeat others' past mistakes and so you know how to address these concerns.

Activating This Talent in Others

- Those with this talent can anticipate the future. Be sure to place them in situations where you can use that ability.
- Offer opportunities where they can share their vision.
- They will be very useful when a group needs to embrace change. They can help others overcome their concerns and learn to become energized by the new.

PROCEDURAL

EQUALIZING

PROCEDURAL THINKING

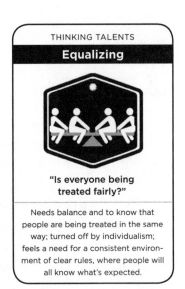

THINKING TALENTS

Equalizing

"Is everyone being treated fairly?"

Needs balance and to know that people are being treated in the same way; turned off by individualism; feels a need for a consistent environment of clear rules, where people will all know what's expected.

Activating Your Own Talent

- At the beginning of a project, ask for clarity about the expectations of group members and the "rules" or processes ahead.
- Help create rules if they haven't been defined and apply rules when needed.
- Be the one who pinpoints each person's contribution at the completion of a project or activity.

- Understand that it's not always possible to be fair and that this can be very challenging for you.

Developing Your Resources

- Partner with people who have strong Seeking-Excellence or Particularizing talents. They can remind you when individual differences can enhance the process or outcome.

Activating This Talent in Others

- Ask people with this talent to recognize each person's contribution at the completion of something.
- They are most comfortable with predictable routines and may have trouble with change. Ask them how they've coped with change in the past.
- These people may be very sensitive to others receiving perceived "special favors" or exemptions. Ask them to help create rules and regulations or to be involved in situations where rules must be applied.

FOCUSING

PROCEDURAL THINKING

Activating Your Own Talent

- Ask others to give you goals with timelines and then let you figure out how to achieve them.
- Explain to others how to check in on your progress—otherwise, you may feel that they don't trust you to get it done on time.
- Help others who are struggling to get something done. You can help focus a whole group.

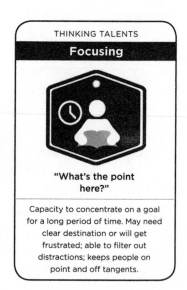

THINKING TALENTS

Focusing

"What's the point here?"

Capacity to concentrate on a goal for a long period of time. May need clear destination or will get frustrated; able to filter out distractions; keeps people on point and off tangents.

- You may have problems if it is not clear what the purpose or goal of a conversation or task is. You'll most likely ask, "What's the point?" Help others to understand that this is a focusing question, not an attack.

Developing Your Resources

- If you tend to get focused to the degree that you lose perspective, take a break with someone with strong Relational or Innovative talents—they can help balance you out with human connection or the big picture.

Activating This Talent in Others

- People with this talent do well with set goals and timelines.
- Assume they will meet your deadline. Ask if and when they want you to check in on their progress—otherwise checking in can be perceived as lack of trust that they'll get the job done.
- Put them with others who are struggling to get something done. They can help focus the whole group.
- They may have problems in a group, in a conversation, or with a task if it is not clear what the purpose or goal is. You might hear: "What is the point of this?" Help them figure out the goal, then step back.

GET TO ACTION

THINKING TALENTS

Get to Action

"What can I do
right now?"

Impatient for action rather
than contemplation. Must make
something happen.

PROCEDURAL THINKING

Activating Your Own Talent

- You always want to do, do, do. Look for where you can appropriately make your own decisions and act upon them.
- New projects, programs, or turnarounds are ideal for you.
- Consider taking a step back from the strategic and analytic aspects of the planning process, or at least understand that it may be difficult for you to sit patiently through these stages.
- If you are feeling antsy, ask others to help you figure out what you can do right away.
- You may need help aiming your action by being aware of strategic priorities.

Developing Your Resources

- Ally with people with strong Strategizing or Thinking-Logically talents. They can provide some ballast, before you blast off into action you may regret.

Activating This Talent in Others

- Those with this talent want to do, do, do. Don't force them into committees or meetings without clear goals or activities.
- They may need assistance with aiming action to align with strategic priorities.
- They're great at spurring others out of talk and into action, but they may come across as impatient or intimidating at meetings. Encourage them to remain aware of this, and to

access their other strengths in situations where Get to Action is not called for.

HAVING CONFIDENCE

PROCEDURAL THINKING

THINKING TALENTS

Having Confidence

"What, me worry?"

Knows he or she is able to deliver. Self-assured; no one can tell this person what to think. Alone has the authority to come to conclusions.

Activating Your Own Talent
- You are most effective when you're in control.
- Explain to bosses that you do best if allowed a lot of leeway in actions and decision-making.
- Understand that you may misjudge your capacities, and ask others to point it out immediately if you do.
- Confidence is contagious, so let it show, but temper any tendency toward arrogance, because not only does it turn people off but you may also be perceived as self-righteous.

Developing Your Resources
- We can't all know everything, so practice saying "I don't know" and asking for help when you need it; this can actually increase people's trust in what you do know.

Activating This Talent in Others
- Those with this talent are at their most effective when they believe they are in control of their world.
- They like to create strong outside boundaries and then have a lot of autonomy within those boundaries when it comes to actions and decision-making.
- These people can calm challenging situations with employees or customers with their sense of assurance.

- Understand that they may have an overinflated sense of their abilities. Be sure to give fact-based feedback.

PRECISION

PROCEDURAL THINKING

Activating Your Own Talent

- Be aware that you tend to ask a lot of questions in order to understand precisely how to do something and that others may find this annoying. Explain to others that questioning things is part of your process in order to do things exactly.
- If an event or organization is chaotic, take the lead in planning and organizing it.
- If forced to be in a situation that requires flexibility, devise a set number of routines that you're comfortable with, each appropriate for a certain situation.

> THINKING TALENTS
> ## Precision
>
> "How can I order this chaos?"
>
> The world needs to be predictable; imposes structure, sets up routines, timelines, and deadlines; needs to feel in control; dislikes surprises; impatient with errors. Control is a way of maintaining progress and productivity.

Developing Your Resources

- Offer to lend your talent to people who have Loving Ideas, Strategizing, or Innovation talents. Rather than seeing these people as dreamers, create success for both of you by using your talent.

Activating This Talent in Others

- People with this talent may ask a lot of questions to understand exactly how to do something.
- If an event or organization is chaotic, ask them to take the lead in planning and organizing it.

- Always give them advance notice of deadlines and try not to surprise them with sudden changes in plans or priorities. Surprises are distressing.
- Don't ask them for gut instincts. These people need to think things through in a rigorous way.
- If they are forced to be in a situation that requires flexibility, encourage them to devise a set number of comfortable routines, each appropriate for a certain situation.

RELIABILITY

PROCEDURAL THINKING

Activating Your Own Talent

- You define yourself by your ability to live up to your commitments. It's intensely frustrating for you to be around people who don't.
- If forced to rush an action or decision, you may be concerned about how the quality of your work will suffer. Ask for more time and, if that's not possible, learn to accept that you cannot always be responsible for everything.
- Be aware that you may be uncomfortable trying something new, because you want to do it right the first time. Identify your concerns and get help working through them.
- Be careful not to take on too much—you are not responsible for the whole world. Let others help you let go when necessary.

> **THINKING TALENTS**
>
> **Reliability**
>
> **"How can I do this right?"**
>
> Excuses and rationalizations are not acceptable; has to take responsibility for anything committed to; reputation for conscientiousness and dependability. Easily frustrated by what is perceived as others' irresponsibility.

Developing Your Resources

- Partner with someone with a strong Precision or Focusing talent; he or she can help you to stay on track one step at a time so you don't get overwhelmed.

Activating This Talent in Others

- Those with this talent pride themselves on the ability to deliver on time every time, and they may have trouble with others who are not equally responsible.
- They want to do everything "right" and will push back if they feel quality is suffering in the attempt to move quickly.
- Be aware that they may be uncomfortable trying something new, because they haven't learned yet how to do it "right." Ask them to identify what the concerns are and help work through them.
- When one project is over, ask them what new responsibility they'd like to take on.
- Help them to not take on too much or feel overly responsible for things that are not within their control.

TAKING CHARGE

PROCEDURAL THINKING

Activating Your Own Talent

- Look for situations where you can be in command.
- You most likely do not want to be supervised too closely. Let your boss know what's most effective in working with you.
- Work on being assertive rather than aggressive or offensive. Ask for feedback on this.

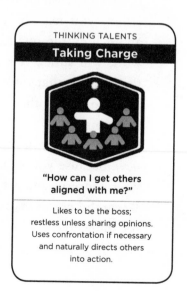

THINKING TALENTS

Taking Charge

"How can I get others aligned with me?"

Likes to be the boss; restless unless sharing opinions. Uses confrontation if necessary and naturally directs others into action.

Developing Your Resources

- Partner with people with strong Feeling-for-Others or Enrolling talents; they can help you get people on board as you initiate action.

Activating This Talent in Others

- Look for situations where those with this talent can be in command. They will naturally take command anyway.
- They will not like to be supervised closely.
- If they start bossing others around inappropriately, meet them head-on. Confront the problem directly and then move forward.
- Avoid power struggles; never threaten them unless you are prepared to take action.
- Their assertiveness is part of what makes them powerful. Help them learn to be assertive rather than aggressive.

THINKING BACK

PROCEDURAL THINKING

Activating Your Own Talent

- Ask others to explain the thinking that led to a particular decision. You need to understand the context in order to move forward.
- Be the one to inform the group about what happened in the past regarding an issue.
- When you're stuck, recall a similar situation from the past. What did you do that could help now?

THINKING TALENTS

Thinking Back

"How is the past a blueprint for the present?"

Looks back to understand the present and future; the present alone is confusing. May have trouble getting oriented to the new, and needs to understand the context of something in order to move forward.

Developing Your Resources
- Partner with those with a strong Thinking-Ahead talent; their focus on future possibilities can keep you from getting stuck in the past.

Activating This Talent in Others
- Those with this talent need to understand the context for any new initiative or action.
- In groups, turn to them to review past actions that could inform the current situation. If you don't ask, they will do it anyway.
- When they're stuck, ask them to recall a similar situation in the past. What did they do that could help now?

RELATIONAL

BELIEVING

RELATIONAL THINKING

Activating Your Own Talent
- Actively clarify what is important to you and seek roles that support these values.
- State your family commitments clearly to teammates, bosses, etc., and ask that they understand, appreciate, and honor these commitments.
- Find ways to serve others in the situation in which you find yourself.
- Help your organization articulate and live out its values.

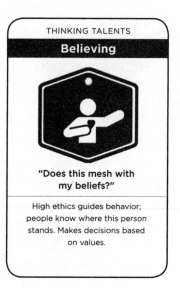

THINKING TALENTS
Believing

"Does this mesh with my beliefs?"

High ethics guides behavior; people know where this person stands. Makes decisions based on values.

Developing Your Resources

- Partner with people who are strong in Feeling for Others, especially if you're in a situation where you think everyone should believe in something as strongly as you do. People with the talent Innovation may help you to find creative ways to put your values into action.

Activating This Talent in Others

- Discover their values and find a way to tie them to the work to be done. Individuals with this talent will not do anything that violates their values.
- You don't have to share their values, but you do need to respect the fact that they have them.
- They will have a natural orientation to serve.

CONNECTION

RELATIONAL THINKING

Activating Your Own Talent

- Be a connector of people: "You have to meet so and so."
- Look for chances to show how a particular idea is linked to others.
- Find ways to connect with other connectors—book clubs, spirituality groups, or affinity groups.

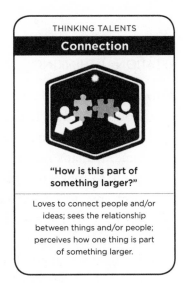

THINKING TALENTS

Connection

"How is this part of something larger?"

Loves to connect people and/or ideas; sees the relationship between things and/or people; perceives how one thing is part of something larger.

Developing Your Resources

- Get help when you need to think linearly rather than in a web. People with Procedural thinking talents may be able to help you.

- Partner with people with a Storytelling talent. They can help you find the right words and examples to express to others your "felt sense" of connection to ideas, people, or experiences.
- You might need help focusing on a given part of your thinking or narrowing down your ideas.

Activating This Talent in Others

- People with this talent perceive the connection between ideas and therefore may have trouble focusing on any given part.
- Give them support to think linearly rather than in a web.
- They are great at connecting individuals or groups.
- They excel at showing different people how each relies on the others.
- Ask them to explain how a particular idea is linked to others.

CREATING INTIMACY

RELATIONAL THINKING

Activating Your Own Talent

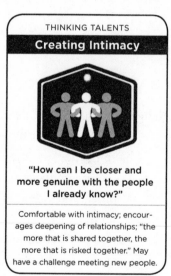

THINKING TALENTS

Creating Intimacy

"How can I be closer and more genuine with the people I already know?"

Comfortable with intimacy; encourages deepening of relationships; "the more that is shared together, the more that is risked together." May have a challenge meeting new people.

- You do well in teams that stay together for long periods of time. If that's not possible, find ways to make one-on-one connections to each new team member to increase your comfort level.
- Recognize that you prefer developing deep relationships; understand that meeting and greeting new people in casual settings may be challenging.
- Minimize networking requirements, if possible.
- Even when your schedule is hectic, maintain your connec-

tions with your friends. You need contact with people who know you intimately in order to thrive.

Developing Your Resources
- Practice good communication skills and develop your ability to give clear, clean feedback.

Activating This Talent in Others
- Understand that meeting and greeting new people may be challenging for individuals with this talent, especially in groups. They want to know more about people than "name, rank, and serial number."
- They are likely to struggle in organizations where roles are formal or demands for casual networking are high.
- They do well in teams that stay together for long periods of time.
- Utilize their talent by allowing them to mentor others.

ENROLLING

RELATIONAL TALENT

Activating Your Own Talent
- Try to find ways to meet new people every day.
- Find activities where you can be a goodwill ambassador for ideas you want to promote, or enlist others to help you do this.
- Look for chances to sell something you believe in.

THINKING TALENTS

Enrolling

"How can I relate to this new person?"

Enjoys challenge of meeting new people and getting in their good graces; enjoys developing rapport, breaking the ice, making a new connection, then moving on.

Developing Your Resources
- Ally with people whose talent is Creating Intimacy or Feeling for Others. They can help secure the relationships you initiate.

Activating This Talent in Others

- Those with this talent are great at selling, meeting, and greeting.
- Use them when you want to enlist others in the organization in a new plan or idea.
- They may struggle with maintaining close relationships with customers or teammates. Put them in a position where they can sell an idea or product and move on.

FEELING FOR OTHERS

THINKING TALENTS

Feeling for Others

"What are people feeling now?"

Senses emotions in those nearby; shares their perspective in order to understand their choices; hears the unvoiced questions; anticipates others' needs.

RELATIONAL THINKING

Activating Your Own Talent

- Help others to get in touch with how those around them are feeling.
- Ask others to allow you to express how you feel about decisions that affect you.
- Explain that you may cry or seem highly emotional, and encourage others not to overreact.
- Find positive, optimistic people to be around. Being around negative feelings may bring you down.

Developing Your Resources

- Partner with people who have strong Get-to-Action or Taking-Charge talents. They can help you to take needed action while balancing your desire to protect others' feelings.

Activating This Talent in Others

- Ask those with this talent how they think others are feeling, particularly when you want to take the pulse of a group.

- Before making a decision that affects them, ask how they feel about it. For them, emotions are a factor to be included.
- Recognize that they may cry at work when moved by sadness or happiness.
- They may make decisions instinctively rather than logically. Ask what their gut sense is.
- They don't like to hurt people's feelings, so provide safe ways for them to be honest or give feedback without being put on the spot.
- They will "catch" the feelings of others and so do better with upbeat people.

INCLUDING

RELATIONAL THINKING

Activating Your Own Talent

- Take the lead in welcoming new people into a project or team.
- When there are group functions, make sure that everyone is included.
- Understand that others don't necessarily think this way and that your perspective is valuable.

THINKING TALENTS

Including

"How can I stretch the circle wider?"

Desires to make others part of the group so as many as possible can feel its support; no one should be on the outside looking in; accepting, nonjudgmental.

Developing Your Resources

- If you have to share "bad news" or difficult information with others, use your natural empathy, but partner with someone who is good at getting to action or taking charge; otherwise, you may be tempted to put off being the messenger.

Activating This Talent in Others

- Those with this talent are interested in making everyone feel part of a group. Ask them to take the lead in welcoming new people into a project or team or at large events.
- Ask them to think about the implications on other people of whatever you're doing; they may think of people whom you have not thought of.

MENTORING

RELATIONAL THINKING

Activating Your Own Talent

- Find formal and informal opportunities to mentor someone.
- Volunteer to give praise and recognition to others.
- Be aware that you may feel compelled to keep helping a struggling employee, even when it's appropriate to give up.

THINKING TALENTS

Mentoring

"What can help others grow?"

Sees potential in others; every person is a work in progress; goal is to help others achieve success; searches for signs of growth in others.

Developing Your Resources

- Partner with someone with a strong Particularizing talent; he or she can help you identify where people's individual strengths lie so you can develop them from there.

Activating This Talent in Others

- Give people with this talent the opportunity to help others.
- They are great when put in charge of employee recognition programs and preparing employees to grow for future assignments.
- Because of their growth orientation, they may keep trying to help a problem employee long past the point when others would have given up. You may need to help them see that.

OPTIMISM

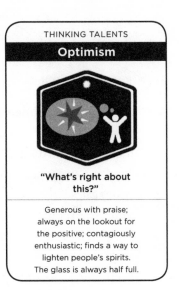

THINKING TALENTS

Optimism

"What's right about this?"

Generous with praise; always on the lookout for the positive; contagiously enthusiastic; finds a way to lighten people's spirits. The glass is always half full.

RELATIONAL THINKING

Activating Your Own Talent

- Understand that your positive energy is a gift to clients, teammates, etc.
- You may need help in seeing potential pitfalls in a situation. You will have a tendency to underestimate them.
- Be the one who creates celebrations.

Developing Your Resources

- Help others to understand that your enthusiasm and optimism are not necessarily "pie in the sky" thinking. Partner with people who can help you create a full vision and those who can help you accomplish it.

Activating This Talent in Others

- Find ways for those with this talent to interact with customers, as they will paint an exciting picture of your organization.
- The glass is always half full for them. Help them to see potential pitfalls in a situation that they are not naturally aware of and strategize about how to respond.
- They may have trouble being around negativity and do better in positively focused situations.

PARTICULARIZE

RELATIONAL THINKING

Activating Your Own Talent

- Ask to mentor or coach, formally or informally.
- You're a great resource on what colleagues like, what's important to them, how they are unique, as well as their strengths and weaknesses.
- Volunteer to come up with ideas for gifts for teammates or bosses.

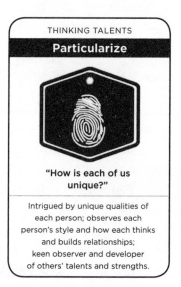

THINKING TALENTS

Particularize

"How is each of us unique?"

Intrigued by unique qualities of each person; observes each person's style and how each thinks and builds relationships; keen observer and developer of others' talents and strengths.

- Be aware that while recognizing uniqueness in others is easy for you, knowing how you feel and what you want may be challenging. Ask yourself: "If I were thinking of someone else in this situation, what would I think they needed?"

Developing Your Resources

- Use your talent to help others understand that diversity is not about just gender, race, or other "obvious" differences, but truly about the unique ways that individuals have of thinking and expressing themselves in the world.

Activating This Talent in Others

- Turn to people with this talent when you're having trouble understanding someone else or getting what you need from someone. They will likely know where the other person is coming from.
- Ask them to mentor or coach. They will have a knack for spotting how each person learns a little differently.
- They are a resource on what other people like, what's important to them, how they are unique, as well as on a person's talents and limitations.

- Count on them to come up with ideas for presents for team-mates or bosses.

PEACEMAKING

RELATIONAL THINKING

Activating Your Own Talent

- Recognize that you may be un-comfortable with conflict.
- If people are fighting, volunteer to help make peace. You're good at helping others find areas where they do agree.
- It may be very hard for you to disagree with someone or stand up for yourself. For the sake of harmony, you may tend to go with the flow no matter what. When you find yourself in this situation, consult with your other thinking talents to make sure you're using all of your-self.

THINKING TALENTS

Peacemaking

"Where is the common ground?"

Looks for areas of agreement; holds conflicts to a minimum; prefers to search for consensus; will modify own direction in service of harmony.

Developing Your Resources

- Learn communication and conflict-resolution skills and prac-tice them so that you can find ways to resolve conflict with-out confrontation. Otherwise, you may simply avoid all conflict situations.

Activating This Talent in Others

- Those with this talent struggle in conflict situations. Don't expect them to be comfortable confronting others.
- If other people are disagreeing or fighting, ask those with this talent to help make peace. They are good at helping others find areas where they do agree.
- Don't expect them to disagree or stand up for themselves.

For the sake of harmony, they may go along no matter what.

- Because of their desire to harmonize, it may be very difficult for them to take action without help.

STORYTELLING

RELATIONAL THINKING

THINKING TALENTS
Storytelling

"How can I bring these ideas to life with a story?"

Needs to explain by painting vivid pictures until others are inspired to act.

Activating Your Own Talent
- Help others understand that your tendency to be creative with facts when telling a story does not mean that you are untrustworthy or "all show."
- Explore ways that your story-telling abilities can be developed within the context of the business.
- Help others to make their pre-sentations to teams, bosses, and/or clients more engaging through storytelling.

Developing Your Resources
- Be aware of others' reactions to the stories you use. Refine and reuse ones that work; discard ones that don't and develop new, more effective ones.

Activating This Talent in Others
- Understand that those with a natural Storytelling talent are not liars—they are creative with facts to fit the story.
- Explore how their storytelling abilities can be used in your organization.
- Ask them to help others make more-engaging presentations to teams, bosses, and/or clients.

TALENTS IN ALL QUADRANTS

GOAL-SETTING

CROSS-QUADRANT THINKING

Activating Your Own Talent

- Volunteer for situations that require extra work.
- Explain to others that you like to be busy and are motivated by a concrete goal to work toward.
- Make sure to find tangible ways to measure progress.
- Help others understand that you need big targets and stretch assignments—goals you believe are worthy of your efforts.

THINKING TALENTS
Goal-Setting

"What can I accomplish today?"

Daily drive to accomplish something and meet a goal. Every day starts at zero and must achieve something tangible. There is a perpetual whisper of discontent.

Developing Your Resources

- Partner with people with strong Precision or Focusing talents. These people can help you develop benchmarks for progress and keep you on track.
- You may have trouble feeling satisfied with an achievement. Make it a goal to learn to be satisfied before looking for the next big goal.

Activating This Talent in Others

- Those with this talent like to stay busy and are motivated by a challenging, concrete goal to work toward.
- Whatever they're doing, they need a way to measure progress and success so they can track achievement. They may have trouble experiencing a sense of satisfaction with success.
- When they finish a task, they will be much more motivated if you give a new goal that stretches them, rather than time off, for instance.

- Any goal must be perceived as worthy for them, so help them set big targets.

HUMOR

CROSS-QUADRANT THINKING

THINKING TALENTS

Humor

"What is amusing about this?"

Enjoys seeing the humor in situations. Can lighten tense moments and puts self and others at ease with laughter.

Activating Your Own Talent

- You can lighten any situation, which is great in groups or team settings that need levity.
- Let others know that your joking is not a challenge to their authority.
- Use your humor in constructive ways—it can be a valuable medium in written communication and making speeches.

Developing Your Resources

- Notice when you use humor as a defensive strategy or as a way to protect yourself from emotions; recognize that humor is not appropriate in all settings or situations, and draw on your other talents in these instances.

Activating This Talent in Others

- Look to those with this talent to lighten a situation.
- Include them in group or team situations where the humor can be a valuable asset.
- Be aware that they can't help joking, so don't take it as a challenge to your authority.
- Encourage them to use humor in constructive ways—it can be a valuable medium in written communication and making speeches.

- Don't forget that they have other thinking talents, although they may be overshadowed by the constant jokes; look for ways to utilize those as well.

THINKING ALONE

CROSS-QUADRANT THINKING

Activating Your Own Talent

THINKING TALENTS

Thinking Alone

"What can I think about now?"

Poses questions to self and tries to figure them out; constant mental hum; needs to be alone to think to come up with an answer; dislikes being put on the spot to respond.

- Let others know that you don't do well with making snap decisions. You need time to think through all the pros and cons.
- Ask for advance notice before you'll be required to take action or make a decision.
- Be sure to set aside designated time in your schedule for Thinking Alone.
- As much as possible, let others know when you will get back to them with your opinion/decision, rather than leaving them hanging.

Developing Your Resources

- Deliberately build relationships with people you consider to be "big thinkers." Spending time with them will nourish and inspire you in your thinking process.

Activating This Talent in Others

- Don't expect people with this talent to make snap decisions. Give them time to think through all the pros and cons.
- Whenever possible, give them notice far in advance of an action or decision that will need to be made.

- Encourage them to take alone time, when they can simply muse.
- Engage them in discussions about their strengths. They will enjoy the chance to think about themselves.

WANTING TO WIN

CROSS-QUADRANT THINKING

Activating Your Own Talent

THINKING TALENTS

Wanting to Win

"Am I better at this than everyone else is?"

Compares performance to that of others; likes measurement to facilitate comparison; competition is invigorating.

- Let your boss know that you're motivated by competitive situations. You need to be able to compare yourself to others in order to be at your best.
- Create your own contests if the organization doesn't offer them.
- Recognize that not everyone sees situations in a win–lose way.

Developing Your Resources

- Take time after a "win" to evaluate how and why you won: Which behaviors and attitudes worked for you? Which didn't? What can you learn from this?
- Have an ally who is good at Feeling for Others. He or she can help you understand how your attitude and process may affect others and can help you minimize the potential of alienating others in your quest to win.

Activating This Talent in Others

- People with this talent naturally want to beat others in competition. So set up contests for them—they are highly motivating. If you want even greater performance, pit them against others with this talent.

- They speak in competitive language—it's all about winning or losing for them.
- If they start competing inappropriately with teammates, give them some external goal to compete for.

APPRECIATIONS

For our partners in love, who stand with us every minute:
Andy Bryner and David Peck

For those who stand behind us and have made this possible:
Milton Erickson, M.D.
Richard Kuboyama
Edith and William Mechanic
Joan Sapiro
Dr. Peter and Jeri McArthur
Heather McArthur and John Stevenson
Megan and Kieran Cuddihy
Michelle, Richard, Logan, Hunter, and Taylor Laver
Ken, Susan, Morgan, and Brendan Dall

For those who stand next to us in collaboration:
Julie Grau
Jessica Sindler
Laura Van der Veer
Mary Jane Ryan
Hamilton South

Suzy Amis Cameron
Pat Dunn
Jeff Dunn
Jim Holland
Al Carey
John Vieceli
Simone Amber
Andrea Beard
Trece Swanson
Robin Marrouche
Jacquelyn Zehner
Joan Selix Berman
Judy and Pete Siracusa
Harmony Hallas
Sara Bresee
Camp Truth
Telemark, Hula, and Mobi

And for those who will follow us and whose future we bless:
Ana Li McIlraith
Elspeth and Grace Stevenson
Ayla and Kai Cuddihy
Kate Laver
Abby and Grace Swanson
Samira Marrouche
Hannah Lutzker
Penn Bresee
Rose, Claire, Jasper, and Quinn Cameron

BIBLIOGRAPHY

Ackerman, Diane. *An Alchemy of Mind: The Marvel and Mystery of the Brain.* New York: Scribner, 2004.

Annis, Barbara, and Keith Merron. *Gender Intelligence: Breakthrough Strategies for Increasing Diversity and Improving Your Bottom Line.* New York: Harper Business, 2014.

Banks, Amy, M.D., and Leigh Ann Hirschman. *Four Ways to Click: Revise Your Brain for Stronger, More Rewarding Relationships.* New York: Tarcher, 2015.

Begley, Sharon. *Train Your Mind, Change Your Brain: How a New Science Reveals Our Extraordinary Potential to Transform Ourselves.* New York: Ballantine Books, 2007.

Blake, John. "What the Tributes to Dave Brubeck Missed." CNN [video post]. www.cnn.com/2012/12/21/us/dave-brubeck-appreciation/.

Buckingham, Marcus, and Donald O. Clifton. *Now, Discover Your Strengths.* New York: Free Press, 2001.

Cameron, Kim S., Jane E. Dutton, Robert Quinn (eds.). *Positive Organizational Scholarship: Foundations of a New Discipline.* Oakland, CA: Berrett-Koehler Publishers, 2003.

Comer, James P. *Leave No Child Behind: Preparing Today's Youth for Tomorrow's World.* New Haven: Yale University Press, 2004.

Commission on Children at Risk. *Hardwired to Connect: The New Scientific Case for Authoritative Communities.* New York: Institute for American Values, 2003.

Cooperrider, David, Diana Whitney, and Jacqueline Stavros. *The Appreciative Inquiry Handbook: For Leaders of Change.* Oakland, CA: Berrett-Koehler Publishers, 2003.

Covey, Stephen R. *The Seven Habits of Highly Effective People: Powerful Lessons in Personal Change.* New York: Simon & Schuster, 1990.

Covey, Stephen R. *The Speed of Trust: The One Thing That Changes Everything.* New York: Free Press, 2006.

Davidson, Richard, Ph.D., and Sharon Begley. *The Emotional Life of Your Brain: How Its Unique Patterns Affect the Way You Think, Feel and Live—and How You Can Change Them.* New York: Hudson Street Press, 2012.

De Pree, Max. *Leadership Is an Art.* New York: Doubleday Business, 1989.

Desimone, R. "Neural Synchrony and Selective Attention." International Joint Conference on Neural Networks, 2009, 683–84.

Dobson, Terry, and Victor Miller. *Aikido in Everyday Life: Giving in to Get Your Way.* Berkeley: North Atlantic Books, 1994.

Doidge, Norman. *The Brain That Changes Itself: Stories of Personal Triumph from the Frontiers of Brain Science.* New York: Penguin Books, 2007.

Dweck, Carol. *Mindset: The New Psychology of Success.* New York: Random House, 2006.

Feldenkrais, Moshe. *Awareness Through Movement: Easy-to-Do Health Exercises to Improve Your Posture, Vision, Imagination and Personal Awareness.* New York: Harper One, 2009.

Frankl, Victor E. *Man's Search for Meaning.* New York: Pocket Books, 1997.

Freed, Jeffrey, and Laurie Parsons. *Right-Brained Children in a Left-Brained World.* New York: Simon and Schuster, 1998.

Friedman, Thomas. "Collaborate vs. Collaborate." *New York Times,* January 12, 2013.

Gallwey, Timothy. *The Inner Game of Work.* New York: Random House, 2000.

Goertzel, Victor, Mildred George Goertzel, Ted Goertzel, and Ariel M. W. Hansen. *Cradles of Eminence: Childhoods of More Than 700 Famous Men and Women.* Tucson: Great Potential Press, 2004.

Goleman, Daniel. *Social Intelligence: The New Science of Human Relationships.* New York: Bantam Books, 2001.

Griffith, Mary. *The Homeschooling Handbook.* New York: Three Rivers Press, 1999.

Hannaford, Carla. *Smart Moves: Why Learning Is Not All in Your Head.* Salt Lake City: Great River Books, 1995.

Hartmann, Thom. *Attention Deficit Disorder: A Different Perception.* Nevada City, CA: Underwood Books, 1997.

Hawkins, Jeff, and Sandra Blakeslee. *On Intelligence: How a New Understanding of the Brain Will Lead to the Creation of Truly Intelligent Machines.* New York: Times Books, 2004.

Herrmann, Ned. *The Creative Brain.* Lake Lure, NC: Brain Books, 1995.

Hillman, James. *The Soul's Code: In Search of Character and Calling.* New York: Random House, 1996.

Hock, Dee. *Birth of the Chaordic Age.* Oakland, CA: Berrett-Koehler Publishers, 2000.

Isaacson, Walter. *Einstein: His Life & Universe*. New York: Simon & Schuster, 2008.

Jegede, Faith. "What I've Learned from My Autistic Brothers." TED Talk, November 2012, www.ted.com/talks/faith_jegede_what_i_ve_learned_ from_my_autistic_brothers.

John, E. Roy. "Neurometric Evaluation of Brain Function in Normal & Learning Disabled Children." International Academy for Research in Learning Disabilities Monograph Series, Number 5. Ann Arbor: University of Michigan Press, 1989.

Kabat-Zinn, Jon. *Coming to Our Senses: Healing Ourselves and the World through Mindfulness*. New York: Hyperion, 2005.

Kahneman, Daniel. *Thinking, Fast and Slow*. New York: Farrar, Straus and Giroux, 2011.

Kanter, R. M. "Collaborative Advantage: The Art of Alliances." *Harvard Business Review* 72, no. 4 (July–August 1994): 96–108.

Kounios, John, and Mark Beeman. "The Aha! Moment: The Neural Basis of Solving Problems." Creativity Post, November 11, 2011. www.creativity post.com/science/the_aha_moment._the_cognitive_neuroscience_of_insight.

Langer, Ellen J. *Mindfulness*. Boston: Da Capo Press, 1989.

Markova, Dawna, Ph.D. *I Will Not Die an Unlived Life: Reclaiming Purpose and Passion*. Berkeley: Conari Press, 2000.

Markova, Dawna, Ph.D. *The Open Mind: Exploring the 6 Patterns of Intelligence*. Berkeley: Conari Press, 1996.

Markova, Dawna, Ph.D. *Random Acts of Kindness*. Berkeley: Conari Press, 2002.

Markova, Dawna, Ph.D. *Think-Ability*. Park City, UT: Professional Thinking Partners, 2002.

Markova, Dawna, Ph.D., and Andy Bryner. *An Unused Intelligence: Physical Thinking for 21st Century Leadership*. Berkeley: Conari Press, 1996.

Markova, Dawna, Ph.D., and Anne Powell. *How Your Child Is Smart: A Life Changing Approach to Learning*. Berkeley: Conari Press, 1992.

Markova, Dawna, Ph.D., and Anne Powell. *Learning Unlimited: Using Homework to Engage Your Child's Natural Style of Intelligence*. Berkeley: Conari Press, 1998.

Miller, Jean B. *Toward a New Psychology of Women*, 2nd edition. Boston: Beacon Press, 2012.

Palmer, Parker. *A Hidden Wholeness: The Journey Toward an Undivided Life*. San Francisco: Jossey-Bass, 2004.

Palmer, Wendy. *The Intuitive Body: Discovering the Wisdom of Conscious Embodiment and Aikido*, 3rd edition. San Francisco: Blue Snake Books, 2008.

Paul, Annie Murphy. *The Cult of Personality: How Personality Tests Are Leading Us to Miseducate Our Children, Mismanage Our Companies, and Misunderstand Ourselves*. New York: Free Press, 2004.

Pink, Daniel. *A Whole New Mind: Why Right Brainers Will Rule the Future*. New York: Riverhead Books, 2006.

Pinker, Steven. *How the Mind Works*. New York: W.W. Norton, 1997.

Ratey, John J. *A User's Guide to the Brain: Perception, Attention, and the Four Theaters of the Brain*. New York: Vintage, 2001.

Remen, Rachel K., M.D. *My Grandfather's Blessings: Stories of Strength, Refuge and Belonging*. New York: Riverhead Books, 2001.

Rosen, Sidney. *My Voice Will Go with You: The Teaching Tales of Milton H. Erickson*. New York: W.W. Norton, 1982.

Ryan, M. J. *Trusting Yourself: How to Stop Feeling Overwhelmed and Live More Happily With Less Effort*. New York: Broadway Books, 2004.

Sawyer, Keith. *Group Genius: The Creative Power of Collaboration*. New York: Basic Books, 2007.

Senge, Peter, C. Otto Scharmer, Joseph Jaworski, and Betty Sue Flowers. *Presence: Human Purpose and the Field of the Future*. Cambridge, MA: Society for Organizational Learning, 2004.

Shifflet, C. M. *Ki in Aikido: A Sampler of Ki Exercises*, 2nd edition. San Francisco: Blue Snake Books, 2010.

Shlain, Leonard. *Leonardo's Brain: Understanding Da Vinci's Creative Genius*. Lanham, MD: Lyons Press, 2014.

Siegel, Daniel. *The Developing Mind: How Relationships and the Brain Interact to Shape Who We Are*. New York: Guilford Press, 1999.

Siegel, Daniel, and Mary Hartzell, M.ED. *Parenting From the Inside Out: How a Deeper Self-Understanding Can Help You Raise Children Who Thrive*. New York: Tarcher, 2003.

Stone, Linda. "Why Email Can Be Habit Forming." Huffington Post, November 17, 2011. www.huffingtonpost.com/linda-stone/why-email-can-be-habit-fo_b_324781.html?.

Taylor, Shelly E. "Biobehavioral Responses to Stress in Females: Tend and Befriend, Not Fight or Flight." *Psychological Review* 107, 3 (July 2000), 411–29.

Turkle, Sherry. *Alone Together: Why We Expect More from Technology and Less from Each Other*. New York: Basic Books, 2011.

Tutu, Desmond. *No Future without Forgiveness*. Colorado Springs: Image Books, 2000.

Wallace, B. Alan, Ph.D. *The Attention Revolution: Unlocking the Power of the Focused Mind*. Somerville, MA: Wisdom Publications, 2006.

Wheatley, Margaret. *Finding Our Way: Leadership for an Uncertain Time*. Oakland, CA: Berrett-Koehler Publishers, 2005.

INDEX

Page numbers of illustrations appear in italics.

ABOUT THE AUTHORS

DAWNA MARKOVA, Ph.D., is the CEO emeritus of Professional Thinking Partners, an organization that teaches collaborative thinking to CEOs and senior executives around the world. Internationally known for her research in the fields of learning and perception, she is a former senior affiliate of the Society for Organizational Learning, originated at MIT's Sloan School of Management, and the co-author of the international bestseller *Random Acts of Kindness*. She lives in Hawaii.

ANGIE MCARTHUR is the CEO of Professional Thinking Partners and co-founder of SmartWired and the Smart Parenting Revolution, organizations dedicated to helping youths and the adults who support them. As an expert in communication and learning styles, she has developed strategies for authors, corporations, CEOs, and the ongoing Executive Champions' Workshop. She also spearheaded the Worldwide Women's Web, a 2001 research initiative to support developing and retaining women in corporate leadership roles. She lives in Park City, Utah.

ABOUT THE TYPE

This book was set in Sabon, a typeface designed by the well-known German typographer Jan Tschichold (1902–74). Sabon's design is based upon the original letter forms of Claude Garamond and was created specifically to be used for three sources: foundry type for hand composition, Linotype, and Monotype. Tschichold named his typeface for the famous Frankfurt typefounder Jacques Sabon, who died in 1580.